THE NEW MIDDLE AGES

BONNIE WHEELER, *Series Editor*

The New Middle Ages is a series dedicated to pluridisciplinary studies of medieval cultures, with particular emphasis on recuperating women's history and on feminist and gender analyses. This peer-reviewed series includes both scholarly monographs and essay collections.

PUBLISHED BY PALGRAVE:

The Vernacular Spirit: Essays on Medieval
Religious Literature
    edited by Renate Blumenfeld-Kosinski,
    Duncan Robertson, and Nancy Warren

Popular Piety and Art in the Late Middle Ages:
Image Worship and Idolatry in England
1350–1500
    by Kathleen Kamerick

Absent Narratives, Manuscript Textuality, and
Literary Structure in Late Medieval England
    by Elizabeth Scala

Creating Community with Food and Drink in
Merovingian Gaul
    by Bonnie Effros

Representations of Early Byzantine Empresses:
Image and Empire
    by Anne McClanan

Encountering Medieval Textiles and Dress:
Objects, Texts, Images
    edited by Désirée G. Koslin and Janet
    Snyder

Eleanor of Aquitaine: Lord and Lady
    edited by Bonnie Wheeler and John
    Carmi Parsons

Isabel La Católica, Queen of Castile: Critical
Essays
    edited by David A. Boruchoff

Homoeroticism and Chivalry: Discourses of Male
Same-Sex Desire in the Fourteenth Century
    by Richard E. Zeikowitz

Portraits of Medieval Women: Family, Marriage,
and Politics in England 1225–1350
    by Linda E. Mitchell

Eloquent Virgins: From Thecla to Joan of Arc
    by Maud Burnett McInerney

The Persistence of Medievalism: Narrative
Adventures in Contemporary Culture
    by Angela Jane Weisl

Capetian Women
    edited by Kathleen D. Nolan

Joan of Arc and Spirituality
    edited by Ann W. Astell and Bonnie
    Wheeler

The Texture of Society: Medieval Women in the
Southern Low Countries
    edited by Ellen E. Kittell and Mary A.
    Suydam

Charlemagne's Mustache: And Other Cultural
Clusters of a Dark Age
    by Paul Edward Dutton

Troubled Vision: Gender, Sexuality, and Sight in
Medieval Text and Image
    edited by Emma Campbell and Robert
    Mills

Queering Medieval Genres
    by Tison Pugh

Sacred Place in Early Medieval Neoplatonism
    by L. Michael Harrington

The Middle Ages at Work
    edited by Kellie Robertson and
    Michael Uebel

Chaucer's Jobs
    by David R. Carlson

Medievalism and Orientalism: Three Essays on
Literature, Architecture and Cultural Identity
    by John M. Ganim

Queer Love in the Middle Ages
    by Anna Klosowska

Performing Women in the Middle Ages: Sex,
Gender, and the Iberian Lyric
    by Denise K. Filios

Necessary Conjunctions: The Social Self in
Medieval England
    by David Gary Shaw

Visual Culture and the German Middle Ages
    edited by Kathryn Starkey and Horst
    Wenzel

Medieval Paradigms: Essays in Honor of Jeremy
duQuesnay Adams, Volumes 1 and 2
    edited by Stephanie Hayes-Healy

False Fables and Exemplary Truth in Later
Middle English Literature
    by Elizabeth Allen

Ecstatic Transformation: On the Uses of Alterity
in the Middle Ages
    by Michael Uebel

ANTIMERCANTILISM IN LATE MEDIEVAL ENGLISH LITERATURE

Roger A. Ladd

ANTIMERCANTILISM IN LATE MEDIEVAL ENGLISH LITERATURE
Copyright © Roger A. Ladd, 2010.

First published in 2010 by
PALGRAVE MACMILLAN®
in the United States—a division of St. Martin's Press LLC,
175 Fifth Avenue, New York, NY 10010.

Where this book is distributed in the UK, Europe and the rest of the
world, this is by Palgrave Macmillan, a division of Macmillan Publishers
Limited, registered in England, company number 785998, of Houndmills,
Basingstoke, Hampshire RG21 6XS.

Palgrave Macmillan is the global academic imprint of the above companies
and has companies and representatives throughout the world.

Palgrave® and Macmillan® are registered trademarks in the United
States, the United Kingdom, Europe and other countries.

ISBN: 978–0–230–62043–8

Library of Congress Cataloging-in-Publication Data

Ladd, Roger A.
    Antimercantilism in late medieval English literature / Roger A. Ladd.
        p. cm.—(The new Middle Ages)
    Includes bibliographical references.
    ISBN 978–0–230–62043–8
    1. English literature—Middle English, 1100–1500—History and
criticism. 2. Literature and society—Great Britain—History—To 1500.
3. Mercantile system in literature. 4. Economics in literature. 5. Social
history—Medieval, 500–1500. I. Title.

PR275.S63L33 2010
820.9'3553—dc22   2010007920

A catalogue record of the book is available from the British Library.

Design by Newgen Imaging Systems (P) Ltd., Chennai, India.

First edition: September 2010

10 9 8 7 6 5 4 3 2 1

Printed in the United States of America.

CONTENTS

ACKNOWLEDGMENTS

Sections of almost every chapter have been presented at conferences over the past decade or so, and I appreciate the valuable feedback from the audiences at many sessions of the International Congress of Medieval Studies and the Illinois Medieval Academy, as well as conversations at the international meetings of the John Gower Society and the New Chaucer Society. Portions of Chapters 4 and 5 have been previously published. Some of the material in Chapter 4 appeared in a very different form in my article "The Mercantile (Mis)Reader in *The Canterbury Tales*," from *Studies in Philology*, volume 99, no. 1, copyright © 2002 by the University of North Carolina Press, used by permission of the publisher (*www. uncpress.unc.edu*). Some material in Chapter 5 is adapted from my article "Margery Kempe and Her Mercantile Mysticism," *Fifteenth-Century Studies* 26 (2001): 121–41. Vicky Wells at the University of North Carolina Press and James Walker at Camden House/Boydell & Brewer have my lasting gratitude for their gracious permission to reprint this material. My scholarly debts are too great to name, but I especially appreciate the mentorship of my dissertation committee, A. N. Doane, Donald Rowe, Maureen Mazzaoui, and my director Sherry Reames. I also thank my wife, children, and extended family, who have all learned not to ask about medieval merchants.

CHAPTER 1

AN INTRODUCTION TO LATE MEDIEVAL
ENGLISH LITERARY MERCHANTS

Powerful commoners in an age of aristocrats, international operators in an age of dangerous travel, city-dwellers within a predominantly rural population: merchants were a paradox in medieval society, and wielded power and influence far in advance of their social status. Literary scholars have only recently started to give merchants the attention they deserve, and while much work has been done by historians of the medieval economy, to date only a few historical studies have been dedicated entirely to English merchants as a social group. Literary scholarship rarely focuses directly on merchants outside the work of Geoffrey Chaucer or the York Mercers' Play.[1] Some recent work has been done on the intellectual history of the concept of trade, but no one has undertaken a comparative study of the position of merchants in late medieval English literature, and this book begins to fill that gap.[2] While I suspect that much scholarly aversion to merchants arises from class-guilt on the part of scholars who desire to launder our own middle-class origins, the simplicity and descriptive power of the three-estates model itself have enabled its dominance as a paradigm. If we imagined that the three estates were a universal ideology of the Middle Ages, reliance upon that model might at least seem true to period values, but Georges Duby argues convincingly that the ideology of the three estates was never universally descriptive, but was instead a contingent social model created for France around the year 1000.[3] It is the lasting ideological power of this imagined social structure that impinges on my study of literary representations of merchants, their sins and virtues. Despite the historical contingency of the three-estate theory, it is remarkable how it still permeates the study of medieval literature, and not just that of estates satire. Although historians have long since abandoned the three estates as a descriptive model, even literary criticism that does not overtly discuss class generally follows medieval satirists by organizing itself around one or another of the three estates, with a strong historical preference for the thicker discursive legacies of the clergy and aristocracy. More recently, study of the peasantry has been lifted by the rising tide of Marxist criticism. Without listing and categorizing all of medieval literary criticism, a glance at a few key branches of criticism should suffice to show why merchants have been given such short shrift.

Transcending the Three Estates of Literary Scholarship

Two approaches to medieval literature have focused primarily on the clerical estate. The earlier of these schools, "historical criticism" (better known as Robertsonianism), grounds most medieval literature in the ideology of the clerical estate. As noted opponent E. Talbot Donaldson argues tellingly, such a theory posits that "all serious poetry written by Christians during the middle ages promotes the doctrine of charity by using the same allegorical structure that the Fathers found in the Bible."[4] Regardless of its merits, such an approach can be problematic, as when Robert P. Miller, in his useful *Chaucer: Sources and Backgrounds*, adheres so closely to Robertson's methodology that he privileges medieval clerical ideology of estate. This leads Miller to foreground Augustine among aristocratic texts relating to chivalry, and to limit the third estate to that proverbial clerical symbol of it, "Plowmen."[5] Miller's facilitation of Augustinian exegesis thus ignores Chaucer's systematic divergence from a clerical ideology of estate in his highly expanded "third estate," which includes his Merchant, Franklin, Man of Law, Reeve, Shipman, Physician, and so on. While Chaucer does present a traditional commoner with his virtuous Plowman, an exegetical focus solely on that undeveloped figure of an ideal laborer misrepresents Chaucer's treatment of the third estate in that poem. The more current vein of clerically oriented criticism is not as clearly labeled as exegetical criticism, but it bears a distinct style and focus, studying both medieval theology and popular piety. Lee Patterson makes a good case for this approach as an alternative to psychoanalytic criticism in his detailed repudiation of the latter.[6] Work on theology has included studies of anticlericalism and nonexegetical interpretations that still explore scholastic and other clerical intertexts of medieval literature, and this critical model reveals productive linkages between literature and faith.[7] The influence of Marxist criticism has also made recent work on popular piety more aware of the complex structures of medieval society, and critics like David Aers have interrogated late medieval piety in terms of the third estate, but we still tend to see the "third estate" as meaning the agricultural peasantry.[8] As a result, we too often neglect much of the increasingly influential urban population.

Work on the aristocracy has had a similarly narrow focus, though it comes as close as any scholarship to discussing merchants. One could argue that the primarily aesthetic criticism of the past aspires to an essentially aristocratic ideal (at least on the part of the critic), as for example when E. Talbot Donaldson uses terms like "high" and "low" quite casually.[9] The most prominent work directly concerned with aristocratic tastes, though, remains Richard Firth Green's *Poets and Princepleasers*, which assimilates the merchant estate to the dominant tastes of the aristocratic court.[10] Green recognizes the difficulty of applying modern class terminology to the Middle Ages (see below), when he refers to the "*so-called* middle-class readership in the fifteenth century."[11] Some of Paul Strohm's work similarly represents "aristocracy studies," as his interest in the crown in particular has led him to study of the chronicles and royal ritual practice.[12] Larry Scanlon and Janet Coleman both study the aristocracy and "middle class," Scanlon in terms of power relations, and Coleman in terms of reading tastes (see below).[13] Like Green, Scanlon and Coleman both discuss the problem of the "middle class," if not of the merchant estate, and Strohm effectively avoids three-estate theory in *Social Chaucer*. Scanlon cautions against reading the term "middle class" as analogous to "its modern American connotations of the majoritarian or average,"[14] and he synthesizes Green's and Coleman's conceptions of audience. As with Strohm's "middle strata," Scanlon's description does not, however, distinguish between the rural "middle class," consisting of those individuals ranging from the highest peasants to the modest gentry, and the urban bourgeoisie generated by the upper levels of the guild system.[15] An interest in the rural "middle class" leads, though, to the final type of criticism, which characterizes the estates: analysis of the peasantry. The best example of this work remains Steven Justice's *Writing and Rebellion*,[16] which traces their appearance as producers of texts. Many scholars who follow the other two estates, particularly Aers and Strohm, share Justice's interest in the peasantry. This focus on the proto-proletariat leaves little room for a discussion of the "merchant class," except as it appears as a foil to the interests of the peasantry. Kellie Robertson's recent *The Laborer's Two Bodies* has a somewhat more nuanced approach to merchants in her discussion of "common profit," but merchants remain secondary to her main focus on the problem of labor and its representation.[17] This is not to say that any of these studies *should* have been about merchants, but merchants only occasionally appear in such studies, and are often folded into a larger "middle class." This gap is problematic, because it is not at all clear that it is based on any coherent reasons to neglect the mercantile estate—instead merchants have simply been missed, because literary scholars have focused their interests on the traditional estates, and touched so briefly on the "middle class" that its complex structure has not been addressed.

While I share with Justice or Green a focus on a single estate, this book's focus on merchants breaks from this unstated reliance of scholars of English literature on the idea of the three estates, in the hope of supporting further work on merchants and issues of trade. Like any scholar of a particular estate group, I must first focus on that genre which discusses estate overtly: estates satire, defined loosely to include William Langland's *Piers Plowman*, John Gower's *Vox Clamantis* and *Mirour de l'Omme*, and Geoffrey Chaucer's *Canterbury Tales*. Important work has been done on estates satire, but it either focuses on a specific author, like Jill Mann's *Chaucer and Medieval Estates Satire*, or relies on outdated theories of genre, like S. M. Tucker and John Peter, both of whom Paul Miller criticizes for anachronism.[18] A few scholars follow an estate through the satire, such as Penn Szittya or Wendy Scase, just as there have been studies on individual Chaucer pilgrims, but there has not yet been a study of merchants.[19] While Lianna Farber touches on representations of trade (three Chaucer tales, a Henryson fable, *St. Erkenwald*, and "London Lickpenny"), her literary analysis supports her paradigm of late medieval attitudes toward trade, rather than using that paradigm to read the texts.[20]

My examination of merchants through these texts then shows fault lines in late medieval English estates satire. Since they directly address late medieval concerns about the gap between the idealized and observed social orders, breakdowns and seeming contradictions in those texts' presentation of a social structure reveal traces of competing ideologies of social relations. Specifically, two opposed but related ideologies directly addressed merchants as an estate- grouping. On the one hand, the church's historical resistance to the money economy encouraged a construction of the Seven Deadly Sins that stressed Avarice's danger, associated merchants with that sin, and opposed the growth of the profit economy.[21] This ideology reinforced the three-estate model, which in its most conservative form excluded merchants, who officially neither fought, prayed, nor labored with their hands, though many merchants probably did all three from time to time. On the other hand, society as a whole was increasingly dependent on the profit economy. For example, Edward III relied on the wool trade to finance the Hundred Years' War, and the church was fully involved in the English profit economy through the wool production of its lands. Great abbeys like Rievaulx and Fountains even took payment for their wool harvests years in advance.[22] Competing with the church's theoretical antimercantilism was economic necessity and the increasing interdependence of national economies. As the English crown increasingly relied on customs income, it sought to maximize the necessary wool profits.[23] Calais was as much a source of income as it was a foothold for Plantagenet ambitions in France, and foreign relations with the Low Countries had at least as much to do with trade as with dynastic politics. Determining the trajectory of the emergent ideology implicit in the rise of trade represents much of my focus. In response to this complex economy, the church placed the blame for profit onto professional merchants, and associated that blame with an abiding sense of spiritual decay, seen most clearly here in *Piers Plowman*. It is this laying of blame that is the basis of satiric representations of the merchant estate, while at the same time those representations contain within them traces of an emergent pro-trade ideology. An examination of satirized merchants thus requires us to explore this tension between residual and emergent ideologies, without succumbing to the teleology that the pro-trade position was destined to prevail.[24] This conflict should help us better to understand how these satiric texts fit into their cultural context as part of a dialogue between these competing ideologies.

Were a reading of satire my only point, however, I would miss an important perspective on this period of transition between competing visions of trade and economic reality. If we look at merchants only as objects of satire, it is all too easy to forget that merchants were more than just types—they were also real people, beset by ideological conflict over their profession, and no doubt aware of their estate's rhetorical role in this debate. Nothing makes ideologies more visible than conflict between them. Although they are rarely considered as a potential audience for literature, medieval merchants were literate, often articulate, and hardly insulated from the conflict between antimercantile and protrade ideologies. It would strain credulity to suggest that many merchants believed themselves damned, but estates satires and sermons certainly implied that they were.[25] Logically, then, there should have been some mercantile reaction to this ideological conflict, and indeed there are several fifteenth-century texts or groups of texts with clear enough mercantile ties. Margery Kempe presents a "merchant-class" response to the spiritual demands of her time, and there are many anonymous poems with a mercantile bent, such as the *The Libelle of Englyshe Polycye*, "The Childe of Bristowe," and the Pseudo-Chaucerian "Merchant's Tale of Beryn." Finally, the York Mercers' "Last Judgement" responds directly to the problem of salvation for merchants. While none of these texts can be read as "the merchants' response to the satirists," they allow a window into a mercantile subjectivity. Within these constructions of a merchant subject-position are traces of merchants' ideological response to antimercantilism, a response also found in Langland and Gower: charity, both institutionalized and personal, both material and spiritual, seems to have allowed merchants to neutralize the blame placed upon them by antimercantile satirists. This is not to say, however, that antimercantile satire had gone away by the time of my fifteenth-century texts, as Kempe seems to have internalized the lessons of antimercantile satire, and because such an antimercantile poem as "London Lickpenny" survives in manuscripts dated to around 1600.[26]

This book does not, however, attempt to settle every possible connection between economic ideology and these texts, nor do I want to imply that any of the texts here are solely concerned with the conflict between pro- and antimercantile ideologies. As a result, my focus varies substantially, both because of the varying ideologies engaged by and embedded within those works, and because some texts are more compartmentalized than others. The encyclopedic poems of John Gower, for example, address a wide variety of social issues, and because Gower demonstrated wide interests, my discussion of his work can address only specific sections of his two satires. Similarly, Geoffrey Chaucer's wide-ranging oeuvre renders absurd the notion that the *Canterbury Tales* is primarily about merchants, so I use the wealth of past work on estates satire in the *General Prologue* to frame a reading of that satiric mode, following its trajectory in *The Merchant's Tale* and *The Shipman's Tale*. *Piers Plowman*, on the other hand, has long been done a disservice by the lack of careful critical attention to its later sections, particularly in terms of Langland's argument concerning the material world and merchandise. As a result, my examination carries my analysis of Langland's vision of social structure throughout the poem. With the fifteenth-century texts, the lack of generic continuity between those nonsatiric texts makes those chapters somewhat more independent of each other than those on Langland, Gower, and Chaucer. More specific claims are possible with the individual anonymous poems, as I read texts that speak directly to the issues confronting the merchant estate. My reading of Kempe examines her generic expectations in a spiritual biography in relation to her stated conceptions of her own estate. Finally, my study of the York Cycle looks primarily at the "Last Judgement" play, in part because we can link the play texts to guild ideologies only in the case of guilds that had real power in the city oligarchy that controlled that play text. I must emphasize also that this categorization of texts as by or about merchants remains artificial. As I discuss later in this chapter, the flexibility of the merchant estate as a category means that a very large portion of the urban population could be conceived of as potentially "merchant class," and Gower, Chaucer, and Kempe could conceivably be included in that social grouping.[27] How one groups merchants within a larger society remains problematic; for example, a traditionally Marxist treatment of them would generally consider merchants as part of those who "live off the surplus product of peasant labour," with inevitable conflict.[28] In the absence of large-scale industrial development, the imposition of a modern base/superstructure model can be expressed only in terms of agricultural production,[29] so Rodney Hilton's grouping of merchants with the economic elite makes sense in his analysis of the 1381 Rising. Estates satirists, on the other hand, generally wedged merchants into the commons: Jill Mann lists the estates described by a number of satires, and only five of her twenty-two examples omit merchants.[30] Mann's satires, including John Gower's *Mirour de l'Omme* and *Vox Clamantis*, all lump merchants together with the rest of the third estate.

The Commons' Profits: How to Define an Estate Which Is Not One

Given, then, the need to define "merchants" more effectively, the remainder of this introduction will outline the estate of merchants, discussing in detail just who medieval merchants were, and will discuss several theological issues that dominate literary treatments of them. It will conclude with a brief discussion of merchants as a potential literary audience. Fortunately the limitations of traditional models of class or estate are addressed in large part by recent work in economic history. Christopher Dyer, for example, helpfully provides a useful table of "the social hierarchy in late medieval England," which lays out distinct urban and landed/rural hierarchies, dividing the latter into clerical and lay, and emphasizing the ties between similar ranks within those competing hierarchies.[31] At the top of the urban hierarchy, merchants had direct relations with those at comparable levels of the rural and clerical hierarchies. The 1381 Rising itself reinforces the idea that merchants' social position lay somewhere between estates satire's placement of them with the commons and Hilton's placement of them with the landowning elite. Neither noble, clerical, nor foreign like London's slaughtered Flemings, English merchants were not the focus of peasant hostility as such.[32] This indifference suggests that the rebels did not necessarily share Hilton's sense of the commons' natural opposition to merchants. Despite the prominence of powerful merchants like Sir William Walworth or Sir Nicholas Brembre, the Rising's ideological focus on rural issues of land use and relations between tenants and landowners[33] elided the economic reality that tied merchants to those hated landowners.

On the other hand, the merchants involved made their own loyalty clear: Wat Tyler was killed by the Mayor of London, fishmonger Sir William Walworth, and two grocers and former mayors, Sir Nicholas Brembre and Sir John Philpot, were knighted along with Walworth for their support of the king during the Rising.[34] With their ties to the aristocracy as wealthy financiers and civic leaders, merchants as a social group were neither noble nor exactly common, and could be associated with either nobles or commons by different ideological discourses. The examples of the knighted Walworth, Brembre, and Philpot show what public figures merchants could be, and how successful merchants could be partially assimilated into the traditional estate of knights or more commonly into the gentry.[35] Brembre's rivalry with draper John de Northampton became a national issue, which ultimately drew in John of Gaunt, Duke of Lancaster and uncle to the king.[36] The Rising targeted Gaunt, but did not go after his merchant clients. Certainly Brembre's perception of his own estate and his resulting activities affiliated him with the aristocracy: he loaned £2970 to Richard II at one point, and at his death, Brembre left "property in London worth nearly £60 a year, [and] manors in Kent and [Middlesex]."[37] When tried for treason by the Lords Appellant in the 1388 Parliament, he offered and was denied the very knightly trial by combat,[38] and was tried with "five confidants of the king."[39] Sir Nicholas Brembre clearly represents a superlative sort of merchant, in that he was friendly with the king and was referred to familiarly as "Nichol" in John of Gaunt's records of currency transactions.[40] Accepting the exceptionality of a figure like Brembre or Walworth still leaves or even begs the question, who were the merchants, exactly?

We can get some handle on this question by contrasting the worldly prominence of merchants like Brembre or Walworth to a brief outline of the most morally exemplary medieval merchants, those very few who attained sainthood. This move involves a contradiction of sorts, because a common trait of those rare holy merchants seems to have been their abandonment of trade. St. Godric of Finchale, for example, started out in the late eleventh century as a beachcomber and then a pedlar, becoming a moderately successful merchant and ship owner. He later became a hermit, though he returned to trade briefly to support himself at a hermitage near Whitby; eventually he settled at Finchale.[41] He is remembered primarily for his poetry and devotion to the Virgin Mary, and for having performed austere penance, including a hairshirt and metal breastplate.[42] His Marian poems bear little direct relation to his early profession, though his prayer to St. Nicholas (patron of merchants along with sailors, criminals, and children) to "bring vs wel þare" could reflect either his mercantile travels or his many long pilgrimages.[43] Significantly for this study, the life of

Godric also shows that material charity was not always seen as a necessary or successful antidote to trade, particularly among those following the Egyptian ascetic tradition that associated avarice with the material world.[44] In an episode that emphasizes Godric's rejection of the material world, he is nearly tempted into avarice by a demon that uses his desire to support "pauperes vel inopes" [the poor and needy] to convince him to dig for buried treasure. Only when pygmy demons emerge from the excavation and begin to hurl smelly things at him does Godric realize his error, and chastise the demons:

Ecce, quod vestrum est percipite et possidete; pecunia thesauri vestri vobiscum sit in perditione; nam nihil quod vestrum, vel mundanæ pompæ sit, habere desidero, sed Christi confixus Cruci, Illum solum quæro.

[Behold, grab and take what is yours; may the wealth of your treasure be with you in perdition; for nothing do I desire to have of yours, or even of worldly pomp, but Christ transfixed on the Cross, him alone do I seek.][45]

Aside from showing the saint's power to resist demonic temptation, this story reflects the thoroughness of Godric's rejection of the worldly life, presenting even charity as a distraction from his isolation as a holy hermit.

Dying only twenty years after Godric, St. Homobonus similarly rejected a life in trade, but in his case material charity became one of his main saintly attributes. André Vauchez explains that "the features which are most characteristic of his lay status were his great charity, which won him the titles 'father of the poor' and 'comforter of the afflicted.' "[46] The centrality of charity to Homobonus's sanctity also resembles that of a better-known merchant saint, St. Francis of Assisi, though the mendicant Francis shows more kinship with Godric's abandonment of material wealth. In common with Godric, both Homobonus and Francis seem to have seen trade as something to reject, in Francis's case to the point of naked beggary. Similarly, a fourteenth-century Italian follower of St. Catherine of Siena, Giovanni Colombini, "had himself whipped...asking his followers to shout denunciations of his past business practices."[47] In all of these examples, trade stands in for the material world, which the individual must abjure before attaining spiritual success. The renunciation varies somewhat, but none of these men advocated trade, and only Homobonus seems to have been taken as a patron of merchants.[48] Although merchants were not excluded from sainthood, it was extremely rare, and one could not be a merchant and a saint at the same time.

More typical merchants are somewhat harder to pin down, in terms of their social standing. Obviously a merchant career required initial funds with which to buy merchandise, but the urban estate of merchants was never entirely distinct from either the gentry or the craft guilds. The relationship between rural and urban estates was complex, because successful guildsmen became merchants, successful merchants tended to buy land outside of town, and children of the rural gentry often moved to town and joined the estate of merchants through apprenticeship or marriage.[49] The crown's policy of distraint for knighthood, in which individuals with sufficient annual income (some years forty pounds per annum) were often compelled to accept knighthood, would also have tended to turn successful merchants into knights, though distraint was not enforced in London.[50] Over all, the interaction of a variety of social groups formed the merchant estate, which consisted primarily of the successes of the guild system and failures of the gentry, individuals able to slip into and out of the gentry and crafts with their success or failure. The rural gentry, prosperous rural commoners, and urban craftsmen regularly provided a replacement population to make up for the depletion of families inevitable to medieval urban life. Aspiring to join the merchant estate or having a family fortune created by a merchant ancestor do not necessarily imply, however, a persistent sense of estate solidarity between those currently working as merchants and the rest of the "middle class."

Despite the prominence of some merchants on the line between gentry and trade, like Sir Nicholas Brembre, it would be a mistake to characterize the estate of merchants as "people like him." While medieval England thronged with prosperous and powerful wool merchants, mercers, pepperers, fishmongers, and so on, it also had a plenitude of lesser merchants, ranging from craftsmen in their shops and chapmen with packs all the way up to powerful figures like Brembre. The key to the social range of merchants and their distinction from similarly prosperous rural gentry comes from a single social institution, the *franchise*, or the freedom of a town. As we can see in the examples of Brembre, Walworth, and Philpot, in London there was not a single Merchants' Guild that defined one as a merchant in the later Middle Ages, though several guilds were primarily mercantile.[51] Brembre and Philpot, grocers (sellers of bulk spices, dyes, and other commodities), traded in wool as well, while fishmongers like Walworth could also grow wealthy by investing in wool the profits of London's dependence on fresh and preserved fish.

Instead of there being a single guild of merchants, the franchise in general diffused the term "merchant" throughout the crafts and urban gentry by allowing a citizen with the franchise of a given town to trade in almost any commodity, at the same time that it labeled any trader a "merchant."[52] Craft guilds allowed one route to the franchise, but not the only one. For example, in London, the craft guilds collectively with the council of Aldermen controlled access to the franchise and thus to trade, and by the fourteenth century the franchise was available through inheritance, paying a fee (redemption), or through apprenticeship.[53] While in early fourteenth-century London purchasing the freedom from ward aldermen was the more common model (72 percent of freedoms in 1309–12), by mid-century the guilds had used the "Great Charter" of 1319 to gain control of most entries to the franchise.[54] The franchise allowed the estate of merchants to include successful craftspeople, who might then occupy the same social stratum as a member of the gentry who bought the franchise. That status could then be inherited. The franchise also granted the potential for, if not the promise of, a wide variety of merchant activity often unrelated to the craft in which an apprentice had succeeded. Sylvia Thrupp explains that while there were distinctly named crafts, in practice "a man who was described as a citizen and goldsmith might have been a wageworker, an independent craftsman with his own small shop, or a great merchant and financier with his fingers in many lines of business besides that of manufacturing articles of precious metal."[55] Thrupp provides examples of individuals trading far outside their crafts, as "anyone whose credit was good might take a plunge;"[56] a "merchant" might thus be any individual with a franchise in some municipality.[57] At the same time, many who could have defined themselves as "merchants" chose not to, preferring their guild identity as did the fishmonger Walworth, or other terms such as Brembre's insistence on his knighthood. The primary limitation on the spread of the estate of merchants was the limited urbanization of medieval England. Dyer explains that "a developed merchant class was confined to thirty or so of the larger towns, both ports and regional centres of trade."[58] Edward Miller and John Hatcher show the extent of the English inland and overseas trade in the Middle Ages, which blanketed Britain and northern Europe.[59] James Masschaele also calculates that roughly half of England's exported wool was produced by the peasantry independently from large manorial estates,[60] which would have required substantial mercantile effort to gather together all the wool. London also generally acted as the distribution point for overseas goods throughout England.[61]

The result of this diffusion of mercantile activity among citizens of towns, then, is that almost any urban citizen could conceivably become a merchant of some sort, great or small. Clearly it would require substantial ability and luck to grow wealthy, and the practice in London of allowing the franchise to be inherited or purchased would mean that powerful families could sometimes skip the apprenticeship process, but ultimately a merchant could have begun from anywhere on a fairly large social spectrum: "London apprentices...represented almost every social group in the kingdom, paupers and nobility excepted,"[62] and many were the children of gentry. This detail explains some of the confusion with John Gower's social position, because as either a member of the gentry or a merchant, he could easily have generated the documents that suggest he was the other. The line between merchant and gentry was never entirely clear, in part because of family relations where "a quarter of the wives of fourteenth-century aldermen whose parentage is known were the daughters of country landowners,"[63] and "marriages between gentry and mercantile families were not unusual."[64] Merchants also presented themselves like gentry, as they often bore coats of arms,[65] and "a merchant who enjoyed a large and regular income was regarded...in much the same light as a gentleman of equivalent wealth."[66] Given the potential for disaster in trade, less successful merchants had substantial downward mobility, as well.

The Charitable Guilds

Reliance on guilds as an avenue to the franchise further complicates this picture, because the concept of the guild was itself highly variable, including at the same time trade organizations, religious fraternities, and convivial fellowships. Traditionally scholars divided guilds into craft guilds and religious guilds, but Virginia Bainbridge explains how this distinction arises primarily from historiography of the late nineteenth century, and the difference between the economic and constitutional history approach of Toulmin Smith and the more sentimental ecclesiastical and social history approach of Herbert Westlake. Such an approach fails to account, she argues, for "religious elements [that] were part of the corporate life of all types of guilds. Their mixture of religious and secular activities defies their simple classification as essentially either secular or religious."[67] Certainly the craft guilds of large cities like London or York carried out religious activities along with their governing of their trades, and were dedicated like noncraft guilds to individual saints or divinities. For example, the Grocers of London were dedicated to St. Antonin,[68] the Tailors of London were dedicated to St. John the Baptist,[69] and the Mercers of York were dedicated to the Holy Trinity.[70] On the other hand, it could be difficult to tell that a specific guild was in fact related to trade, especially outside London. For example, the Gild of the Holy Trinity of Bishop's Lynn was not a craft guild, but did have a merchant membership and a direct political role in Lynn.[71] Guilds also generally had similar ordinances, focusing on regular meetings, livery, an oath, devotion to a saintly patron, perhaps charitable activities, and regulation of a craft if necessary. London craft guilds, for example, generally included clauses about "the election of masters or wardens," "the search...for defective goods," "the making and marketing of goods," "the acceptance and training of apprentices," and "excluding non-members from working in the craft."[72]

This similarity in ordinances between guilds with or without a craft is further complicated by the ordinance form itself, and its overt goal of idealizing the association of its members. This idealization could perhaps be an application of civic power, as Heather Swanson argues that the ordinance form was part of the mechanism by which York's mercantile oligarchy imposed guild divisions on the workers of York. She suggests that guild ordinances "were not intended to reveal the economic structure of the town, but rather to reflect the order that the authorities wished to see imposed on society, a hierarchical and above all male-orientated [sic] order."[73] While her argument for the artificiality of York's guild structure is not entirely convincing (see chapter 6), her warning about the ideological function of ordinances is valuable. Bearing in mind that these ordinances reflect an ideal self-conception for the guilds, it is still striking how regularly mercantile guild ordinances include provisions for different sorts of charity. Such an emphasis certainly accords with individual practice on the part of medieval English merchants. Thrupp describes "the custom of setting aside at least a third of a man's movables...as a kind of voluntary death duty for pious and charitable purposes."[74] She may overstate the extent to which such a practice was voluntary, as Barbara A. Hanawalt explains that London law required property to be divided such that a third "was for the testator to dispose of for the good of his soul," a third was for children or heirs, and a third for a widow's dower.[75]

Voluntary or not, this practice could leave heirs in an uncomfortable or even dire financial position, which suggests that the Mayor and Aldermen behind such a law weighed the salvific benefits of charitable bequests above the clear difficulties those bequests caused for impoverished heirs. While merchants often lacked clear male heirs,[76] such bequests would also mean that mercantile success could not easily be inherited, encouraging an ethos that merchants should be self-made. This emphasis on personal charity also served another function. Given the church's traditional distaste for the profit economy (see later discussion), such bequests would also help to make restitution for any sins of financial practice. Given the sustained clerical debate over permissible financial practice, regular personal charity functioned as a sort of heavenly insurance, just in case. As Thrupp puts it, a merchant's "priest would tell him that worldly standards should at this point [death] give way before humility and piety: he should spend his money on alms, not on vain [funeral] display. Torn between the habits of a lifetime and a fear that his priest might be right, the merchant either compromised or left the problem to his executors."[77] This material charity was also integrated into the guild system itself. For example, the Mercers of York integrated a hospital into the structure of their guild, which institutionalized the guild members' collective charity. The Mercers kept the Hospital of the Holy Trinity, and their ordinance integrates the management of the hospital with the management of the guild itself, with the master of the hospital subordinate to the guild's master.[78] In London, the aldermen ultimately took over administration of "the hospital of St. Mary of Bethlehem," though that situation was fairly complicated.[79] The Grocers of London had no charitable institution, but they did explicitly sponsor charity as a guild: they promised in their 1375 ordinance to pay 10d. yearly apiece to support the guild's priest, and to support charity for impoverished members and others in the community.[80] It was particularly common for such charity to have been directed at the needy within the guild. The London "Ordinances of the Weavers' Fraternity, 1378–79" promises that the guild will pay "in caas ony brother or suster of the brotherede falle into swych poverte thorw Godes ordinaunce and nought thorw his owen defaute."[81] The fourteenth-century London White-Tawyers' ordinance promised the same, as did the London Grocers' 1376 ordinance.[82] Fourteenth-century ordinances of both the Drapers and Mercers of London mandated the use of guild dues for alms to impoverished members of those guilds, while the Drapers' ordinance provided for burial of poor brothers at the guild's expense, and encouraged brothers to leave money in their wills in exchange for which the surviving brothers would pray for their souls.[83]

Such policies were ultimately self-serving, but the practice of caring for impoverished brethren would act as an insurance policy, reinforce group solidarity, and reassure guild members that they were adequately charitable. Solidarity was particularly important, and guild rules elsewhere in Europe required members to attend member funerals, making the guild act as a "support system in time of grief."[84] Ordinances of noncraft guilds were similar in their charitable provisions. The ordinance of the Gild of St. Katherine, Aldersgate, for example, required the same support of impoverished brothers, while the guild dues were explicitly for the purpose of "almesse."[85] According to Steven Epstein, the fact that most craft guilds were also religious guilds led to these similar practices in craft and noncraft guilds, which combined their business activities with religious activities.[86] Charitable activity also spread beyond the guilds themselves, as "frequently the guild attended to the needs of the urban poor."[87]

What is less clear is how effective such efforts were at relieving the misery of the urban poor. Judith M. Bennett describes the institution of "charity ales," another form of poor relief which made up for the need left after the "empowered rich helped the impotent poor."[88] These ales, where the recipient of charity sold personally produced ale to his or her neighbors at inflated prices, allowed a great deal of money to be raised within the estate of the relatively poor. The necessity for them argues that guilds' efforts to aid the poor were limited in scope. This view of guild charity is increasingly influential, as Ben R. McRee points out recent challenges to the efficacy and scale of guild charity made by Caroline Barron and Miri Rubin. Such recent work suggests that individual charitable grants were small, and that promises of assistance far outweigh evidence of actual assistance. McRee argues that poor relief was only one of many goals of guild relief programs, and that such charitable activities worked also to "protect the public reputations of the organizations that sponsored them" and to "strengthen gild solidarity by reinforcing the sense of mutual obligation among gild members."[89]

These latter goals were particularly determined by the social status of the guild itself, as McRee explains that among those guilds presenting returns in 1388–89, at least, the guilds that supported their impoverished members were those "whose ambitious goals and high public profiles set them apart from other fraternal organizations."[90] Such charity seems to have gone hand in hand with solidarity-building activities, since such guilds' "returns mentioned public processions, burial services, masses in honor of their patron saints, special rules governing behavior of their members, and the existence of liveries symbolizing organizational solidarity far more often than did those of other fraternities."[91] Also, because these guilds were so high-profile, they tended not to have to give very much aid to members,[92] which might explain why the York Mercers' ordinances stipulate both member assistance *and* a hospital with a wider pool of people to assist. When we recall McRee's observation that charitable guilds were "overwhelming urban in origin,"[93] it becomes clear that those guilds which best fit his model of the most charitable guilds are those guilds which were also the most likely to be made up of successful merchants, those urbanites with ambition, social standing, and money. Although the charity of these guilds provided only a small portion of the charitable resources available in the Middle Ages, which included "hospitals, help-ales, monastic alms, family aid, individual acts of charity, handouts to mourners at funeral and obit services, and parish assistance,"[94] such charity clearly performed a necessary ideological function. While guild charity did not cure poverty, it did go far to address medieval merchants' need to be charitable.

The Trouble with Merchants: The Antimercantile
Position and the Rules of Trade

This need arose directly from the church's response to the medieval rise
of commerce and money in general, and the tension between this charity
and the church's censure of much mercantile practice forms the subject
of much of this book. The church's response to the economy was complex, though. On the one hand, the church had long owned much of the
productive land available, roughly 25 percent in 1430, and thus dominated the agricultural economy.[95] Churchmen also played a powerful role
in the money economy, as for example they were not above disputes
about their rights to tithes,[96] and the movement of papal tithes drove the
international banking that brought church income from far-away places
like England.[97] Despite the church's implication in the money economy,
though, many theologians remained ideologically uncomfortable with
money. Richard Newhauser makes it clear that theologians found avarice
deeply troubling from the very beginnings of Christian thought, with
an ongoing tension between ascetic abandonment of material goods and
almsgiving as the solutions to greed.[98] Closer to the period of this study,
Lester K. Little outlines the ideological conflict created by the shift from
a gift-based model of exchange to a profit-based economy, so that the
traditional ban on usury coincided with clerical discomfort with money
in general. This discomfort is the main source of the antimercantile ideology, which this book traces through late medieval English literature.
Little explains its origins, arguing that during the transition to a money
economy "money was seen as an instrument of exchange that had devil-like, magical powers of luring people and then of corrupting them,"
powers ultimately associated with avarice.[99] This association is clearest
for Little in satiric portrayals of that sin in the visual arts. Images range
from a "small crouching figure, his distorted mouth open, at the ready
to devour, while he retains the matter accumulated in moneybags" to "a
rather distinguished-looking person, both handsome and well-dressed,
but with a moneybag pulling at his neck and with a dragon-serpent lurk-
ing nearby or a grotesque devil right behind."[100] The "rich man" had
similar iconographical attributes, so that "when the rich man dies, we see
under the bed his moneybags with big, slimy serpents coiled about them.
The rich man's soul, moreover, is poked into a gaping hell mouth by a
devil who gleefully wields a pitchfork."[101] Little also cites a variety of textual examples of this moral opposition to commerce, including Honorius
of Autun and Peter Lombard.[102] The story of St. Godric finding dung-
flinging demons of avarice instead of buried treasure (see earlier) would
also fit into this tradition. All of these examples date to the eleventh and

twelfth centuries, rather than the period of my study, but these visual representations of money as a dead weight drawing the possessor to hell would have remained quite visible in church architecture. The satirists I study here show in their straightforward links of merchants to avarice that the antimercantile ideology embodied by these images had discursive currency long after Honorius of Autun, Peter Lombard, and Godric of Finchale were gone.

On the other hand, the estates satire view of money, which kept alive an earlier association of money with greed, was not always shared by later theologians who discussed trade. Indeed, the development of the theory of the just price shows how sophisticated the church's view of economics could be. Edwin S. Hunt and James M. Murray explain that Albertus Magnus and Thomas Aquinas developed the concept of the just price in the thirteenth century,[103] a concept that allowed market prices to dominate. This is not to say, however, that this theory was perfect, as it allowed both challenges to the fairness of almost any price, and justification for almost any shift in price. N. J. G. Pounds explains that the theory tried both to posit an appropriate price for a commodity and the labor involved to bring it to market, and to allow for a variable market price, by balancing use value and demand against the occasional need for price regulation.[104] The contradictions within this theory reflect contradictions within the church's approach to the economy, and go back very early. Lianna Farber traces conflict over value and pricing to Augustine of Hippo's schema of natural and economic values: natural value would be "an absolute scale that works according to God's creation," while economic value derived from utility.[105] The latter type of value develops into the "just price," but the shadow of the former continued to haunt economic theorists. In practical terms, as Hunt and Murray explain, elements in the church that were involved in the economy "favored a flexible approach, while its theologians viewed the rising tide of business as a threat to morality deserving greater, not less, control."[106] Just price theory created anxiety because of its failure clearly to balance rising demand against price gouging, but in practice it adapted to fit mercantile realities.

We see a similar ambivalence to money and merchants' potential to gain it dishonestly in the common satiric concern with exchange, chevisance, and usury. The example of exchange allows us to see how the needs of antimercantile ideology created a gap between the definitions of key economic terms used by antimercantile and promercantile discourses. Jill Mann outlines how "an overwhelming number of satirists associate [merchants] with fraud and dishonesty," and how monetary exchange "was often connected with shady or illegal dealings;" similarly, the term "chevisance" is often "a simple euphemism for usury," and

Mann shows its affiliation with the term "exchange" in Chaucer's *General Prologue,* Gower's *Mirour de l'Omme* and in *Piers Plowman.*[107] "Chevisance" had quite a range of meaning, including a loan with or without usury, a stratagem, acquisition, and sustenance.[108] Although "exchange" lacked the semantic range of "chevisance," there was much more to it as an economic concept than the antimercantile ideology might allow. Kenneth S. Cahn shows how exchange was one of many practices developed to generate credit within the usury prohibition, so that the link between exchange and usury was not as straightforward as satirists might suggest. Cahn explains that there were two sorts of exchange common in the late Middle Ages, "manual exchange," or the direct exchange of one currency for another, and "merchant's exchange" or *cambio reale,* a form of short-term, nonusurious loan that Hunt and Murray term the "bill of exchange."[109] Manual exchange was not practiced in late fourteenth-century England,[110] but the bill of exchange was fundamental to international trade, for it freed merchants from the necessity of transporting bulky specie.[111] It was not, however, generally usurious in the modern, exploitative sense of that term. The bill of exchange "made it possible for one party to receive a sum of money in one currency in one place on one date and repay it in another currency at another place at a later date."[112] Thus, a merchant could "sell" Flemish currency (shields) in London, be paid in English currency (pounds) on the spot, but not have to deliver the shields to an agent in Bruges for a month or two. Each currency was generally worth a little more in its country of origin, so on average this practice yielded a roughly 12 percent annual profit for the lender.[113] The borrower thus paid for the privilege of using the currency for a few months, and avoided the risky shipping of bullion.

While such bills of exchange did not function as modern credit to increase the money supply substantially, they did much to facilitate international financial transactions, and were eventually used by "the great institutions of church and government."[114] There was still room for fraud in this exchange, lending some currency to exchange's regular appearance in satirical literature, and not all merchants were blameless. Still, the satires' discourse of condemnation was more a result of the church's critique of the dangerous power of money than an indication of necessarily shady practice. There was moral ground to condemn some exchanges, such as "dry exchange," in which the regular practice of a business loan would be used to cover usury by creating an imaginary delivery overseas. This practice, which Cahn points to in *Piers Plowman,* helps to account for the use of the term "exchange" as a marker of dishonesty.[115] Satirists presented this potential for abuse as the norm, though, and combined it with concerns about money in general, because such an interpretation of exchange fits the needs of antimercantile discourse, which described the worst possible mercantile activity and attributed it to the entire estate. While this practice fits the rhetorical needs of estates satire, the distance between practices observed by satirists and those determined by the ideology surrounding the individual estates has not always been clear in the case of merchants. Satiric examples of issues like exchange show how the church's worries about merchandise had expanded from specific clerical concerns with money to a more widespread mistrust of merchants.

Actual usury, on the other hand, never had the clerical acceptance that the bill of exchange eventually found, with the result that the accusation of usury remained the most powerful critique available to satirists. Certainly the ambivalence of the term "chevisance" contributed to the blurred line between licit exchange and usury, so that the collocation of exchange with usury provides much of the former's satiric negative connotations. Usury itself was clearly defined, however, and John Noonan links the church's reasoning for the ban to its distaste for money as "technically fruitless and useless."[116] Noonan insists that usury was defined as lending for interest, rather than necessarily including other purely monetary practices like exchange,[117] but satiric depictions of finance blurred those definitions. The problem of an absolute definition of usury was obvious to medieval merchants, as it lumped consumption loans in with the productive loans necessary for economic growth.[118] The church eventually accepted a distinction between good and bad lending, so that canon law eventually distinguished between business and "distress" loans, with only the latter to be condemned.[119] The practice of the English church courts reinforced this distinction between usurious and business loans. R. H. Helmholz explains that while English canon law used a strict definition of usury, and the law provided for excommunication of offenders, such an interpretation was not generally enforced.[120] Instead, only conspicuous loans with high interest were challenged, and "the English church courts prosecuted only...lenders who had entered into relatively small transactions, and at relatively large rates of interest."[121] The evolution of business practice allowed by this pattern of (non)enforcement was economically necessary, but this gap between law and enforcement led to a situation where any successful merchant could conceivably be accused of practices that could be strictly defined as usury, even if he had not made any distress loans, and did not consider himself a usurer. These issues were then further complicated by the fact that Italians came to dominate international finance and credit, and were often favored by the English crown in exchange for loans. The Italian companies were extremely unpopular in London, and Italians were occasionally the victims of violence and murder at the hands of London merchants.[122]

20   ANTIMERCANTILISM IN LITERATURE

Caught between the demands of their commerce and the church's skepticism of their financial practice, merchants occupied an uncomfortable ideological position. As D. Vance Smith characterizes "later antimercantile discourse," merchants were represented in "two irreconcilable ways": both "at the heart of fourteenth-century society," and "condemned...because of what was seen as a precedent set by Christ and because of their involvement in potentially usurious practices."[123] As Christians, they could not escape theological challenges to their practices, while as not entirely voluntary financiers to the crown,[124] the foremost English merchants were under substantial pressure to make enough to offset royal loans that stood little chance of being repaid. At the same time, the king routinely played them off against their Italian rivals. The rewards of merchandise were potentially high, as Sir William de la Pole's son, Michael, wound up the Earl of Suffolk, and many merchants rose to become prosperous rural landowners.[125] Still, constant concerns about financial and spiritual security took their toll, and merchants' practice of leaving so much to charity reflects this anxiety. Conditions were changing slowly, however. As we will see, even the more directly antimercantile satires of the late fourteenth century bore within them traces of the emergent acceptance of trade, while by the late fifteenth century, mercantile emphasis on charity had entered the mainstream of popular piety through didactic poetry and the cycle drama.

Reading (Like) Merchants?

The development of this ideological dialectic within fourteenth- and fifteenth-century English literature then begs the question of just how involved those merchants were with the textual culture that sought to chastise or encourage them. Fortunately this question is growing easier to answer than it once was, though evidence remains less than abundant. The main avenues of inquiry here involve address to merchants as an inscribed audience, evidence of mercantile ownership of literary manuscripts, and inquiry into the interconnecting social and professional networks of authors, scribes, and merchants.[126] A sustained study into mercantile reading habits is long overdue, but some preliminary conclusions can be drawn here. In terms of merchants as an inscribed audience, my analysis in the following chapters will address this question more directly for the specific texts under discussion, some of which are more overtly aimed at merchants than others. One fundamental principle guides all such discussions, which is that there seems little point in any writer addressing the failings of a social group in depth and detail without some corresponding expectation that the group under discussion would somehow receive that correction; for a group known to be literate and able to afford books, why would any author not address that group directly? This question can remain an actual question because of the relative dearth of hard evidence about actual ownership of literary manuscripts. There is some evidence of mercantile ownership of Chaucer and Gower manuscripts, though more in the fifteenth century. Though mercantile tastes in general seem to have run toward religious texts, others—mercers, for example—did own literary books: Thomas Roos owned a copy of *Piers Plowman*, Thomas Crisp a copy of the *Confessio Amantis*, and William Fetiplace owned a Chaucer manuscript.[127] William Caxton, the printer, was a mercer, and Anne F. Sutton attests to the "high incidence of mercer book-ownership."[128] Sylvia Thrupp similarly suggests that mercantile tastes ran toward religion and history, but that mercantile demand drove the book market.[129] The manuscript miscellanies that contain the "Childe of Bristowe" poems certainly meet this mercantile taste, and the manuscript with the "Childe of Bristowe" itself also contains Chaucer's *Prioress's Tale*.[130] The sole manuscript of the York Cycle was the town's official register,[131] though as a performed text its audience would have included anyone who saw the plays. Unfortunately it is harder to tie most of the other texts examined in this book to an initial mercantile readership; Chaucer manuscripts date to the fifteenth century,[132] and while the manuscript of Gower's *Mirour de l'Omme* dates to the late fourteenth century, there are no indications of its medieval ownership.[133] The sole manuscript of *The Book of Margery Kempe* belonged to a Carthusian priory,[134] and manuscripts of *Piers Plowman* tend to lack ownership markings, though the "educated laymen of modest background" whom A. V. C. Schmidt includes in the poem's initial audience could well include modest members of the merchant estate.[135] Still, it is important to remember that it is generally understood in manuscript studies that we have only a fraction of the manuscripts copied; we should not assume that a lack of abundant evidence for initial mercantile readers precludes their existence.

The probability of such an audience also goes up in the light of recent work on the scribes who actually created the manuscripts. While not all London scribes can be named, it is clear that those who can be often worked both for the guilds and as literary copyists. The most notable of these is undoubtedly Adam Pinkhurst, a member of the Scriveners' Company, scribe of the Hengwrt and Ellesmere manuscripts of *The Canterbury Tales*, and scribe and account keeper for the Mercers' Company.[136] Pinkhurst also produced a *Piers Plowman*, Chaucer's *Boece*, part of a *Confessio Amantis*, and at least parts of another *Canterbury Tales* and Chaucer's *Troilus and Criseyde*.[137] A contemporary of Pinkhurst, "Scribe D," worked on a *Confessio Amantis* manuscript with Pinkhurst and Thomas Hoccleve, as well as a *Piers Plowman* manuscript; "Scribe D" was more of a Gower specialist than Pinkhurst or Hoccleve, though, and seemed to work primarily for civil servants.[138] Pinkhurst was not the only scribe with both a mercantile and literary body of work; the "Hammond scribe," working in the fifteenth century, copied authors including Hoccleve, Lydgate, Chaucer, legal documents, and a collection of guild-oriented documents including a translation of Oresme's *De moneta*, and documents on the rights of the franchise.[139] More prominently, the authors Hoccleve and Thomas Usk were both professional scribes themselves; Usk worked for the Goldsmiths' Company, and while Hoccleve was primarily a Clerk of the Office of the Privy Seal, his work involved receipts for royal transactions with merchants.[140] Admittedly five men do not make a reading community, but especially for the London poets, Langland, Gower, and Chaucer, whose work at least sometimes shared scribes with the guilds, we can draw a direct line between the mercers and the poets through a single man, Pinkhurst. Perhaps Pinkhurst was exceptional, and Chaucer shared the mercers' desire to hire the best. Given that Usk knew Chaucer's work,[141] and these other scribes all copied Chaucer, Gower, or Langland professionally, it seems more likely that there was no absolute division between literary scribal work and other scrivening for hire. This common market means that merchants, whose work required literacy and whose success allowed for the purchase of books, also clearly had access to the full range of London literature. One did not have to know the author to read something—one had to know the right scribe.[142] Merchants were never a primary audience for writers like Langland, Gower, or Chaucer, but it would be a mistake to discount them as part of the original audience.

CHAPTER 2

LANGLAND'S MERCHANTS AND
THE MATERIAL AND SPIRITUAL ECONOMIES
OF *PIERS PLOWMAN B*

In 1949, E. Talbot Donaldson dismissed William Langland's satire on medieval merchants, characterizing it as entirely conventional: "cheating, along with a disposition to keep shops open on Sundays and holy days, is the occupational hazard incurred by tradesmen. . . . But so long as they trade fairly, and make distribution of their profits in good works, Truth, and the poet of all three texts, bear them no ill will and promise them heaven at the last."[1] While *Piers Plowman B* does often follow the antimercantile estates satire tradition, though, Langland transcends conventionality by questioning the very possibility and necessity of honest trade in Christian society. Langland goes beyond the simple opposition of trade and alms cited by Donaldson, applying this tension between trade and charity to contrasting worldly and spiritual economies. For Langland, merchants best embody the irresolvable conflict between the often contradictory necessities of the material and spiritual worlds. He complicates mercantile language by expanding on a technique from the New Testament as he, in James Simpson's terms, "consistently uses economic imagery to describe spiritual relations;"[2] his description of the two economies constantly intermingles. The poem presents worldly economics as *both* antithetical to *and* implicated in the success of the spiritual economy, and these economies overlap when material economics functions as a metaphor for the spiritual enterprise of salvation. This shifting use of mercantile language and characters creates a persistent tension between Langland's traditional disdain for worldly profit and his emphasis on the hoped-for (and forever deferred) success of Piers's metaphorical plowing.

Throughout his long poem, Langland models his complicated relationship with the material world outside his visions, a material world of which he does not entirely approve, but for the problems of which he retains much sympathy. F. R. H. Du Boulay associates Langland's emphasis on social order and stereotypes of estate with the turbulence of the times, and a desire for people to keep in their places.[3] This characterization of Langland's social conservatism has become somewhat commonplace, particularly because of David Aers's readings of the half-acre passage in terms of the Statute of Laborers, seeing that section of the poem reinforcing "gentry legislation and their parliamentary petition against 'vagrant' labourers."[4] While Langland's approach to the poor is more complicated than simple class resentment and conservatism, Aers's and Du Boulay's description of what Ralph Hanna recently labeled the "Langlandian nostalgic imaginary"[5] seems apt, and has driven materialist approaches to *Piers Plowman*. Seen in this light, merchants belonged by their very nature to an unstable estate, one defined by a potential for both spectacular success and abrupt failure, and one that relied on the very instability Du Boulay suggests as problematic for Langland. Langland taps into the deep distrust of merchants and merchandise preserved by the satiric tradition to analyze the sin inherent to involvement in the profit economy, while at the same time retaining merchandise as a powerful metaphor for spiritual enterprise. The poem is not about trade per se, but much of its message relies on economic discourse and imagery.

The Merchant Sin: Coveitise

We see the problem with merchants most directly, of course, in the poem's two merchant sinners: Coveitise and Haukyn. Coveitise is clearly a figure from estates satire, and his sins are a catalogue of mercantile malpractice. The poem also singles Coveitise out from the other sins, because of his lack of a purely spiritual penance. Only Coveitise among the Seven Deadly Sins gets the response from Repentaunce, "Thow art an vnkynde creature—I kan þee noȝt assoille / Til þow make restitucion" (B.V. 269–70),[6] a response in line with the church's position on the sins of usury and theft.[7] Coveitise is the only sin with a trade,[8] and it is also evident that Coveitise practices direct fraud. His behavior clearly exceeds the loosening of the restrictions on mercantile financial practice advocated by Peter John Olivi, and thus fits neatly into such catalogues of sin as the one in Thomas Aquinas's *Summa Theologica*.[9] Coveitise's skill at stretching out cloth to sell more of it (B.V. 205–10) directly cheats a system of just price, by creating an increase through dishonesty, and this fraud matches guilds' concerns with consistent measures. In *Piers Plowman*'s own terms, Coveitise's constant misuse of measuring denies Conscience's "mesurable hire" (B.III. 256) when "ten yerdes or twelue tolled out þrittene" (B.V. 210). Similarly his wife Rose's pound that "peised a quarter moore / Than...whan I weyed truþe" (B.V. 213–14) directly contradicts both the just price and fair measure, and she commits fraud when "peny ale and puddyng ale she poured togideres" (B.V. 216). Such mercantile malpractice allows Langland to associate excessive profit with usury in the person of Coveitise, both sins signifying increase at the expense of others through the desire for money.

This linkage of fraud and just price theory to the separate problem of the usury ban allows Langland to imply a greater connection between the two than was required by medieval economic theory. When Repentaunce follows up his first questions about restitution by asking Coveitise, "Vsedestow euere vsurie?" (B.V. 236), the merchant replies with a list of economic practices inclusive of associated sins (B.V. 238–52).[10] This list of economic practices includes most forms of medieval credit subsisting around the edges of usury, and also involves mistreatment of money itself. There is something vaguely blasphemous about lending "for loue of the cros" (B.V. 240) on the reverse of silver coins. Coveitise "pares" or clips "the hevyeste" coins (B.V. 239), makes loans in order to gain the collateral, "to legge a wed and lese it," (B.V. 240), and hides loans inside the purchase of his own "chaffare" from people "to bene hire brocour after" (B.V. 243–44).[11] Coveitise also violates crown control of specie both by clipping and in "eschaunges and cheuysaunces" (B.V. 245) of different currencies, and he defrauds the Church by embezzling Peter's Pence and participating in advanced banking practice through the paper transfers of funds in "Lumbardes lettres" (B.V. 247). Finally, and perhaps most transgressively, he has loaned to knights in the name of the problematic "maintenance" (B.V. 249).

This term approaches the heart of the sins associated by *Piers Plowman* with usury and abuse of money in this context, because "maintenance" implicates money in the problem of class transgression and the instability of one's estate. As Howard Kaminsky points out, one of the most common uses in this period of the term "estate" was in "a formula used very often in a grant of revenues or other rights to an individual [which] justified the grant as necessary to help the recipient 'maintain his estate.'"[12] Presumably those landowners unable to convince the crown to support their estates had recourse to loans, so that borrowing to "maintain" oneself in this modern sense of the term would be socially acceptable. We see the danger in such loans, though, in records of merchants becoming landowners by acquiring manors as security on defaulted loans.[13] Although we cannot know what bills the former owners of such manors had to pay, loans to landowners potentially undermined the social hierarchy. We see these fears of social instability even more clearly in other usages of the term "maintenance" that Langland plays upon here. Schmidt explains "maintenance" in the modern sense used by Kaminsky, in his note that "Greed bought the 'protection' of lords, or less probably, lent them money to enable them to maintain their position."[14] Contemporary definitions of "maintenance," though, ranged from collective abuse of the law courts to the increasing practice of lords retaining gangs of men outside the normal limits of feudal holding of retainers.[15] Paul Strohm explains that these extrafeudal gangs were often characterized by livery and transgressions of their social position.[16] The livery given these men might represent how usury made "many a kny3t boþe mercer and draper" (B.V. 251), while that line also suggests a violation of estate boundaries. Langland thus establishes the sin as a divisive force in the community. Coveitise's customers also share his sin, for the most part. Lords borrowing for love of their armed gangs could hardly be free of avarice, and the ready availability of borrowed funds amplifies the social disturbance made possible by all forms of maintenance.

This suggestion of aristocrats as both victims and accomplices emphasizes one reason usury is particularly negative for Langland. Not only does usury abuse the poor through loan-sharking, so that Coveitise has "as muche pite of pouere men as pedlere haþ of cattes" (B.V. 254), but "maintenance" reveals how unstable the feudal estate structure had become. Usury might allow aristocrats to maintain their standard of living, and money borrowed for maintenance of liveried men would allow lords to increase their power, but the upward and downward movement enabled by usury reveals the rotten core of late fourteenth-century feudalism. These moments when Langland seems most conservative in his estate ideology suggest one reason Coveitise is so disturbing: the usurer acknowledges and even lives off of the instability of estate in late feudalism as he makes knights into mercers and drapers, either selling their clothes to pay debts or giving their men illicit livery, while appearing to allow them to stay knights or even gain political power out of proportion with their estate. Smith also points out that the language in this section of the poem echoes the language of a 1363 royal writ against usury, which similarly blurs the line between lending and trade.[17] The implications of Langland's satire thus expand further when we consider how Coveitise's practices overlap with basic mercantile finance. Labeling mercantile exchange and "Lumbardes lettres" of credit as usury helps to cement the link in Langland's economics between usury and trade in general, because these practices were necessary to international trade, and were not unique to merchants.

What sets Langland's treatment of mercantile sin apart from most other estates satires, though, is that Langland is willing to suggest the

abandonment of trade altogether. Coveitise, and through him the merchants he represents, can only find salvation in Langland's spiritual
system through Repentaunce's advice: "marchaundise, leue it!" (B.V.
285). The poem here emphasizes "restitucion" (B.V. 228) and charity or
Largenesse.[18] Here Langland most clearly states the opposition between
mercantile malpractice like fraud and usury and their antidote, charity,
when Repentance asks Coveitise "hastow pite on pouere men þat borwe
mote nedes" (B.V. 253). Coveitise's response that he has "as muche pite
of pouere men as pedlere haþ of cattes" (B.V. 254) establishes the dialectic between charity and trade that will dominate Langland's use of
trade and its language throughout the poem. Repentaunce's citation of
Augustine here outlines the heart of Coveitise's problem: "non dimittitur
peccatum donec restituatur ablatum" [The sin is not forgiven until the
stolen goods are returned] (B.V. 272a).[19] This context links Coveitise's
profit directly to theft, for which the church unequivocally required restitution.[20] Repentaunce distinguishes restitution from charity when he
argues that the possession of stolen goods precludes charitable donation:
"were I frere of þat hous þer good feiþ and charite is, / I nolde cope us
wiþ þi catel, ne oure kirk amende, / Ne haue a peny to my pitaunce of
þyne,.../ And I wiste witterly þow were swich as þow tellest" (B.V.
264–68). Langland establishes the spiritual economy alongside the dangerous material one through the economics of restitution. Repentaunce's
plan of possible salvation for Coveitise, if he "wite neuere to whiche ne
whom to restitue" (B.V. 290), negotiates between these economies: the
sinful merchant can launder his goods through the spiritual economy by
giving his ill-gotten gain to the bishop, because the bishop can "answere
for [him] at þe heiȝe dome" (B.V. 293). Because of his office, the bishop
can "yeue a rekenyng: / What he lerned yow in Lente,.../ And what he
lente yow of Oure Lordes good, to lette yow fro synne" (B.V. 294–96).
    Langland's puns here, which rely on words having both worldly and
spiritual meanings, emphasize the overlap of economic and spiritual language: the bishop *lends* Lent, and exchanging *goods* for *good*, God's *caritas*
allows God himself to become Coveitise's spiritual *and* material creditor,
through the bishop's "rekenyng." The material economy provides a metaphor for the spiritual process of redemption, at the same time terms such
as *lent* and *good* accurately describe the spiritual process Langland suggests. James Simpson suggests one way to read this overlap of language;
he ties the paradox of the language of profit describing salvation to biblical uses of mercantile language along with the polemical tradition of the
Franciscans.[21] While Simpson concludes that Langland consistently uses
spiritual economic imagery to reject the material profit economy,[22] his
analysis might take more account of the slippage involved in Langland's

punning style. On a first reading this passage follows Simpson's model, so that the shift from *goods* to *good* might not necessarily satirize the bishop as a usurer, because the lending of divine grace doesn't come from the bishop but from God himself. The type of divine money-laundering Repentaunce suggests here does seem potentially within the range of a Bishop's cure of souls. One must wonder, however, how safe a solution this ultimately presents, given Langland's complaint in the Prologue that bishops should not handle accounts, and that "drede is at þe laste / Lest Crist in Consistorie acorse ful manye!" (B.Prol. 98–99) for their economic involvement. In a poem where the church's own problems with money abound, we must remember that while a bishop might have the spiritual authority to avoid the taint of finance, there can be no guarantee of immunity. Any solution that requires a reliable prelate is subject to abuse and hence flawed within the world of *Piers Plowman*. This mercantile language does not pun in only one direction: just as *goods* become *good*, *good* can become a *good* to be sold. We will see further overlap of the sins to which merchants and ecclesiastics are prone in the other primarily mercantile figure in the poem, Haukyn, who works for the Pope.

A Sinful Merchant: Haukyn

By Passus B.XIII, the poem has mostly moved away from estates satire material, and Haukyn receives very different solutions to Coveitise's problems. Still, while Piers Plowman himself symbolically rejects the material economy at B.VII.118, that world returns in the body of Haukyn. Stella Maguire characterizes the poem's movement from the internal world of Passūs B.VIII–XII back into more worldly terms through Haukyn's function as a figure, arguing that Haukyn is the "embodiment" of the more material world of the poem's earlier passūs.[23] Although at first Haukyn seems positive, he soon reveals that he is particularly susceptible to sin. As John Alford explains, "he is described first as a minstrel, then as a waferer, beggar, merchant, money lender, and plowman; and he is indiscriminately prey to all the deadly sins, so that the value of a 'characteristic' weakness is quickly lost as each vice in his portrait gives way to another."[24] We see Haukyn's virtues in that he hates "ydelnesse" (B.XIII. 239), and he works for Piers (B.XIII. 238), but Maguire argues that these virtues themselves represent a subtle challenge to the material world. Thus, according to Maguire, Langland "build[s] up as favourable a picture as possible of this particular narrow form of Active Life, and then show[s] how inadequate it is to keep man from hell or to bring him to heaven."[25] Haukyn's profession itself is of course necessary to the Eucharist, as "alle trewe trauaillours and tiliers of þe erþe, / From Mighelmesse to Mighelmesse I fynde hem wiþ wafres" (B.XIII. 240– 41), so that it seems perhaps a licit form of trade. Still, Haukyn invites suspicions of his business when he goes on to explain how he finds "payn for þe Pope and prouendre for his palfrey," but is paid only with "a pardon wiþ a peis of leed and two polles [*heads*] amyddes!" (B.XIII. 244–47). This exchange is not quite simony, but its mixing of the material and spiritual economies, exchanging a *good* for *goods*, emphasizes the extent to which the church was tied up in the material economy. Haukyn's *wished-for* exchange, a "personage...of þe Popes ʒifte" (B.XIII. 246) does imply the simony of buying a benefice, so that Haukyn at least desires to commit that sin, though papal preferments were only about 50 percent successful in this period.[26] Given the relatively small scale of Haukyn's attempted simony, exchange of food for pardon underlines the extent to which this exchange is satirical; bribery with Eucharistic wafers is particularly blasphemous. The problematic nature of pardons themselves further complicates this little transaction. Piers's "pure tene" of Passus VII (B.VII.115) should leave us suspicious of pardons in general. If pardons signify clerical greed, with this exchange Haukyn and his Pope implicate each other.

Our suspicions of Haukyn's motives gain further textual support when the waferer wants more. He explains his desire for "a salue for þe pestilence" (B.V. 249) from the Pope, with which he would be "prest to þe peple, paast for to make, /...founde I þat his pardoun / Miʒte lechen a man" (B.XIII. 251–54). Haukyn's desire to cure plague seems commendable, but his fantasy of having access to the magic inherent in "the power þat Peter hymself hadde" (B.XIII. 255) shows that, like Simon Magus, he does not really understand the nature of the Church's power. Haukyn's undermines pardons' invocation of limited papal power by using the reader's skepticism of their healing power to challenge their pardoning power. If Haukyn cannot understand Papal power, Popes who sign those pardons may not understand it either. Haukyn's power fantasy also recalls Coveitise's stretching of cloth and Glotoun's over-conviviality, since Haukyn wishes he could increase the pope's payment for food in terms of being "buxom and busy aboute breed and drynke" (B.XIII. 252) for the papal court. This overlap of vicarious gluttony and direct avarice reinforces how Haukyn unites the sins in a single personification, and the poem uses a common desire for excessive increase to link those sins.

This variety of sins becomes clearer with Haukyn's soiled coat, which leaves no doubt that this mercantile waferer stands for all sinners in the material world. The mixture of other sins with mercantile discourse, and the desire behind many sins, characterizes this section of the poem. As "eche a maide þat he mette /...to þe werke yeden, / As wel fastyng dayes and Fridaies and forboden nyʒtes, / And as lef in Lente as out of

Lente, alle tymes yliche—/ Swiche werkes with hem were neuere out of seson"(B XIII. 345–51), Langland here casts lechery in the terms of a commonplace sin of the guilds, as merchants and craftsmen were traditionally criticized for a "disposition to keep shops open on Sundays and holy days."[27] Translating lechery into "work," this passage extends that basic tendency to include Lent and the nighttime work that was periodically a scandal in London.[28] The poem shows both the dangers of mixing the categories of sins, and the primacy of desire in sin. Langland continues this pattern, as he links lechery back to covetousness with his "vnkynde desiryng" (B.XIII. 355) and a description of mercantile malpractice. This passage uses traditional estates material for avarice, as the "false mesures" (B.XIII. 359) and "menged...marchaundise" (B.XIII. 362) recall Coveitise's mercantile fraud, and loaning for "loue of the wed" (B.XIII. 360) recalls Coveitise loaning "for loue of þe cros, to legge a wed and lese it" (B.V. 240). Haukyn similarly claims that his avarice blocks charity: "If I kidde any kyndenesse myn euencristen to helpe, / Upon a cruwel coueitise my conscience gan hange" (B.XIII. 389–90). Haukyn's suggestion that "conscience" *prevents* good works is particularly perverse, as is his statement that he aimed "Þoru3 gile to gaderen þe good that ich haue" (B.XIII. 370). This mixture of the language of trade and salvation puns on *good*, emphasizing the point with *g* alliteration like the line "moore to good þan to God þe gome his loue caste" (B.XIII. 357). This slippage between *good* and *goods* reminds the reader how easy it can be to confuse the two: both charity and avarice love the *good*, after all. This mixing continues when "into wanhope he worþ and wende nou3t to be saued" (B.XIII. 407), recalling Coveitise's moral collapse at the prospect of restitution.[29] Haukyn's admission that this wanhope leads people to do "non almesdede" (B.XIII. 413) further characterizes these overlapping sins as potentially mercantile.

   One implication of this conjunction of charity with the moment when material sins are collapsing into mercantile covetousness is that, just as the mercantile Haukyn reflects all material sinners, perhaps charity can remedy material sins. Thus, when Will explains that the rich should have "beggeres bifore hem" (B.XIII. 440), followed by "the pouere for a fool sage sittynge at þi table" (B.XIII. 444) and "a blynd man for a bourdeour, or a bedrede womman / To crie a largesse tofore Oure Lord, your good loos to shewe" (B.XIII. 448–49), the poem presents charity as a remedy for material success in general, not just mercantile success. Langland's use of the mercantile as a figure for the material helps to explain why Conscience revises Repentaunce's earlier absolutism concerning avarice. Where Passus B.V could suggest that merchants' sins might be unabsolvable, here the sacrament of confession seems up to the challenge of the sins of an *Activa Vita*. Langland cannot totally dissociate the mercantile

elements from his model for the *Activa Vita*, though, and Haukyn cannot distinguish between good and goods, spiritual and material success.
The very pragmatism of Conscience's model of (mercantile) redemption
concedes too much to the necessity of worldly life that Passus B.XIV will
deny, and for that reason a focus on charity as a material activity cannot
stand in this part of the poem.

Langland addresses this lingering mercantility in his model of the
Activa Vita when Pacience challenges any reconciliation between spiritual and extra-spiritual aspects of life, and the need for any sort of worldly
economy at all. As David Aers suggests, the ascendance of Pacience in this
scene attempts to transcend the "densely textured, complicated world"
of the more material portions of the poem.[30] Pacience's image of eating
of a "pece of þe Paternoster" (B.XIV. 49) for sustenance underlines the
profound difference between this Passus and the worldly Passūs B.V–VII:
here the route to salvation is purely symbolic. With the explanation to
Haukyn that Charite dwells "Ther parfit truþe and poore herte is, and
pacience of tonge— / There is Charite þe chief, chaumbrere for God
hymselue" (B.XIV. 100–101), Pacience directs the waferer to poverty and
a "poore herte" rather than to giving alms. Where Conscience argues
that a charitable wealthy person can cancel out dangerous profit by giving it away, Pacience argues that a poor person opts out of the exchange
system altogether, and like Piers leaving his plow, exits the worldly economy. Thus poverty, rather than eleemosynary charity, is the antidote to
the Seven Deadly Sins united in the merchant Haukyn (B.XIV. 215–60;
275–319). The poor can compete with merchants here as a symbol of the
material economy, because while a merchant's material success makes
virtue more difficult, poverty's material failure directs the soul's attention toward spiritual things, at least in theory. As Pacience points out in
highly economic terms, there was never a rich man "þat he ne dredde
hym soore, / And þat at þe rekenyng in arrerage fel, raþer þan out of
dette" (B.XIV. 106–7). With this emphasis on "rekenyng," "arrerage,"
and "dette," the material discomfort of defaulting on a debt transfers
to the much greater discomfort of coming up short at the Judgment.
While there remains the possibility for merchants to fulfill their half of
the contract with Truth and be "oute of dette," Pacience doubts that they
will. By this point in the poem, successes in the material and spiritual
economies are mutually exclusive. While this opposition will not resolve
the basic conflict between spiritual and material economies, it does help
explain Langland's sustained interest in the poor, both as a focus for charity and as a group with a potential spiritual advantage. The vivid details
of Hunger in Passus B.VI and Nede in Passus B.XX also remind us that
Langland fully understood material poverty.

Poverty and charity do have something in common, of course, at least on a superficial level, and Lawrence Clopper argues that the poem equates the two at times.[31] Both virtues contradict the profit economy, and they also represent two of the main organizing principles of the mendicant movement; their conjunction necessarily invokes the controversy over mendicancy and questionable begging. While merchants and mendicants seem natural opposites, Langland uses both to address the problem of materiality. Like his portrayals of merchants, Langland's mendicants have traditionally been read as negative, though in the case of the latter scholars now rarely assume that estates satire material is necessarily historically descriptive. Penn R. Szittya characterizes Langland's reliance on antifraternal tropes in his depictions of mendicants, which Clopper refines by suggesting that *Piers Plowman*'s criticisms were shared by Franciscans' critiques of their own order, and he points out that Szittya's list lacks some commonly external antifraternal accusations.[32] The controversy over friars matters here because of the nature of begging. Langland uses mendicancy in Passus B.XIV as a problematic figure for rejection of the material economy in favor of the spiritual. Szittya shows that scorn for the friars leads traditional antifraternal satire to some odd conclusions about poverty, though, when he points to Langland's scorn for (able-bodied) beggars, who "live off the labor of others and contribute nothing to the common good."[33] Such scorn would also apply to the friars, who, if they begged unnecessarily, essentially robbed their donors of the opportunity to be charitable.[34] The poem's own complex relationship with the material world mirrors the problem of poverty and begging, as it refuses to present either voluntary poverty or wealth as a permanent solution to the world's spiritual ills. Szittya classifies able-bodied friars as undeserving poor,[35] while Clopper uses a Franciscan distinction between solicitous begging, a sign of greed, and begging for genuine need, to include non-solicitous friars who simply prayed for alms and accepted only subsistence in the category of deserving poor.[36] Neither scholar emphasizes, though, the self-contained economic system of alms and begging.

Pacience ultimately praises those who are "poore of herte" (B.XIV. 195), and a person who "for Goddes loue leueþ al and lyueþ as a beggere . . . / And put hym to be pacient, and pouerte weddeþ, / The whiche is sib to God hymself" (B.XIV. 264–73). Will observes at the end of Passus B.XIII that "riche men sholde / Haue beggeres bifore hem, þe whiche ben Goddes minstrales" (B.XIII. 440), and Clopper points out that the latter term translates the Franciscan self-description as *joculatores dei*.[37] If those who succeed in the material economy must slough off their success, if "ye riche [must] haue ruþe, and rewarde wel þe poore" (B.XIV. 145), the rich require people to whom they can give, who must also be deserving

or nonsolicitous. There must be poor people, because poverty is seen as
a moral good in itself, because the poem ratifies the social hierarchy, and
because those not fortunate enough to be poor require the poor in order
to cleanse themselves of their wealth. The catch is that since poverty and
charity both resist the sins of the worldly economy, Haukyn's weeping at
the conclusion of Pacience's sermon reminds us how the necessities and
complications of material life make a pure focus on *caritas* and poverty
"of herte" difficult. Langland is momentarily absolutist in his asceticism,
but also aware of the distastefulness of that position. Haukyn's weeping
recapitulates Roberd the Robbere's tears: " 'So hard it is,' quod Haukyn,
'to lyue and to do synne. / Synne seweþ vs euere,' quod he, and sory gan
wexe, / And wepte water with hise eighen and weyled þe tyme / That
euere he dide dede þat deere God displesed" (B.XIV. 322–24). Haukyn
seems taken aback by the difficulty of renunciation at the same time
he acknowledges Pacience's position. There is an important difference
between his tears and Roberd's, though: Haukyn has made the first step
to Dowel in its formulation as confession within this vision. He sighs for
his lack of poverty and cries, not from despair, but because "euere he
dide dede þat deere God displesed" (B.XIV. 325). As we remember from
B.XIV. 17, contrition of the heart is how Conscience and Pacience both
define Dowel. Since Haukyn confesses his sins in detail, he demonstrates
both the local Dowel and Dobet, *contricio* and *confessio*, and as the dream is
cut off, he prepares himself for Dobest, the "satisfaction through prayers
and good works."[38] Since Coveitise did not receive absolution and penance, there remains the possibility that Haukyn will not make it to *satis-
faccio*; like one's own, Haukyn's spiritual fate remains unknown.

Several features do remain in common between Haukyn and Coveitise
that allow us to draw some intermediate conclusions about Langland's
portrayal of merchants. Both figures embody sin and implicate their profession and estate. Langland manipulates traditional conceptions of merchants as an inherently sinful estate; like the friars, merchants transgress
estate stability through their own success and their competition with
groups like the gentry or the secular clergy. The poet may be conventional in his scorn for merchants and their profession, but not by accident.
The estates satire tradition allowed Langland to explore a fundamental question of Christianity: how to reconcile the needs of the material economy which merchants ostensibly exist to meet with the more
important but less immediate demands of the spiritual economy. Since
Langland uses Haukyn to fold sins besides avarice into the *Activa Vita*,
Haukyn intersects the material and spiritual economies of the poem. As
a wafer-selling merchant, he is fully implicated in material life, and he
faces the same sins as any soul. The fact that he sells Eucharistic wafers

reminds us of the interconnection of the spiritual and material economies. Regardless of their estate, Langland's readers face Haukyn's problems, and the memory of Coveitise's inability to make restitution underlines those problems' immediacy. Although Haukyn shares Coveitise's mercantile stereotypes, his merging of those stereotypes with other sins as a more general emblem of material life extends mercantile satire to the basic problem of materiality.

Antimercantilism Without Merchants: Conscience and Usury Theory

If Coveitise and Haukyn allow Langland to apply antimercantile discourse to the problems of spiritual living in the material world, what happens when that discourse erupts into other conflicts between material and spiritual economies in the poem? This conflict appears primarily in Conscience's debate with Mede, the Pardon scene, and the search for Charity. The tension between spiritual and material economies drives much of the poem's approach to the problem of salvation. From its beginning, *Piers Plowman* attacks the European economy's dependence on money, what Lester Little characterizes as that "instrument of exchange that had devil-like, magical powers of luring people and then of corrupting them."[39] We see this problem of money in connection with fourteenth-century politics directly with Mede and the many urban references in her part of the poem, but Langland throughout refers to merchants as embodiments of trade and hence of avarice and worldly sin.[40] For example, Gyle hides from Drede as merchants "bishetten hym in hire shoppes to shewen hire ware, / And apparailed hym as a prentice þe peple to serue" (B.II. 214–15). Although specific merchants are not Langland's focus before Passus B.V, as a general class they make a useful figure for his discomfort with money, and they provide a target for concern about the sinfulness that material existence makes it impossible to avoid.

The key defining moment for Langland's early treatment of money comes when Mede defends herself by explaining that "alle kynne crafty men crauen mede for hir prentis" (B.III. 225). Theologie had previously defended her by arguing that "*Dignus est operarius* his hire to haue" (B.II. 123), and by claiming that "Mede is a muliere, a maiden of goode / And myȝte kisse þe Kyng for cosyn and she wolde" (B.II. 132–33). Mede's and Theologie's position, that exchange in the form of wages forms a virtuous model for the money economy, does show the extent to which economic theory in the fourteenth century described a morally implicated system.[41] We can see that Langland continued to wrestle with the central problem of the morality of economic exchange, in that in the C-text, to further divide good and bad *mede*, he renames the former *mercede*. In the earlier formulation, Conscience distinguishes between licit and illicit payment or reward, the "two manere of medes" (B.III. 231) which will become "'mede' and 'mercede,'—and both men demen / A desert for some doynge, derne oþer elles" (C.III. 290–91): the permissible sort is the reward from God through grace, available to him "þat ne vseþ noȝt þe lyf of vsurie / And enformeþ pouere men and pursueþ truþe" (B.III. 240–41). This mention of usury does not appear in the C-text; Martyn Miller explains that Langland constructs a "grammatical metaphor" of *mercede* as a direct relation, "one in which a pronoun and its antecedent agree in gender, case, and number" and *mede* as an indirect relation, "in which agreement is limited to gender and number," so that agreement between deed and reward is more exact with *mercede*.[42] Grace is far more integral to the fine distinction between *medes* in the B-text, with the difference between *mede* and *mercede* in the C-text being construed as that between reward given "bifore þe doynge" and that given "When þe dede is ydo," which is "a manere dewe dette" (C.III. 292, 303–4).[43]

Lacking the term *mercede*, in the B-text Conscience explains the difference between *mede* that God "graunteþ in his blisse / To þo þat wel werchen while þei ben here" (B.III. 232–33), and "anoþer mede mesurelees, þat maistres desireþ: / To mayntene mysdoers mede þei take" (B.III. 246–47). Conscience sharply differentiates between earthly and heavenly rewards, with the implication that rewarding the good is God's business and involved with grace, refuting Mede's earlier insistence that earthly kings must use *mede* to reward and keep feudal loyalty: "it bicomeþ to a kyng that kepeþ a reaume / To yeue men mede þat mekely hym serueþ— /...Mede makeþ hym biloued" (B.III. 209–12).[44] Langland will stress grace as the only acceptable *mede* later, when he discusses charity, and here Conscience opposes spiritual rewards granted in God's "blisse" to the more suspect rewards of maintenance (B.III. 247). As it will with Coveitise, "maintenance" appears at a moment when the power of money is most suspect and *mede* hardest to define, and this invocation of maintenance undermines Mede's earlier suggestion that kingship requires gift-giving *mede*. We also see Langland's concern with the power of money through the repugnance of his imagery here: the admonition that "he þat gripeþ hir gold...Shal abien it ful bitter, or þe Book lieþ!" (B.III. 250–51) recalls Little's descriptions of personified Avarice holding tightly to his money bags.[45] David Aers also argues that Langland adds to this repugnance with the misogyny of the marriage metaphor here, and he associates Langland's contempt for Mede with "the profit economy...pervading social relations and spiritual relations;"

thus, according to Aers, Langland renders greed, money, and the economy itself vividly obscene.[46]

Langland does mediate or at least shift this repugnance somewhat, though, when Conscience goes on further to separate "mede" and "mesurable hire" by asserting "That [which] laborers and lowe lewede folk taken of hire maistres, / It is no manere mede but a mesurable hire" (B.III. 255–56). This move separates Mede's and Theologie's theory of wages from the debate over her sinfulness, though Clare A. Lees argues that the poem cannot separate Mede fully from the issue of marriage.[47] Still, Conscience's hair-splitting economic definition of several types of payment shifts Passus B.III away from the desire for Mede to the more esoteric world of medieval economic theory. Key here is Conscience's assertion that "in marchaundise is no mede, I may it wel auowe: / It is a permutacion apertly—a penyworþ for anoþer" (B.III. 257–58), which suggests Langland's vision of a perfect material economy. A "penyworþ for anoþer" does not necessarily entail profit, and "mesurable hire" is what the *operarius* is *dignus* of (B.II. 123), a separate issue from the simony of "Preestes and persons þat plesynge desireþ, / That taken mede and moneie for masses þat þei syngeþ" (B.III. 252–53). Conscience defends merchandise as separate from *mede* (and significantly also from *mede* in the form of divine grace), but in very limited terms that blur the scholastic distinction between dishonest usury and potentially honest merchandise. Divine *mede* is available only to him "þat ne vseth no3t þe lyf of vsurie" (B.III. 240), so that Conscience ties the problem of money specifically to the usury ban. This move makes sense, since the sin of usury came from its purely monetary increase, not from the more concrete (and more clearly necessary) exchange of money for goods.[48]

There remains, however, the question of to what extent the "permutacion...[of] a penyworþ for anoþer" represents an invocation on Langland's part of the "just price," or whether it instead applies an inelastic natural value to merchandise. As D. Vance Smith points out, "the notion of what a pennyworth might be, of what modes of commensuration come into play in order to make one equivalent to another, is anything but straightforward."[49] With just price theory, the church tentatively recognized the contingency of a market price on material conditions surrounding sale, so that the just price was never too closely defined. In its specificity, though, Conscience's strict exchange of a "penyworþ" seems at best a limited version of that theory.[50] Since Conscience specifies an amount for his example of exchange, in the "penyworþ" that recalls the purely monetary nature of usury, Langland here shifts from a scholastic emphasis on contingent value to one on money as an inelastic marker, though of course a "peny*worþ*" implies the value of a penny rather than

the actual coin.[51] The term *permutacion* complicates this issue: as Schmidt
points out in his Everyman edition note, "Conscience does not recognize legitimate *profit* in trade (*lucrum*), which was allowed by the theologians; but he may imply it under *permutacion*."[52] Schmidt's parallel-text
note suggests that Langland is "presupposing not 'exactly equal exchange
value' but a 'just price' for goods that takes proper account of the labour
that went to producing them."[53] Langland's choice of words may itself be
informative; scholastic theorists as far from each other's positions as John
Duns Scotus and Aquinas prefer the term *commutatio* for "exchange."[54]
The Oxford English Dictionary (OED) and Middle English Dictionary
(MED) agree that *permutacion* is the Latinate term adopted in fourteenth-
century English, but Latin lexicographical evidence suggests that the
monetary connotations of Classical *permutatio* had subsequently shifted
to *commutatio*, so that *permutatio* here is not the obvious term.[55] If we
accept Schmidt's reading of the passage, and see Langland as enough of
a Latinist[56] to attempt to shift Latinate diction for exchange, *permutacion* allows Langland to distance himself from scholastic economic theories that use *commutatio*, and thus to differentiate his preference for equal
exchange from the increasing acceptance of economic contingency.

In Conscience's emphasis on an equal exchange of value, expressed in
terms of coinage, we can see how Langland's treatment of trade in general
invokes the more straightforward problem of usury through his emphasis
on money.[57] This approach opposes the work of Olivi, who extended the
licit contingency of just price theory to mercantile lending, and that of Duns
Scotus, who "legitimized the idea of equality in exchange *secundum rectam
rationem* defined according to human use rather than the inherent value of
the things exchanged,"[58] emphasizing the element of risk in the just price.[59]
Still, given that Olivi's work was banned after his death, and Duns Scotus
was opposed into the fifteenth century, Langland's retention of what Joel
Kaye calls "the old ideal of strict mathematical equality" is hardly an indication of unorthodoxy.[60] The fact that Mede raised the problem of merchandise in the first place also helps to explain why it will be so hard to redeem a
merchant in the poem, because even sophisticated economic theorists were
somewhat vague on the distinction between reasonable profit, built into the
just price, and the obscene power of money embodied by Mede.[61]

The Pardon for Merchants

The tension between the material and spiritual economies demonstrated by Mede's debate with Conscience underlines the difficulty for
any commercial sinner to find redemption. Coveitise's failed confession
brings this issue to a crisis, but the early parts of the Pardon scene make

another attempt to address the problems raised by the material economy. Langland's model of restitution through episcopal mediation in Passus B.V failed to address the problems of simony and the church's overinvolvement with money. In Passus B.VII, the poem shifts that intervention to more abstract terms through Truth's letter to merchants. The Pardon scene remains one of the murkiest moments of the poem, though. Before taking the letter as a genuine suggestion for how merchants can find redemption, we must first decide whether Truth's letter is part of the Pardon, and then whether or not the Pardon has any validity. There remains no critical consensus on its validity, and there remain emphatic arguments against the validity of pardons per se, arguments supported by Haukyn's later treatment of a papal pardon. On the other hand, only if the Pardon retains some validity can the letter of Truth present even a temporary solution to the conflict between earthly reality and spiritual needs, because only a true pardon can answer the question of how to get to heaven. The answer to this apparent contradiction, that the poem needs a pardon here but distrusts pardons in general, can be found in the way that Langland regularly moves between different solutions to the same problem, what David Aers characterizes as "a dialectical process in which arguments and positions are often developed with sympathy and depth even when, especially when, they are to be superseded."[62] Just as Langland's model of confession moves from Roberd the Robbere's despair to Haukyn's penitent tears, and just as Dowel, Dobet, and Dobest change radically throughout the poem, the Pardon represents a thesis in search of its antithesis, an experiment that need only work locally in the poem. Langland here posits a Pardon from an impeccable source, and then works out the ramifications of this particular form of clerical intervention. Piers's tearing of the Pardon then ends the experiment, by reducing the Pardon to the most basic terms, "do yvel" and "do wel."

Robert Adams argues for the Pardon as positive, fitting its emphasis on good works (*doing well*) into a context of Langland's more general interest in the question of "grace versus works."[63] Adams interprets the Pardon as God's "declaration...that He will consider all genuine efforts at good deeds to be worthy of grace[, which] constitutes a most generous pardon,"[64] so that for Adams the Pardon represents more an invocation of the need to navigate between grace and works than the faulty rejection of grace that it represents for opponents like Malcolm Godden and Denise Baker.[65] Traugott Lawler expands on Adams's idea with his concept of repentance as "'the silent middle term' of the pardon;...It is precisely God's acceptance of repentance that makes the pardon a pardon."[66] If we accept Adams's and Lawler's interpretations of the Pardon as an implicit reminder of the need for both grace and repentance, it fits right into the

problem of how merchants could find salvation, since the need for restitution inhibits grace. As the poem considers heavy reliance on works,
although of course not to the exclusion of the grace implied by Truth's
agency in writing the Pardon, it seems only natural for Truth's letter to
elucidate the Pardon's focus on works as they connect to grace.

The letter does, however, present a somewhat different version of the
Pardon for merchants than for other estate groups. The letter replaces a
Pardon they cannot have, because merchants have ignored Repentaunce's
order of "marchaundise, leue it" (B.V. 285), and "þei holde no3t hir holiday as Holy Chirche techeþ, / And for þei swere 'by hir soule' and 'so
God moste hem helpe' / Ayein clene Conscience, hir catel to sell" (B.VII.
20–22). This denial of pardons in general to merchants presents an equivocal vision of their estate. Where the actual Pardon, if we accept Adams's
reading, promises grace and salvation to any who try to do well, doing
well and especially proper penance[67] must be much more specifically
laid out for merchants. The details of Truth's letter would also apply to
anyone involved in any form of trade, since its focus on material charity
would include clergy, gentry, or others who were involved in buying and
selling. These unpardonable merchants swear inappropriately and work
on Sundays, but their sins are almost incidental to their work, unlike
Coveitise's usury and fraud: here the poem presents mercantile sins distinct from those of Coveitise, and Langland uses this reference to merchants to create some of the distance between Coveitise and Haukyn, at
the same time that, as Derek Pearsall argues, he experiments with the
Church's response to merchandise in his time.[68]

The Pardon merchants' relative superiority to Coveitise does not help
their case with Truth, though. They are refused an easy way out of their
sin, a pardon a pena et a culpa, and Langland's focus on repentance is
individualized for merchants through a letter under Truth's "secret seel"
(B.VII. 23), instructing merchants to go about their business, but then to
perform a number of charitable works:

> amende mesondieux [hospitals] þerwiþ and myseisé folk helpe;
> And wikkede weyes [bad roads] wi3tly hem amende,
> And do boote to brugges that tobroke were;
> Marien maydenes or maken hem nonnes;
> Pouere peple and prisons, fynden hem hir foode,
> And sette scolers to scole or to som oþere craftes;
> Releue religion and renten hem better. (B.VII. 26–32)

Part of what is compelling about these lines is their improvement on
Repentaunce's use of a bishop as a middle-man: Truth here allows a

dispensation for charity without drawing the church into money-laundering. The amending of "wikkede weyes" also suggests the extent to which this catalogue of charitable behavior is both material and abstract. While Schmidt glosses this phrase in context to mean repairing roads, it also through puns on "wicked" and "way" refers to the Pardon itself, as amending one's wicked ways also means to stop doing evil. While Langland outlines a difficult and expensive path to salvation for merchants, though, he also casts Truth's letter in the form of a contract, where merchants get salvation in exchange for their charity (B.VIII. 33–36). James Simpson's theory of Langland's economic language is useful here, as he argues that "Langland often chooses to use such images precisely at moments when he is specifically rejecting a profit economy in the earthly realm."[69] This "contract" represents just such a moment. The difference between economies is brought into sharp relief, because although the letter seems to offer an exchange of salvation for charity, it hardly represents an even exchange of a "penyworþ for anoþer," since the grace offered here is vastly more valuable than merchants' charity. Still, the letter does repeat the quid pro quo of the Pardon proper: "*Et qui bona egerunt ibunt in vitam eternam; / Qui vero mala, in ignem eternam*" (B.VII.110a). While it is not an even exchange, neither is any promise of salvation.

At the same time that it offers salvation to merchants without episcopal involvement, the letter directly recalls Matthew 25 and the parable of the talents: since those who do not invest their talents will lose them, virtue must be an active enterprise, and the most active material form of virtue must be charity. *Piers Plowman* here emphasizes the peril of a life without material good works, and the biblical intertext adds the sting, just as the second line of the Pardon consigns to eternal hellfire those who "do yvel." In particular, the biblical parable uses commercial language to support the notion of divine "profit" advocated in Truth's permission to buy and sell, as "he that had received the five talents, went his way, and traded with the same, and gained other five" (Matt. 25.16), later to be rewarded with "the joy of thy lord" (Matt. 25.23).[70] Similarly, "Pouere peple and prisons fynden hem hir foode" recalls "For I was hungry, and you gave me to eat...I was in prison, and you came to me" (Matt. 25.35–36) This passus does not focus on prisoners elsewhere, so that the inclusion of "prisoners" here directly recalls this biblical description of charity.[71] Langland uses the Bible's worldly economic language of spiritual redemption through the Corporal Works of Mercy, and Truth's instruction to merchants to donate all of their profits underscores the extent to which the spiritual economy succeeds directly at the expense of the material economy. If we then recall the guild classes' reliance on charitable activity in their ordinances and bequests (see chapter 1), we see that Langland here taps into an opposition between trade and charity, which was clear even to the traders of his time, and all the more so to those like himself who distrusted merchandise. His opposition of charity to mercantile greed is quite conventional, but *Piers Plowman* goes well beyond the guilds' commitment to charity as Langland eventually refuses any compromise that will encourage trade.

Redefining Charity

A discussion of Langland's use of charity as an antidote to material sins first requires a brief look at Langland's use of the slippage inherent in the word *charity* in this period between *caritas* and alms. Janet Coleman provides a useful distinction, arguing that Langland ultimately comes to stress the *caritas* meaning of charity, linking it with grace: she argues that the poem makes a distinction in Passus B.XV between "the grace/ charity one merits through good deeds done naturally and promised by the generosity of God's covenant with man, and that grace/charity which saves absolutely and is given to the righteous man who not only seems to do good works but has been judged worthy by God and thus elected to salvation absolutely."[72] Coleman's reading here in terms of William of Ockham's theory that *caritas* was God's response to the choice of the will "to do the good"[73] underlines the importance of the material world to Langland's theology. Even though the poem will ultimately move charity beyond the physical, as one will know Charite "but þoruȝ wil oone" (B.XV. 210), the poet's need to explain that works and words alone do not make charity/*caritas* reminds us that the sufficiency of the material world retains a problematic fantasy. Perhaps the lesson to be learned from the widespread nature of historical mercantile alms-giving is that some merchants *did* expect material largesse to save their souls. While the clergy seek to know Charite through grace, merchants are likely to have only their anxiously performed works, and be doubly unable in Langland's theology to achieve true charity.

The poem's shift by Passus B.XV away from merchants to a state of grace depends greatly on Langland's establishment in the first seven passūs of the more material conception of charity as alms, and as an antidote to sin. In the Pardon scene, for example, Langland experiments with the notion that giving back the profits *might* be enough to bring merchants, and through them any participants in a profit economy, close enough to a state of grace. Then, starting with Haukyn's emotional contrition, Langland approaches a far more complex concept of charity than merchants held: while guild ordinances requiring prayer clearly acknowledged a need for grace, merchants' physical donations suggest a preference for alms as an action to be balanced in a divine ledger against previous profits. Langland, however, moves to Charite of the sort found "þoruȝ wil oone." Anima's speech in Passus B.XV explains charity in terms that continue an anticlerical discourse on poverty. This long passage starts with a simple question: " 'What is charite?' quod I þo. 'A childissh þyng,' he seide...Wiþouten fauntelte [*childishness*] or folie a fre liberal wille' " (B.XV. 149–50). Anima's charity here is not the eleemosynary variety, and the "fre liberal wille" (aside from the pun on the author's name) suggests the connection to free will in grace in William of Ockham, as suggested by Coleman. Will himself picks up on this distance between *caritas* and alms, when he asks in return, "Where sholde men fynde swich a frend wiþ so fre an herte?" (B.XV. 151). He follows with the "signature" line "I have lyued in londe,' quod I, 'my name is Longe Wille" (B.XV. 152), but afterward describes a world where one sees occasional alms "to mendinauntȝ and to poore" (B.XV. 154), but he has never met a man who would not "coueite / Thyng þat neded hym noȝt" (B.XV. 159–60). Here the poem directly opposes charity in the sense of *caritas* to the familiar focus on giving to the poor that we have seen in alms, but the language of lending so problematic with Coveitise has reappeared as alms-giving, emphasizing the fine line between positive and negative mercantile practice: those men who give alms also "wollene lene þer þei leue lelly to ben paied" (B.XV. 155). Lending could be charitable, since a virtuously interest-free loan would help a needy person. Even if the donor expected no return, though, this expectation that charity will be paid back may be a criticism of the typical mercantile practice of considering alms as half of a transaction with God, so that the "his" that one "wolde aske after" (B.XV. 159) would reify the taint of finance that the charity was meant to wash away.

Anima certainly implies that charity is not so available to merchants as they may think, as Charite " 'ne chaffareþ noȝt, ne chalangeþ, ne craveþ; / As proud of a peny as of a pound of golde." (B.XV. 165–66). This section clearly distances from a mercantile life the best sort of charity, "þat Poul preiseþ best and moost plesaunt to Oure Saueour" (B.XV. 156), and at this point the poem has made a major step beyond the letter of Truth. This direct rejection of *chaffaren*, or to "engage in business or trade for profit,"[74] directly challenges any connection between literal trade and grace. At the same time, the contrast of "peny" and "pound," "russet" and "scarlet" (B.XV. 166–68), undermines the social distinctions elsewhere so important in the poem. Equating rich and poor removes charity here from the symbiotic alms-giving relationship discussed earlier. Here where Langland describes an ideal spiritual economy, merchants lose their usefulness as a site for reconciling the earthly with the spiritual. We

see that more directly as Anima goes on, "Coveiteþ he noon erþely good
but heueneriche blisse.... Of rentes ne of richesse rekkeþ he neuere"
(B.XV. 175–77). Punning again on *good*, Langland suggests that it would
be misdirected to search for good on earth rather than heaven, and argues
for a complete focus on the spiritual economy. Then, in the line "if he
soupeþ, eet but a sop of *Spera in Deo*" (B.XV. 180), Pacience's advice to
eat the paternoster (B.XIV. 49) shifts to Psalm 41, and rejects materiality.
This metaphoric nourishment shows Langland's willingness at this key
moment to abandon along with merchants his earlier attempts to reconcile the needs of the material and spiritual economies.

    This is not to say, however, that Langland here has completely aban-
doned eleemosynary charity, as Anima explains of Charite that "ouþer-
while is his wone to wende on pilgrimages / Ther poore men and prisons
liggeþ, hir pardon to have; / Thou3 he bere hem no breed, he bereþ hem
swetter liflode, / Loueþ hem as Oure Lord bit and lokeþ how þei fare"
(B.XV. 182–85). In this passage Langland repeats one of the key elements
of the letter of Truth, its use of Matthew 25, but the detail that "he bere
hem no breed" moves Charite from the physical and worldly to the spiritual: within a few lines, "by colour ne by clergie knowe shaltow hym
neuere / Neiþer þoru3 wordes ne werkes, but þoru3 wil oone" (B.XV.
209–10). Charity has transformed from an antidote to trade to something
far more central to salvation, reminding the reader that charity represents
a universal spiritual need. Subsequent focus on action in the physical
world in the poem explicitly represents part of *caritas* rather than a material counteraction to a particular sin. Also, as Wendy Scase points out,
this view of charity resembles Pacience's view on poverty, as both require
"giving to beggars with no expectation of a return; not trading; not asserting one's rights; taking no pride in money, nor in clothing; being heedless
of property; [and] trusting in God to provide."[75] For Langland, this shift
away from the material, outside world also moves him past merchants
and their *chaffare*, because they and the material economy they represent
have no place here. He has abandoned for now the problem of reconciling
spiritual and material economies through his focus on the overwhelming
needs of the spiritual economy, so the estate that most embodies conflict
between material and spiritual success has become unnecessary.

The Ending: The Return of the Material Economy

The need to balance material and spiritual economies has no place, that
is, until Passus B.XIX. At the end of the poem when Conscience explains
Passus B.XVIII to Will, he returns to Piers's Pardon in the context of
Christ's leaving the keys with Peter the Apostle. Here Langland first uses

the oft-repeated phrase "*Redde quo debes*" (B.XIX. 187). Economic language reappears at a key moment in the form of debt, and redemption in the spiritual economy corresponds yet again to divine repayment. The change, of course, is the context of Passus B.XVIII, which presents the redemptive role of the Crucifixion. Langland has returned for now to the model of exchange, salvation in the form of the unbalanced *commutatio* of worldly works for heavenly grace that characterized Passus B.VII. This stress on how grace represents that which humans gain by virtue of the Crucifixion then leads to the appearance of the *Spiritus Paraclitus* in line B.XIX. 202. Grace, summoned by Conscience, began "þe comune to sompne: / 'For I wole dele today and dyuyde grace / ... Tresour to lyue by to hir lyues ende, / And wepne to fight wiþ þat wole never faille" (B.XIX. 215–19), because "Antecrist" (B.XIX. 220) is coming. The apocalyptic tone here will hold for the rest of *Piers Plowman*. Still, this conception of grace (earlier associated with *caritas*) explicitly applies to everyone. The poem retreats from the absolutism of Passus B.XV here, because several professions receive grace that should be excluded from Anima's formulation of charity. Most significant for this chapter, in the middle of Grace's presentation of a wide variety of worldly occupations including priests, lawyers, agricultural laborers, astronomers, philosophers, and the poor, "some he kennede craft and konnynge of sight, / Wiþ buggynge and sellynge hir bilyue to wynne" (B.XIX. 235–36).[76] In this reappearance of merchants, trade seems to have become (briefly) as morally neutral as manual labor. Because Langland soon collapses this model of the physical world, the problem of integrating it with salvation in the spiritual economy has less immediate importance.

Suddenly, then, we are back on the half-acre, and Grace insists on the social harmony that was lacking in Passus B.VI: " 'Thynkeþ þat alle craftes,' quod Grace, 'comeþ of my ȝifte; / Look þat noon lakke ooþer, but loueþ alle as breþeren' " (B.XIX. 255–56). As this new half-acre progresses, we can see just why it is that the material world has reappeared, and what has changed since Passus B.VI. As Daniel F. Pigg explains, "the second plowing is not limited by the physical boundaries such as those of a manorial estate; its purpose is universal, and its source of power unlimited."[77] In Passus B.XIX, the material economy has become pure allegory, so that the reappearance of merchants is more akin to the use of mercantile language in "*redde quod debes*" (B.XIX. 188, 261, 394; B.XX. 309) than to Passus VI. Merchants still recall the problem of integrating survival in the profit economy with spiritual success, but by Passus XIX the end of the world is so close that material success becomes subordinated to the typological history of the Church, *Unite*. While Will looks twice when presented the paternoster as food (B.XIV. 48) and Haukyn cries at the thought of focusing on the spiritual economy (B.XIV. 320–32), no one in Passus B.XIX seems bothered that the virtues are expected to feed everyone. Merchants are so unexceptional by this point in the poem that when Conscience brings everyone into the barn to hide from Pride, it is prostitutes, lawyers, and summoners who fail to come. Once merchants as a group fade away, there remains only the economic language borrowed by the spiritual economy from the material economy. The repetition of "*redde quod debes*" emphasizes that this part of the poem is concerned with the calling in of the divine debt. We first see this phrase in Conscience's description of God granting pardon "To alle maner men, mercy and forȝifnesse; / To hym, myght men to assoille of alle manere synnes, / In couenaunt þat þei come and kneweliche to paye / To Piers pardon þe Plowman—*Redde quod debes*" (B.XIX. 184–87). Here, *redde quod debes* encapsulates the basic concept of redemption. The phrase reappears in B.XIX. 261, and again occurs in a potentially pro-Papal context as Grace explains, "I make Piers þe Plowman my procuratour and my reue, / And registrer to receyue *Redde quod debes*" (B.XIX. 260–61). This establishment of the new half-acre fits the Pope into a feudal model as divine reeve, responsible for the manor's accounts and management. The economic metaphor of redemption remains subordinate to the overall allegorical context; the material economy lacks the threatening sense of transgression seen earlier in merchants' and friars' dangerous wealth and avarice. Another use of *redde quod debes* in Passus B.XIX shares this containment of sin in the successful economic metaphor for spiritual redemption, as Grace has given Piers the authority to make Eucharistic bread and for people to eat it, "þo þat hadde ypaied / To Piers pardon þe Plowman, *Redde quod debes*." (B.XIX. 393–94). Again, the poem emphasizes the power of the sacraments (and recalls Haukyn), and the assumption seems to be that there will be no real problems in paying off the divine debt.

Then material reality returns to the poem as the divinely ordered social structure of Passus B.XIX collapses in Passus B.XX. While the end of time is not blamed on merchants, it is blamed on the friars, who in the antifraternal tradition came to represent the forces of the Antichrist. We see how the friars in this poem show the threat of material success and material desire to the divine economics embodied by Piers's power in Passus B.XIX, when *Redde quod debes* makes its last appearance in the poem in Conscience's attempt to contain the damage of the Seven Deadly Sins' assault. The dire need for successful confession reminds the reader that the end is near, as Conscience calls for a "leche, þat koude wel shryue" (B.XX. 305), to see "þat Piers pardon were ypayed, *redde quod debes*" (B.XX. 309). Piers's pardon reappears as a reminder of a contract with those involved in the material world, encouraging them to follow a mercantile quid pro quo and trade success in the material economy for success in the spiritual one, while this call to *redde quod debes* reminds those under Conscience's cure that one cannot default on spiritual debts without paying the ultimate forfeit. The subsequent collapse is largely antifraternal with a "leaven" of less directly antifraternal apocalypticism.[78] The anti-Friar *Penetrans-domos* does have his economic moments, as he admits that he comes "for profit and for helþe" (B.XX. 333), and he offers the protection of his order "for a litel siluer" (B.XX. 369). *Penetrans-domos* also becomes a spiritual usurer, charging interest with the "pryuee paiement" (B.XX. 365) he extorts from an unsuspecting Contricion. At the same time, he brings out and encourages Contricion's own greed, much as Coveitise had when he made "many a kny3t boþe mercer and draper" (B.V. 251). Mercantile language in this part of the poem thus shifts to apocalyptic antifraternal satire.[79]

The material economy remains in the poem, as the "litel siluer" that *Penetrans-domos* requires, and with the problem of a group that manipulates that material economy in the name of the spiritual economy, Langland ultimately faces up to the limitations of his various attempts to reconcile the two economies. The false confessor is able to use the mercantile language of debt not as a metaphor for spiritual success, but to engage in simony. Where the poem in Passus B.XV and the new half-acre of Passus B.XIX used mercantile language in the service of the spiritual economy, *Penetrans-domos* shows how that language can lead to the damning misunderstanding that one can pay one's way out of sin. The popularity of pardons and their equivocal role throughout the poem suggested this potential problem with the use of economic terms for salvation, but the end of the poem shows that a deliberate manipulation of *redde quod debes* has the potential to contaminate the entire metaphorical structure of the spiritual economy. While Langland's Passus B.XV analysis of Charity successfully used merchants as a figure for the problem of integrating the material and spiritual economies, the end of the poem reminds the reader that not only can the material economy be a metaphor for the spiritual imperative of salvation, but the inherent flaws of that economy (such as greed, the sloth of despair, and the pride of too much material success) can also infiltrate a theology too dependent on that metaphor, and once penetrated, that theology collapses just as the poem surrenders to the need to start all over again.

What, then, can we ultimately say about the importance of the estate of merchants to this poem? While *Piers Plowman* is encyclopedic in its scope, it consistently questions how an individual can live in the world while still attaining Christian salvation. Langland has many objects of his satire, but with the problem of how merchants can be saved, he faces the greatest degree of interaction between the material economy he satirizes and the spiritual economy to which he wants to direct his readers. Thus, Langland must face the fundamental question of how to reconcile the needs which merchants existed to meet with the needs common to any soul. He could presumably just have declared that all merchants were damned, which was suggested by his satire of Coveitise, but since merchants come, through Haukyn, to recall all individuals implicated in the material economy, he draws back from that most absolute and too-easy condemnation. As a result, the poem might well have been more appealing to a mercantile reader than other satires. Although there is little direct evidence of a merchant-estate readership for the poem (see chapter 1), Langland does acknowledge merchants' spiritual concerns as he uses them symbolically. Throughout the poem he parallels material and spiritual economies, making use of the Bible's economic terminology for the concept of redemption, and he suggests several solutions to the problem of mercantile redemption. The involvement of charity in the most successful solutions to the merchants' problem further presents merchants as a type for sinners in general, but the basic paradox of the spiritual and material prevents Langland from adopting any one solution permanently. The similarity between merchants' and friars' problems with material success further complicates merchants' usefulness as a type for material humanity, and this unresolvable paradox of conflicting material and spiritual success ultimately contributes to the apocalyptic ending of the poem. Before that moment, though, Langland can point out the flaws in a multitude of targets, ultimately suggesting through *Penetrans-domos*' subversion of *redde quod debes* that by his mercantile era, even the Bible's use of economic language poses a threat to the spiritual economy.

CHAPTER 3

THE *MIROUR DE L'OMME* AND GOWER'S LONDON MERCHANTS

Gower might not seem to belong in a study of this sort, because his critical reputation has generally been based on the *Confessio Amantis*, which makes little mention of merchants. Unlike the *Confessio*, the text of Gower's that most directly addresses merchants, the *Mirour de l'Omme* (or *Speculum Hominis* or *Speculum Meditantis*), has long languished in obscurity. Even the discoverer and editor of the *Mirour de l'Omme*, G. C. Macaulay, dismisses that work as crushing Gower's "better part...under mountains of morality and piles of deadly learning."[1] Derek Pearsall shows that avoidance of close engagement with Gower's texts has a long tradition,[2] but despite the astonishing growth in Gower studies in the past few decades, the *Mirour* remains in large part undiscovered country. For those willing to work with Gower's non-English works, the fact that the *Vox Clamantis* has long had an available translation, while the *Mirour de l'Omme* waited until 1992, has led scholars of Gowerian satire to start with the more conventional *Vox*, with the result that the *Mirour* remained largely unstudied until the 1990s.[3] Even scholars who briefly touch on that Anglo-French poem often simply conclude that Gower did not like anybody very much, including merchants.[4] While Gower's satires do critique society categorically by estate, a closer reading of the section of the *Mirour* assigned to merchants reveals that Gower's satire of trade is far more complex in the *Mirour*, the satiric poem most readable for the merchant estate (see later discussion). Thus, while this chapter cannot undertake a comprehensive reading of the *Mirour*, which has a great deal going on beyond satirizing merchants, my reading of the poem's antimercantile satire hopes to open up this poem somewhat, and encourage further detailed study.

Where the *Vox* slightly deviates from a straightforward antimercantile position, the *Mirour* takes a much more thoroughly ambivalent and even apologetic position on merchants. The *Vox* argues in favor of trade as a necessary part of the divine design of the world, and it shares many details with the *Mirour*. The *Mirour's* greater detail and initial rhetorical positioning, though, present a strong conflict between this promercantile vision of trade as necessary to worldly existence, and a more traditional antimercantile ideology. These two positions conflict in the *Mirour* within a context of national pride and widespread concern about foreign merchants, concerns balanced with a thick description of London merchants' malpractice. While Gower ultimately critiques English merchants, his engagement with a mercantile point of view in the *Mirour* presents some of the strongest evidence available for direct merchant involvement in the ideological conflict over merchandise. While the lack of information about the *Mirour's* medieval readership precludes certainty about its initial readership,[5] the poem's direct engagement with merchants' point of view suggests that Gower at least prepared for the possibility that merchants would read his poem.[6]

Gower's Apologetic Critique

We see such a conflict working in the *Mirour* immediately in the opening of the section on merchants. Gower here suggests that the estate of merchants has been ordained by God:

> Si une terre avoir porroit
> Tous biens ensemble, lors serroit
> Trop orguillouse, et pour cela
> Dieus establist, et au bon droit,
> Qe l'une terre en son endroit
> Del autry bien busoignera:
> Sur quoy marchant dieus ordina
> Qui ce q'en l'une ne serra
> En l'autre terre querre doit;
> Pour ce qui bien se gardera,
> Et loyalment marchandera,
> De dieu et homme il est benoit.

[If one country had all goods together, then it would be too proud. And therefore God established, quite rightly, that any one country would properly have need of the others. Thereupon God ordained merchants, who would go seek in another country whatever any one country did not have. Therefore, he who conducts himself well and trades honestly is blessed by God and man.] (*MO* ll. 25189–200)

The *Vox*'s section on merchants opens with similar material, with the surface emphasis of both openings on the licit reasons for trade:

> Quia varias rerum proprietates vsui humano necessarias nulla de se prouincia sola parturit vniuersas, inter alios mundi coadiutores Ciuium Mercatores instituuntur, per quos singularum bona regionum alternatim communicantur....
>
> [Since no single region by itself produces all the various kinds of things necessary for human use, merchants, among others, have been appointed to assist the world's citizens. Through their agency the goods of all regions are mutually shared.] (*VC* 5.654+)

In the *Vox* this justification represents almost the only divergence from a conventional antimercantile satire, and was not itself unorthodox by the fourteenth century. Nonetheless, this passage has supported a school of thought arguing for Gower's "mercantile and bourgeois bias."[7]

Gower's formulation of trade as divinely ordained in both poems is less a sign of "mercantile and bourgeois bias" than it might seem, though. Gower follows scholastic practice in part, and as an indication of how readily available such an idea might have been to Gower, Thomas Aquinas shares it in his more equivocal justification of trade, which presents a succinct approach to trade in line with that of Gower's contemporary Nicholas Oresme, if more conservative than the cutting-edge thirteenth-century work of Peter John Olivi. Aquinas distinguishes between "the exchange of commodity for commodity or of commodity for money, for the maintenance of life," which he associates with households and governments, and "exchange...of money for money, or even of any commodity for money, though now for the sake of making a profit, and this is the sort of exchange that belongs to business men in the strict sense;" he praises the former, and condemns the latter.[8] Coming from outside the estates satire tradition, Aquinas attests to trade's necessity, but retains the church's lingering distaste for the taint of finance in his implicit condemnation of usury in the sinfulness of exchanging "money for money." Gower resists directly linking professional trade to usury, though that sin will come up in his discussion of fraud, and he also avoids Aquinas' specific exemption of those who sell their produce, such as the great monasteries selling their wool, from the culpability of professional merchants and their profits. Instead Gower invokes the divine order without tying estate to the propriety of trade, just as elsewhere in the *Mirour* he lists other estates under Covoitise (*MO* ll. 6505–16), and attacks knights who engage in trade (*MO* ll. 23749–60). Gower focuses on good behavior as the characteristic that makes trade licit, in his emphasis on "qui bien se gardera," and this rhetorical move sets the stage for him briefly to consider virtuous merchants. This is not to say that Gower entirely disengages trade from merchants, since he discusses that estate predominantly in terms of trade. He complicates the sole identification of trade with merchants, though, and he challenges the satiric tradition of deferring economic blame onto merchants when he foregrounds that scapegoating by portraying it in an unexpected context.

Before deconstructing the scapegoating process, though, Gower localizes his vision of trade to England through his choice of commodities, as he describes how different countries have different products:

> Dieus solonc la diverseté
> Des terres ad ses biens donné
> A l'une leine, a l'autre soie,
> A l'une vin, a l'autre blée,
> Et ensi la commodité
> Divide.

> [God has given His goods according to the diversity of the countries: to one He has given wool; to another, silk; to one, wine, to another, wheat. And thus He divides commodities.] (*MO* ll. 25177–82)

Wool remained the primary commodity of the English economy, while wine was a primary English import from France, particularly from English-held Gascony.[9] Wheat was a staple crop in England as elsewhere, and silk long characterized long-distance trade, so that Gower has chosen staple commodities of Northern European trade.[10] The suggestion that a nation with every commodity would be "trop orguillouse" [too proud] (*MO* l. 25191) further complicates this text's relationship to antimercantile ideology, by linking trade to a Deadly Sin. Rather than suggesting that trade causes avarice, though, Gower praises trade's potential antidote to the more socially prominent sin of pride.[11] Similarly distancing trade from avarice, in the *Vox* Gower opposes trade to wrath as he presents trade relations as fundamental to the stability of the state (*VC* 5.669 — 5.670). In both poems Gower ties trade to sin, but presents trade as a social good while initially resisting the expected link of merchants to avarice. Gower shows his awareness of traditional antimercantile associations of trade and sin, but he characteristically rearranges and adapts those terms to create a more equivocal analysis of merchants.

Having established his satire firmly in England, Gower in the *Mirour* departs further from convention with an apology to good merchants prior to launching into his satire:

Et pour cela, si je voir die
As fols ce q'est de leur folie,
Ly sages oms ne se doit mye
Par celle cause coroucer;
Car foy d'encoste tricherie
Du plus notable apparantie
Par son contraire est a louer.
Les bons sont bons, les mals sont mals;
Dont si l'en preche as desloials,
Pour ce ne doit il pas chaloir
As ceaux qui sont en soi loials.

[And therefore (if I am to tell the truth), the wise man should not get angry because of the follies of the foolish; for good faith is to be praised by its contrast to fraud. The good are good; the bad are bad. So if one preaches to the bad, the good should pay no attention.] (*MO* ll. 25218–28)

Gower's simple logic here is highly disingenuous in a poem that spends thousands of lines cataloguing sins and virtues. This suggestion that good and bad people may easily be separated contradicts the central idea of the *Mirour de l'Omme*, and the remark that "As fols ce q'est de leur folie, / Ly sages oms ne se doit mye / Par celle cause coroucer" [The wise man should not get angry because of the follies of the foolish], directly contradicts Gower's own position at the opening of the poem. He had initially presented a traditional vision of satire:

Ainz vuill conter tout voirement
Coment les filles du Pecché
Font que tous sont enamouré
Par leur deceipte vilement.
He, amourouse sote gent,
Si scieussetz le diffinement
De ce dont avetz commencé,
Je croy que vostre fol talent
Changeast, qui meutz au present
Reson en bestialité.

[rather I want to tell very truthfully what the daughters of Sin do to make everyone love them for their vile deceit. Ah, foolish, loving people, if you knew the end of what you have begun, I believe you would change your mad ways, which are now turning reason into brutishness.] (*MO* ll. 13–24)

This initial position matches Paul Miller's characterization of medieval satires, in which "the satirist is motivated by indignation (*indignatio*) . . . which leads to his sudden (*ex abrupto*) outburst against human iniquity.... [He is] a poet who aims to correct with constructive criticism, not to defame with malicious slander."[12] Gower's overall satire demonstrates this indignation.

Since Gower from the beginning indignantly addresses the *Mirour* to the foolish, why does he later suggest that the wise listener should not get angry at fools, distancing himself from his satiric mode before he criticizes merchants? This defensiveness anticipates the possibility of a mercantile audience for this poem, a possibility because many London guilds wrote ordinances in Anglo-French.[13] This contradictory introductory material, both Gower's apology to merchants and his language choice for the poem, inscribes a possible merchant audience. While the mercers' 1393–94 Charter was in Latin, it would be a mistake to overstate merchants' Latinity: the Ovidian Latin of the *Vox* would have been far more difficult than trade Latin, which was directly dependent on London French vocabulary, syntax, and word order, while London French remained a viable dialect.[14] Given their dependence on French and "macaronic Latin,"[15] merchants would have been far more able to read the *Mirour*. Indeed, recent work on Anglo-French usage by London guilds suggests that Gower's hoped-for interaction with such a francophone audience may have been considerably more complicated than previous analyses of the *Mirour* have suggested.[16] Gower's usage of and plays on words which resonate between Anglo-French and Middle English in trade contexts suggests that he expected any mercantile readers to bring the full range of their linguistic and professional experience to a poem sharply criticizing them. Professional scribes' movement between work for the guilds and as literary scribes further suggests mercantile access to literary texts (see chapter 1). This is not, of course, to suggest that merchants were the only possible audience for a poem in Anglo-French, as R. F. Yeager makes a solid case for an initial aristocratic audience ultimately replaced by the brothers of the priory of St. Mary Overie.[17]

Still, a close reading of Gower's use of specific business terms indicates that he expected his readers to understand the business register, which allows him to target his satire very narrowly in this portion of the *Mirour*. Janet Coleman attests to the wide usage of Anglo-French in her study of medieval readers,[18] and William Rothwell has argued tirelessly that reports of the degeneracy of Anglo-French tend to be premature. Merchants and lawyers were major francophone populations; Kathleen E. Kennedy describes fourteenth-century development of "orthographic treatises in Latin" teaching either business or law French, reflecting the need for French in commercial and legal contexts.[19] Rothwell also notes that the usage of Anglo-French was apt to be "intertwined" with that of Latin and English.[20] This mixed linguistic practice suggests the value of looking very closely at cognates in poetic contexts. Indeed, based on Rothwell's work, it is often difficult to differentiate clearly between Middle English and Anglo-French words; he notes both how commonly Anglo-French vocabulary and meaning differ from that of Continental French,[21] and how regularly those Anglo-French terms find their way into Middle English.[22] Laura Wright's work on multilingual business writing also describes this slippage between Middle English and Anglo-French.[23] Gower consistently relies on the overlap in trade terminology between Anglo-French and Middle English. For example, take the now-common English word *customer*: Lisa Jefferson observes that "the meaning of a buyer or purchaser is specific to England,"[24] and it would come up primarily in business contexts. Gower uses the Anglo-French term in just such a context when he describes how Triche as a brewer only supplies good ale at first, "pour acrocher / Qe tu luy soies coustummer" [in order to get you as his customer] (*MO* ll. 26164–65). He uses a business word in a business context, but in his satire there is also no doubt that a customer is really a victim.

Given this complex linguistic situation for the poem, and its potential connection to a multilingual audience, Gower treads a fine rhetorical line when criticizing merchants. He carefully outlines how to practice legitimate trade, which creates a rhetorical space in his poem for morally upright merchants. He insists that "Pour ce vous dy, cil qui sa cure / Mettre voldra pour marchander, / Et son argent aventurer / S'il gaigne, en ce n'est a blamer, / Maisqu'il le face par mesure / Sanz fraude" [Therefore I say to you that he who wants to become a merchant and risk his money is not to be blamed if he earns a profit, provided he earn it in moderation and without fraud] (*MO* ll. 25205–10). Since the *Vox* has no parallel passage, this favorable treatment of trade appears linked to his linguistic choice and hence his audience; the Latin poem much more quickly moves to show how merchants seek ill-gotten gains (*VC* 5.657–62). Thus Gower replaces the good merchants' behavior of the *Mirour* with bad merchants' behavior in the *Vox*, which moves immediately from positive wealth to the "delit en lucre" that both poems ultimately condemn.

If this attention to merchants' sensibilities shows sensitivity to a merchant audience, we could find no more compelling evidence for it than Gower's casual mention of the value of good works in this portion of the poem:

Car chascuns solonc ses travals
Doit son pris ou son blame avoir
Ne sont pas un, pour dire voir,
Marchant qui pense a decevoir
Et l'autre qui par ses journals
En loialté se fait movoir;
Tout deux travaillont pour l'avoir,
Mais ils ne sont pas parigals.

[for each one, according to his works, should receive either praise or
blame. To tell the truth, there is a great difference between a merchant
who intends to deceive and another merchant who is motivated by good
faith in his daily work; both work to gain wealth but they are not at all
alike.] (*MO* ll. 25229–36)

This reliance on good works implicitly recalls the merchants' widespread
self-association with charity, in the form of the charitable works discussed
in the previous two chapters. Elsewhere in the *Mirour*, Gower further
links charity rhetorically with merchants. For example, when describing the virtue of charity Gower exclaims, "O Charité la dieu amye, /
Comme peres sage en marchandie! / Des toutez partz tu prens le gaign; /
Meulx valt donner la soule mie, / Maisque ce vient de ta partie, / Qe
sanzs toi donner tout le pain" [O Charity, beloved of God, what a shrewd
merchant you are! From all sides you get the profit. Better to give a single
crumb provided it comes from you than to give the entire loaf without
you] (*MO* ll. 13285–90). This passage links charity in the sense of *caritas*
directly to an act of largesse, the giving of bread, while using figurative language, "Comme peres sage en marchandie," to link the virtue
to an estate known to demonstrate it ostentatiously. In a similar vein,
Gower's description of alms-giving leans further on the trade metaphor,
explaining that "Qui donne almoisne il se proufite, / Qant il pour chose
si petite / Reprent tant large avancement" [He who gives alms profits
himself when he receives such a large return for such a small thing] (*MO*
ll. 15481–83), and going on to recount the parable of the widow's mites.
Taken together, these passages unite usage of mercantile language, such
as "marchandie," "marchant," "proufite," and "avancement," with a suggestion of an exchange of good works for salvation. Gower does not argue
that good works are sufficient, as he concedes that "Almoisne est doun,
nounpas bargaign, / Car droite Almoisne ne quiert gaign / Reprendre
de s'almoisnerie" [Alms-giving is a gift, not a trade, for proper Alms-
giving seeks to get no gain in return for her alms] (*MO* ll. 15601–3). The
biblical reference, to the widow who gives a small donation in Mark
12.41–44, further insulates Gower from the notion that salvation has a

specific price, a key distinction discussed in the previous chapter. Gower in these earlier passages on charity and largess uses mercantile language not as a critique of trade or eleemosynary charity, but as a metaphor for good works that must be united with "volenté parfite." These passages establish Gower's awareness of the same charitable impulse that was reflected by guild ordinances and merchants' testamentary patterns. In such a context, Gower's statement that good merchants will be known by their good works invokes an entire domain of cultural associations, and these terms of charity and good works thus appeal to merchants' better nature.

Despite this careful positioning in the early lines of the *Mirour*'s critique of merchants, Gower soon returns to his overall satiric project, that bountiful indignation. The shifting of sins of trade onto merchants seen in the earlier sections of *Piers Plowman*, which Gower initially avoids, returns with a twist in the *Mirour*'s approach to merchants. Gower focuses on the figure of Triche, or Fraud, who stands in for merchants throughout Europe, to create a peculiarly English critique of trade:

> Del un Marchant au jour present
> L'en parle molt communement,
> Il ad noun Triche plein de guile,
> Qe pour sercher del orient
> Jusques au fin del occident,
> N'y ad cité ne bonne vile
> U Triche son avoir ne pile.
>
> [Everyone nowadays talks a great deal about one merchant, called Fraud, full of guile. From the Orient to the end of the Occident there is no city or town where Fraud does not amass his wealth.] (*MO* ll. 25237–43)

This passage then lists all of the places where Triche can be found, including Bordeaux, Seville, Paris, Florence, Venice, Bruges, and Ghent (*MO* ll. 25244–51), a list which covers the Mediterranean trade through the Italian and Spanish cities, the wool trade tied to the cloth-making trade of the Low Countries, and the English wine trade centered around Bordeaux.[25] Triche may also be found in "La noble Cité sur Tamise, / La quelle Brutus fuist fondant" [the noble city on the Thames, which Brutus founded] (*MO* ll. 25254–55), both Gower's home and the center of English trade. Gower's estate of fraudulent merchants thus appears dangerously transnational, a trait that Chaucer and Margery Kempe will also associate with merchants. The very Gowerian repetition of the name "Triche" throughout the passage—an effect lost in Wilson's prose translation—reinforces the exotic locales associated with Triche.[26] The passage also makes Triche's sinfulness clear: "il ne chalt par quelle guise, / Ou soit derere ou soit devant, / Son propre lucre vait querant / Et le commun proufit despise" [he cares not in what guise (whether behind or before) he seeks his own lucre, disdaining the profit of the community] (*MO* ll. 25257–60).

Since Triche has his "franchise" (*MO* l. 25250) in these distant cities, but London is placed under his care (*MO* l. 25252), the wording of this passage also recalls the controversy surrounding the hotly debated role of alien merchants in English society, and expresses solidarity with English prejudices against aliens.[27] Elements of antimercantilism are present here, but Gower rearranges the terms to create a semimercantile position. Because the crown tended to favor alien merchants, local merchants often violently resented aliens (see chapter 1). Given the nature of the urban franchise, where one either bought or earned the "freedom" of a city and thus the right to trade in any commodity within city limits, there was no clear legal distinction between a native-born or alien with the franchise, but Londoners knew who was English. Since the crown favored its alien creditors with trade rights, sometimes allowing only aliens to export wool, Londoners had ample ground to resent such merchants, sometimes with individual violence and rioting. While the *Mirour* soon outlines merchants' malpractice in London terms categorized by guild, this catalogue of overseas cities where Triche has his franchise lists those places from which Londoners' greatest rivals came, particularly Venice, Florence, Bruges, and Ghent, and thus encourages readers' own prejudices against aliens. In contrast, the *Vox* refers to overseas cities without any nod to Londoners' resentment of aliens, complaining instead that international trade allows fraudulent merchants to claim that prices are higher overseas, "Ita Parisius Flandria siue dedit" [That's what Paris or Flanders has been paying] (*VC* 5.758).

This association of Triche with alien merchants allows Gower to rearrange the deferral of blame for the sins of the profit economy onto merchants, by pushing that deferral one step further. This construction of antimercantilism uses English merchants' own prejudices to place them in the unaccustomed role of applying the same terms with which they themselves were traditionally satirized. This role reversal foregrounds the scapegoating process of antimercantilism, which blamed merchants for the perception of sin created by late medieval distaste for money, assuming that the reader notices the scapegoating. This rhetorical move offers to a merchant reader the highly tempting possibility that the truly sinful merchants are these aliens who profit from England and take money out of the realm without giving it back. Gower's placement of Triche in Florence especially recalls anti-Italian prejudices familiar from Gower's earlier criticism of Lombards, who "orguil et leccherie / Et covoitise ont plus loé" [value pride, lechery, and covetousness most highly] (*MO* ll. 23237–38).

By mapping the conventions of satire onto English xenophobia, Gower ensures that a Londoner reading this text might briefly reassure himself that he was among the good merchants specifically exempted, and that aliens like the Flemish and Italians were to blame for Triche. Gower thus presents a trap for a merchant reader, whom he will directly attack within a few hundred lines. This initially shifted deferral of blame, like Gower's discussion of good merchants, creates a highly limited space for sympathy with English merchants. Simultaneously, the poem calls attention to the ideological construction of the antimercantile position by displacing the familiar structure of blaming merchants for avarice onto the English desire to blame aliens for fraud, or Lombards for usury. This redeployment of the rhetorical armament of antimercantile satire suggests that the reality of trade in English society was far more complicated than simple satire would suggest. Gower here criticizes and abandons the ideology that has condemned them too simplistically in the past. Far from being what David Aers labels a "bland, conventional criticism of all three estates," the complexity of Gower's satire of merchants reveals the limitations of conventional satire as a lead-in to a more detailed social critique.[28]

The Gloves Come Off

Although Gower uses the rivalry of London denizens and aliens to suggest that some merchants might be less honest than others, his shift to merchants' malpractice leaves no doubt that some sins *are* characteristic of London merchants. Gower first critiques fraudulent measure, a widespread concern. Gower had introduced it under the category of Triche much earlier in the poem, suggesting that "Ce sont q'ont double la balance / Et la mesure en decevance, / L'un meinz et l'autre trop comprent" [These are the ones who have double weight and measure in deceit, one including less, the other more] (*MO* ll. 6553–55), and suggesting a biblical prohibition on "mesure et pois que doublement / Se fait a la commun nuisance" [double weights and measures for the common harm] (*MO* ll. 6563–64). This concern with false measure was characteristic of the antimercantile position that Gower invokes with Triche. This sense that measure should be kept even and that a commodity should be what it seems depends directly on the concept of the just price, which dominates Gower's critique of London merchants. Just price theory's reliance on a fluctuating but more or less natural price that follows no fully understood

pattern (see chapter 1) makes the perception of fraud inherent to a subjec-
tively-defined just price: consumers' desire for the just price to be what
they would rather pay creates the perception of fraud.

Concerns with fraudulent measure were thus part of measuring goods
for sale, and Gower elaborates on the insecurity of measuring when
he discusses the grocers, that guild most intimately associated with
measurement:

> Ascune fois Triche est grossour,
> Mais il ad trop la foy menour
> Endroit de cell avoir du pois
> Quel il engrosse, et au retour
> Le vent par pois du meindre tour
> Q'il n'achata l'avoir ainçois,
> Dont par deceipte le surcrois
> Retient, et l'autre en ad descrois:
> Mais ce que chalt, car son amour
> Triche ad tourné tant sur la crois
> De l'esterling, q'as toutes fois
> Il quiert du bargaign le meillour.

[When he deals wholesale [*is a grocer*], Fraud may handle large transactions,
but he has small honesty in weights [possibly with the implication *the avoirdupois pound is dishonest*]; for he sells goods by a shorter weight than he used
for buying. So he retains as profit the excess weight obtained by deceit,
and his customer suffers the short-weight. But what is more important,
Fraud has concentrated his love on the cross of sterling; consequently he
always seeks the best bargain.] (*MO* ll. 25261–72)

Gower here adds to the commonplace of dishonest weight by associating
it with idolatrous love for "la crois de l'esterling" on the reverse of the
English coinage, presumably at the expense of that of Christ; this is a concern that will reappear later in the poem, and recalls Langland's Coveitise
lending "for loue of þe cros."[29] This term is also more directly monetary
than Wilson suggests with his simple translation "sterling," as "esterling"
was the Anglo-French term used by the English mint to designate the
English silver penny. "La crois de l'esterling" is literally "the cross on the
English penny."[30] More importantly, a detail lacking in Wilson's translation, Gower presents the weight issue in terms of a specific guild, as
Gower's analysis of mercantile malpractice groups merchants just as they
organized themselves, by guild. "Ascune Triche est grossour" should be
translated "when Triche is a grocer," which matters because the grocers
took their name from the "gross" or heavy avoirdupois pound-weight
in which they did most of their trade. Thus, the phrase "avoir du pois"

further ties this passage to the grocers' technical terminology. Through this special "grocer" weight, Gower's accusation that Triche the grocer buys with one weight and sells with another reflects grocers' usual purchase of goods in the 16-ounce pound avoirdupois and sale in the 12-ounce troy pound.[31] Gower's critique suggests that this shift between pounds caused some customer anxiety, and since the grocers themselves seem to have worried about weight standards, Gower targets both grocers' anxieties and their customers' suspicions.

Like the guild terminology of "grossour" and "avoir du pois," "bargaign" was a business term, and Rothwell lists *bargain* among key Anglo-French terms found in the archives of the Grocers' Company, arguing that "the extension of meaning that has given the modern English sense 'goods bought cheaply, for less than their real value' is already present in Anglo-French in the late 14c."[32] "Bargaign" is also familiar from Chaucer, whose Merchant "estatly was ... of his governaunce / With his bargaynes and with his chevyssaunce."[33] Jill Mann makes a convincing case that when paired with terms like *chevisance*, *exchange*, and *usury*, this term was part of the estates satire discourse on merchants,[34] and Gower himself links "Eschange, usure et chevisance" (*MO* l. 25417). In the context of Gower's discussion of grocers, the terms "esterling" and "bargaign" combine traditional antimercantile satire of a merchant seeking the "best bargain" with careful usage of Anglo-French discourse on trade and money, so that the business register of Anglo-French localizes and strengthens his satire. The grocers' own efforts in regulating members' measures suggest that it shared Gower's satiric concern, as articles concerning the grocers in a London city charter of grocer Sir Nicholas Brembre's 1384 mayoralty specifically place the grocers' scales and measures "in custodia proborum et sufficiencium hominum de eadem Ciuitate" [in the custody of honest and sufficient men of the same City].[35] Gower's reference to the grocers, who included such powerful figures as mayors Brembre and Sir John Philpot (see chapter 1), localizes his satire just as specifically as subsequent stanzas' naming of Triche "en mercerie" [in the mercer's trade] (l. 25274), or as a "draper" (l. 25309).

The latter two trades continue the London orientation of Gower's critique of merchants. Despite his initial suggestion that fraudulent merchants might be aliens, Gower attacks powerful guilds by name. Leaders of the grocers, mercers, and drapers all profited from the highly lucrative cloth trade; Gower's mercer sells "litz, courchiefs, penne ostricer, / Cendals, satins, draps d'outre mer" [Beds, kerchiefs, ostrich feathers, silks, satins, imported cloths] (*MO* ll. 25291–92), while the draper sells clothes and cloth for people to use specifically for clothing. The sins of these local cloth traders are also very specific. The mercers come across in Gower's description as rhetorical ancestors of used-car salespeople, with "Q'il ad toutplein du queinterie, / Des buffles et de musardie, / Pour assoter la vaine gent, / Dont porra gaigner lour argent: / Et si parole bell et gent, / Et fait leur bonne compaignie / Du bouche" [for he has plenty of cunning, jokes, and tricks to make vain people foolish, so that he can get their money. And he talks so well and politely and entertains them well with his mouth] (*MO* ll. 25276–82). This particular complaint has more to do with sales technique than actual fraud, although given the context one expects a certain amount of falsehood in the sales-pitch that Gower describes.

Gower's description here calls upon a reader's potential experience as a customer of these mercers, and advises readers how to protect themselves from them. Unlike Mann's description of Chaucer's merchants as "victimless" sinners,[36] the victim of Gower's mercers is in part the reader, whom Gower directly addresses:

Car Triche au point ne se desclose,
Ainçois par sa coverte glose
Te dourra craie pour fourmage.
Tu quideretz par son language
Qe celle urtie q'est salvage
Soit une preciouse rose,
Tant te ferra courtois visage;
Mais si voels estre sanz damage,
En son papir ne te repose.

[For Fraud never reveals himself fully; rather, by his sly flattery he will give you chalk for cheese. You will think by his language that this wild nettle is a precious rose—so courteous a face he will put on for you—but if you will escape unhurt [*without damage*], do not trust yourself to his paperwork.] (*MO* ll. 25300–8)

Gower's use of "te" and "tu" places the reader directly into the experience of mercers' fraud, and makes the vice immediate and personal. The phrase "sanz damage" also portrays the feeling of being cheated as immediate and personal, a feeling reinforced by images like nettles sold as roses, and chalk for cheese. Gower uses this same technique in his description of the drapers, as well, who under-light their wares (*MO* ll. 25321–32). While the mercers' ordinances do not directly address this specific criticism, the 1364 Letters Patent of the drapers acknowledge a general problem of "demy grein" cloth being sold as the more expensive "escarlet."[37] Though the Letters Patent do not attributed this fraud to actual members of the Drapers' Company, this selling of "demy grein" as scarlet would be made easier by poor light, recalling the misrepresentation described by

Gower. More generally, these details match the traditional sins of fraud associated with merchants, since both mercers and drapers mislead their buyers. Gower's images of fast-talking mercers and of drapers' dim shops make that traditional fraud both specific and experiential. This localizing effect complicates Gower's earlier deferral of blame from local merchants to aliens, by establishing mercantile behavior as more complicated than the traditional antimercantile position allows, while still implicating merchants in the sins described by that tradition. He follows convention by criticizing false measure, but fraud involves more than just the injustice of false measure or adulterated silver, because it also necessitates people like the reader getting cheated, and not all merchants practice the same frauds. These merchants' vices affect the implied audience, "tu" and "te," who run the risk of being convinced by flattery that chalk is cheese. Given how many Londoners were involved in trade, and that London merchants were a potential audience for the poem, direct address to the reader also reminds merchant readers what it feels like to be cheated.[38]

The Trouble with the Wool Staple

Gower then further localizes his vision of sinful merchants in the *Mirour* in a passage usually labeled the paean to wool (*MO* ll. 25369–428), a passage which John Fisher sees as patriotic.[39] Fisher unfortunately ignores the role of Triche, and the poem's overt criticism of royal Staple policy, which required all wool to be shipped through a certain port or ports either in England or more commonly on the Continent, typically Calais. This passage, which has no counterpart in the *Vox*, outlines the value of the wool trade to the realm, but it also shows how Triche manipulates the Staple for his own benefit. Gower's references to the Staple in this context thus attack the crown's Staple policy through Triche's involvement. The policy focused the wool trade in a single city to make it easier to control and tax, but it also had the effect of enriching the monopoly of the Staple merchants, the committee of merchants to whom the implementation of the policy was sold.[40] The Staple's appearance here thus casts aspersions on the Staplers which are not entirely clear in Wilson's translation: "Mai il ad trop soubtile aleine / Qant il l'estaple de la leine / Governe, car de son encress / Lors trete et parle asses du pres" [But he has a very keen nose when he checks the staple of the wool, for he is now dealing with and talking about his own profit] (*MO* ll. 25360–64). Wilson's translation of "governe" as the relatively weak "check," rather than the cognate meaning that Wilson uses later in l. 25397, elides the implication that Triche is a Stapler, a suggestion which would have been apparent to a reader familiar with the controversial governing of the Staple. Wilson's translation of the passage makes too little of the slippage between Anglo-French and Middle English in the period, in that both languages had a comparable range of meaning for *governe* in Gower's time: both the *Anglo-Norman Dictionary* and *Middle English Dictionary* list similar meanings of "control" or "manage" for the word. Rothwell also cites the passage's term "encress" for "(accrued) profit" as part of the business register displayed in the grocers' archive.[41]

The passage on wool also makes the leap from specific guilds directly to the main source of London wealth, the bulk wool trade. Since local merchants like drapers and mercers had to deal with big international operators like the Italians, this critique of wool implicates English merchants in the sins of international trade, much as the transparency of Gower's deferral of blame for trade onto alien merchants ultimately implicated London merchants willing to redirect the deferral of blame onto aliens. This attack on the wool trade shares general elements of his initial treatment of Triche, as wool distracts merchants from their proper spiritual devotion, much as the "la crois de l'esterling" had earlier. Extending this notion of idolatrous desire for wool and thus money, he presents it as the "duesse" [goddess] (l. 25370) of merchants, and thus kin to Langland's Lady Mede. Wool is also a source of "fortune" (l. 25372), and an idol of "cristin…paien et Sarazin" [Christian, pagan, and Saracen] (*MO* ll. 15378–79), combining the exoticism of international trade with a sense that it can pull devotees away from any religion. Wool also represents a source of power "en temps du peas, en temps du guerre" [in times of peace and times of war] (l. 25384), a strong statement to make during a war financed in large part by the wool trade. With another reference to the Staple, the passage firmly links Triche to the Staplers, telling "leine":

> En Engleterre tu es née,
> Mais que tu es mal governé
> L'en parle molt diversement;
> Car Triche, q'ad toutplein d'argent,
> De ton estaple est fait regent,
> Est le meine a sa volenté
> En terre estrange, u proprement
> Son gaign pourchase, et tielement
> Nous autres sumes damagé.

> [In England you are born, but many people say widely that you are ill-governed. For Fraud (who is full of money) has got control of your warehouse, and he takes you at his will into strange countries, where he seeks his ill-gotten gains, and thus the rest of us suffer hurt.] (*MO* ll. 25396–404)[42]

Wilson does not quite capture the mercantile register: this time he keeps the cognate with "governé," but translates "ton estaple" as "your

warehouse" despite his earlier translation of it as "staple." This choice
obscures Gower's claim here that the Staple is mismanaged. Gower's
critique of Staple policy works topically, as the controversy over Staple
management was central to London politics in the 1370s. Placement of
the Staple initially helped make Calais financially independent of the
crown,[43] but by the early 1370s the Staple was dominated by grocers
led by Nicolas Brembre, who were challenged by those rivals who purchased licenses to avoid it, led by John de Northampton.[44] This controversy became national, as the king's sale of those licenses drew the
crown into a London feud, and Gower's challenge to the greed behind
the Staple policy ultimately implicates the crown in his critique of merchants. Indeed, regular and unpredictable shifts in the Staple policy
encouraged the perception of merchants as being up to something with
the king, and Gower is not afraid to say so. As with the initial deferral of Triche onto aliens, Gower's attack on the Staple integrates into
satire the criticisms generated by merchants' rivalries. This coopting of
mercantile rivalries thus balances Gower's awareness of the issues that
most exercised the merchant estate with a consistent sense that, while
merchants might be subject to greed, they are hardly unique in that
quality.

Alongside this criticism of national trade policies, the wool passage
then repeats the familiar triplet of negative financial terms: "Eschange,
usure et chevisance, / O laine, soubz ta governance / Vont en ta noble
Court servir" [Foreign exchange, usury, and bargaining go under
your rule to serve in your noble court, O Wool] (*MO* ll. 25417–19).
As Jill Mann points out, the same three terms are linked to Langland's
Coveitise (see chapter 2), and two of the three to Chaucer's *General
Prologue* Merchant (see chapter 4). She explains that "exchange" and
"chevisance" were generally associated with usury in the satire tradition, and consistently bore negative connotations in that context.[45]
While Mann sees these three terms as "professional jargon,"[46] they also
represent a constellation of mercantile practices of which the satirists
collectively disapproved. Rothwell cites Chaucer's use of "chevisance"
as an Anglo-French borrowing,[47] and the word is widely used in Middle
English satire of merchants. There were methods of exchange that were
permissible in Gower's time, and the term "chevisance" has complicated
connotations, but lending money for interest remained forbidden under
canon law. The ban on usury was one of the last elements of the antimercantile position to survive (see chapter 1). Gower's connection of
usury directly to Triche thus makes explicit the link between usury and
merchandise implicit in a general distrust of money, and the *Vox* classifies usury specifically as a sin of merchants:

Hoc scit mercator instanti tempore ciuis,
Qui probat vsuram posse licere suam...
Sic latet Vsure facies depicta colore
Fraudis, vt hinc extra pulcra pateret ea...
Nonne deum fallit cautelis institor ipse,
Talia dum scelera celat in arte sua?

[At the present time the merchant-citizen, who approves of his being able
to put a price on his usury, knows how to do this [create a gloss contra-
dicting the ban on usury]....Thus Usury's face lies hidden, painted with
the hue of Fraud in order that she may hence appear outwardly beauti-
ful....Surely the merchant doesn't deceive God himself with his precau-
tions, when he conceals such evil deeds with his skill?] (*VC* 5.723–32)

The link here between usury and merchandise comes, of course, from
the taint of finance generated by the usury ban, continually placed in
tension with the increasing sophistication of the money economy and
international finance.

Gower demonstrates the staying power of this traditional distrust of
money and monetary transactions most clearly with the *Vox*'s usury passage (*VC* 5.723–32); he is more measured in the *Mirour*'s explanation of
how the temptation of profit leads merchants into dishonest practice:
"Mais quique s'en voet abstenir / Du fraude, Triche ades l'avance, / Siq'en
les laines maintenir / Je voi plusours descontenir / Du loyalté la viele
usance" [But though some abstain from Fraud, Fraud always increases,
so that, in keeping wool going, I see many who cease to observe the old-
fashioned usages of honesty] (*MO* ll. 25424–28). This passage vividly presents the temptations of wool profits. Gower can see the potential profit of
wool as both appealing, when he states that "La terre dont tu es norris /
Par toy puet grande chose fere" [the country in which you are nourished
can do great things through you] (*MO* ll. 25391–92), and threatening in
this passage, where it moves merchants from "la viele usance" of honest
practice to "l'avance" of Triche. While Gower acknowledges the limitations of the antimercantile position in his willingness to connect avarice
with estate groups other than merchants, he retains many of its assump-
tions, such as scorn for usury and a corresponding willingness to apply
that scorn to a common merchant practice like exchange. He does not
stereotype merchants consistently, though, between his acceptance of the
potential positive power of wool's wealth, his willingness to describe
temptation, and his rhetorical technique of placing merchant readers in
the position of criticizing each other.

Those Pesky Lombards

Having now in the *Mirour* attacked national trade policy and the most powerful merchants in England, Gower retreats to his earlier technique of playing upon merchants' prejudices by moving from Londoners and Staplers to an attack on Lombards which has no parallel in the *Vox*. Lombards represented various negative traits to the English, both as the inheritors of the Jewish trade in usury[48] and as representations of tyrants, but for Gower here they are aliens "Q'est ce q'ils vuillont chalanger / A demourer en noz paiis / Tout auci francs, auci cheris, / Comme s'ils fuissent neez et norriz / Ovesque nous" [who...try to claim to dwell in our country just as free [*franchised*] and welcome as if they were born and brought up with us] (*MO* ll. 25433–37). This description plays upon Italian merchants' privileged position in the English economy, but Gower goes on to blame them for taking gold bullion out of the country in exchange for unnecessary luxury goods (*MO* ll. 25441–52), and for subverting the nobility into supporting them instead of denizens (*MO* ll. 25453–64). Gower seems particularly indignant about the fact that "Par leur deceipte et leur conspir / Plus noblement se font vestir / Qe les burgois de no Cité" [They clothe themselves by their deceit and conspiracy more nobly than the burghers of our city] (*MO* ll. 25468–70). This particular criticism seems ideally suited to appeal to a possible merchant audience, by reminding a burgess that he or she is being outshone by aliens, at the same time that the phrase "plus noblement" reminds a reader that those burgesses themselves may have been overdressed in violation of sumptuary laws.[49] A reader may recognize his or her own prejudices in Gower's criticism of the Lombards, but not without getting a dose of it. Gower also caters to merchants here by suggesting that avarice reaches out beyond the merchants into the nobility: "Mais c'est grant honte au seignourage, / Qui nous duissont garder la loy, / De noz marchantz mettre en servage, / Et enfranchir pour le pilage / Les gens estranges trestout coy" [But it is a great shame that our lords, who ought to keep the law for us, are putting our merchants in bondage, and very quietly letting foreigners pillage everything] (*MO* ll. 25484–88). Given that royal favor created the Lombards's privileged position, most English merchants would agree with Gower here. Still, denizens themselves were hardly in a position to cast stones, although many mercers seem to have done so quite literally (see chapter 1). The fact that Lombards could get the franchise of the city of London when English merchants from outside London might not would naturally have been a source of resentment, but it also shows how the concept of nationality in the context of merchants was a troubled one. Since the great sins of the Lombards seem to be supplanting English merchants and taking resources out of England, they represent a particular threat to the conception of the estates as locally interdependent, by undermining the loyalties that the nobility should have to English subjects. Although Gower at some level challenges the idea of the three estates by spending most of his analysis of the third estate discussing lawyers and merchants rather than laborers, this invocation of inter-estate loyalty places merchants in the same position relative to the nobility in which tradition would place peasants.

Antimercantilism Redux

While Gower may seem to be done with merchants at this point, we immediately see how the broad definition of merchants affects Gower's conception of the third estate, as he attributes the same basic sins of fraud to the less purely mercantile guilds, "ceaux qui vivont du mestier et d'artifice" (*MO* l. 25500+), matching the general practice cited by Mann.[50] Triche reappears, and his tricks remain the same. When Gower discusses Triche as a goldsmith, he uses a number of terms that have highly technical meanings in the records of that guild, observing:

> Triche est Orfevere au plus sovent,
> Mais lors ne tient il pas covent,
> Qant il d'alconomie allie
> Le fin orr et le fin argent;
> Si fait quider a l'autre gent
> Qe sa falsine soit verraie;
> Dont le vessell, ainz q'om l'essaie,
> Vent et reçoit la bonne paie
> De l'esterling, et tielement
> Del argent q'il corrompt et plaie
> Sa pompe et son orguil desplaie,
> Et se contient trop richement.

> [Fraud is often a goldsmith, but then keeps not his agreement when, by alchemy, he alloys fine gold with fine silver. Thus he makes people believe that his adulteration is pure gold. So before someone can test the vessel, he sells it and receives a good price paid in sterling silver. And thus, corrupted by silver, he displays his pomp and pride and lives on a very rich scale.] (*MO* ll. 25513–24)

Here Gower seems quite clear how goldsmiths speak. For example, Lisa Jefferson explains that the term "alconomie" is used in the London gold-smiths' records to refer to "a metallic composition, a yellowish alloy, imitating gold;" she refers as an example to "Alkenamye et faux argent" being found in a prosecution for fraud.[51] Gower's description of adulterating precious metals is further complicated by Jefferson's observation that "argent fin" was the guild's technical term for "refined silver."[52] Similarly, the verb "essaier" is a technical term meaning "to assay."[53] Incorporating this jargon into the translation gives a somewhat different sense than Wilson provides: Triche as goldsmith uses a specific alloy mixture known to the trade to adulterate materials refined to the craft standard, and is able to sell vessels made of this adulterated metal before they can be assayed and his fraud revealed. Gower also calls attention here to the irony of exchanging such alloyed silver for pure English coinage, the familiar "esterling."[54] As with the material on grocers, mercers, and drapers, Gower here balances traditional satire with specific reference to dishonest trade practices. The concern with purity in particular is a commonplace regarding gold and silver.[55] Logically enough, the goldsmiths seem to have shared this worry, as their 1327 charter focuses on standards and purity.[56] Perhaps this explains why Gower felt the need to make this particular accusation again: "Mais bien sai q'il fait trop de mal, / Q'ensi l'argent fin et loyal / De sa mixture fait falser" [But I know well that he commits much evil by adulterating fine [refined] honest silver in his mixture] (MO ll. 22528–30). Given that Gower does go to some lengths earlier in the poem to deconstruct the process by which merchants are blamed for the sins of materialism by estates satire, he seems here to use the business register and technical terms to put a local face on satiric generalizations; the Mirour problematizes overgeneralized satire, but models satiric tropes' applicability to local practice.

Once Gower has critiqued a number of local crafts, he then returns to merchants in general, and where his earlier discussion of merchants' malpractice reflected their concerns and brought a potential merchant reader into his poem, he moves here to a much more abstract and allegorical emphasis on merchants' dishonesty, as opposed to dishonest practice, followed by a criticism of merchants' debt. The terms of merchants' dishonesty and bad faith strengthen his earlier critiques:

Q'est ce que je vous dirray plus,
Mais que le siecle est trop confus
Des tieus marchantz especial?
Q'entr'eulx ont loyalté refus,
Si ont le triche retenuz:
De luy ont fait lour governal,
Et de Soubtil le desloial
Ont fait lour sergant communal,
Qui vent les choses a lour us:

Ja Bonne foy deinz leur hostall
Ne puet entrer apprentisal,
Car guile le reboute al huiss.

[What more shall I tell you, except that the world is brought to ruin by such merchants especially? For they have rejected honesty, and have allied themselves with Fraud, whom they have made their governor. And they have made Cunning, the dishonest, their common servant, and he sells things in their way. Good Faith can never take up apprenticeship in their house, for Guile turns him back at the door.] (*MO* ll. 25789–800)

This particular attack is not uniformly antimercantile, since Gower carefully refers to "tieus marchantz" who are dishonest, while he emphasizes the global damage caused as "le siecle est trop confus" by merchants' dishonesty. With greater abstraction, he balances his earlier particularity with a moral and allegorical style, arguing just why dishonest merchants are such a bad thing. At the same time, though, he keeps that moral allegory in a mercantile context: the detail that "Good Faith" cannot be such a merchant's apprentice enhances the personification of "Bonne foy" with the everyday scene of an apprentice entering a master's home, and also seems to invoke *Piers Plowman*, where merchants "bishetten [Guile] in hire shoppes to shewen hire ware, / And apparailed hym as a prentice þe peple to serue."[57] While Gower shifts here to a more formal tone and abstract language, he retains the realities of urban life that made his earlier critiques so specific and aimed at a merchant audience.

Once he has established this allegorical mode, Gower moves on to describe another generalized problem of merchants—debt. He balances his critique of overborrowing with an attack on inflation:

Jadis qant les marchantz parloiont
De vingt et Cent, lors habondoiont
De richesce et de soufficance,
Lors de lour propres biens vivoiont,
Et loyalment se contenoiont
Sanz faire a nully decevance:
Mais ils font ore lour parlance
De mainte Mill; et sanz doubtance
Des tieus y ad que s'il paioiont
Leur debtes, lors sanz chevisance
Ils n'ont quoy propre a la montance
D'un florin, dont paier porroiont.

[When merchants of old talked of twenty or a hundred, they had plenty and abundance of wealth, and lived from their own means, conducting themselves honestly without deceiving anyone. But now they parley about many thousands; and no doubt there are some who, if they paid their debts, would not have left any more than a florin with which to pay.] (*MO* ll. 25813–24)

This rare idea of a golden age of merchandise is not the sort of thing we find in the *Vox*, and this passage shifts the poem's discursive space for morally good merchants to the past. As Gower becomes more abstract and more harsh, he portrays the merchants of his time as inflated beyond their natural limits. His condemnation of great debts makes large-scale merchants who talk in thousands seem literally hollow: the thousands of which they speak are not theirs, leaving them merely braggarts or liars, while the mention of business debts recalls his earlier attack on usury. There also remains some question about whether these debts are necessarily monetary ones. Gower explains that when the merchants are dead, "lors crier / Om puet oïr la niceté / De leur orguil, que povreté / Leur debtes covient excuser" [Then one can weep to hear of the folly of their pride, for poverty has to forgive their debts] (*MO* ll. 25833–36). Given that Gower had earlier stated the need for restitution of dishonest profits (*MO* ll. 6529–40), there remain the questions of whether "poverty has to forgive their debts" in the sense that merchants must be forgiven by their poor victims, and whether mercantile practice might also generate unpayable spiritual debts. Certainly one hears an echo here of *Piers Plowman*'s "*Redde quo debes.*"[58] If these debts are as spiritual as Langland's, then Gower uses the mercantile language which earlier made his examples specific to express the dangers of merchandise in the very language that those merchants might use for their daily business. He thus retains a sense of what a merchant audience needs to hear to understand his message.

This use of mercantile language in the *Mirour* continues with a biblical citation, where Gower uses the business register to discuss the dangers of substituting present happiness for future salvation:

En l'evangile truis escrit
Dieus nous demande quel profit
Homme ad pour tout le mond gainer,
Qant il en pert son espirit:
C'est un eschange mal confit
Pour chose que ne puet durer.
Mais Triche ainçois en marchander
Quiert le proufit de son denier,
Qe tout le bien q'est infinit;
Quique luy doit desallouer,
Il prent du siecle son louer,

Mais au final ne s'esjoÿt.

[In the gospel I find written that God asks us what profit a man has for
gaining the world if thereby he loses his soul. It is a bad exchange for
something that cannot endure. But in trading, Fraud seeks profit for his
money before all infinite good. Blame him who may, he takes his reward
from the world, but in the end he does not rejoice.] (*MO* ll. 25897–908)

This stanza cites Matthew 16.26, "For what doth it profit [*prodest*] a man,
if he gain [*lucretur*] the whole world, and suffer the loss of his own soul?
Or what exchange [*commutationem*] shall a man give for his soul?"[59] Some
of Gower's mercantile language derives from the biblical text, such as
"profit" from "prodest," "gainer" from "lucretur," and "eschange" from
"commutationen," but Gower adds the mercantile language of Triche's
"marchander" and his misplaced priorities of "le proufit de son denier"
(the cross of sterling again) over "le bien q'est infinit." The sting at the
end of that stanza, "mais au final ne s'esjoÿt" recapitulates the previous
stanza's warning of divine "vengance" (l. 25892) and punishment "apres
la mort" (l. 25895). This passage thus supplements biblical commercial
language to apply the problem of salvation in the material world directly
to a context where exchange or "commutatio" represents the fundamental
defining factor of the estate under discussion. Biblical metaphor becomes
real, because it is no longer a metaphor. As we saw in *Piers Plowman*,
the exchange of present good for future damnation overlaps with the
exchange of merchandise, linking profit potentially to damnation.

"Par Argument du Marchandie": The Merchants' Own Words?

At this moment where Gower brings the Bible to bear against the sins
of merchants, he makes the odd move of citing what he claims are merchants' own defenses of their practice. He overcomes their claims so easily that one has to wonder whether his "merchants" are straw men or just
theological unsophisticates. The first "argument du marchandie" (*MO*
ll. 25928–29) is that "qui puet tenir la doulçour / De ceste vie et la des-
voie, / A son avis ferroit folour, / Q'apres ce nuls sciet la vérrour, / Queu
part aler ne quelle voie" [He who can have the sweetness of this life and
turns it away would, in his opinion, commit folly, for afterwards no one
knows truly where we go nor by what way] (*MO* ll. 25916–20). Such a
position directly contradicts the earlier biblical citations, and the lesson
of the verse cited by the poem, Matthew 16.26, depends on the faith
in the Christian afterlife that this hypothetical merchant denies in the
assertion that "no one knows truly where we go." In this context such

doubters damn themselves with their own words. Gower's presentation of a merchant reader's response to his poetry shows that reader missing the whole point of the poem's earlier contrast between positive and negative mercantile behavior. Similarly, the "mercantile" claim in the poem that "Et nepourqant quie les reprent, / Tout lour estat par argument / Du marchandie justefiont" [And yet, whoever reproves them is told they justify all their estate by the argument of 'business'] (*MO* ll. 25927–29) rings overtly false, in the sense that the Gower has already explained repeatedly in his section on merchants that there are specific routes toward merchants' salvation through honesty. Since Gower has gone out of his way to establish in detail that merchandise need not involve fraud, this later suggestion that sinful behavior is part of business seems naive at best. As Gower puts it, "Des marchans ore luy alqant / Le siecle blament nepourqant, / Et l'un et l'autre en sa partie / Vait mainte cause enchesonant: / L'un dist arere et l'autre avant, / Mais riens parlont du tricherie / Q'ils mesmes font en marchandie" [Certain merchants nowadays blame the world, however, and each in turn puts the blame on many a different cause; one says one thing, the other another. But they say nothing of the frauds which they themselves commit in trading] (*MO* ll. 25945–51). The antimercantile shifting of economic blame reappears, but here that deferral is being overtly practiced by merchants to avoid taking responsibility for their sins, a move which extends Gower's deconstruction of that rhetorical approach to merchants' sin.

This argument suggests that sin is the world's fault, just as Londoners want merchandise to be aliens' fault and clerics want greed to be merchants' fault, but in the context of a poem about Reason rescuing the Soul from the World, blaming the world for sin is no excuse. As Gower's satire shifts from merchant practice to merchant thought, he sees the merchants' error more in their approach to their trade than in the details of that trade itself. Where he first addresses merchants' malpractice, he now condemns the attitudes that allow such sins to go on. Gower does return briefly to his earlier semiconciliatory position with the reminder that "chascune art en sa substance, / De ce que donne sustienance / A luy qui de son mestier vit, / Est bonne en bonne governance" [But every craft (by giving sustenance to him who lives from his trade) is substantially good, if it is under good direction] (*MO* ll. 25975–78). After going on at such length on the ubiquity of Triche, though, such a conciliation acts more to underline the extent of merchants' moral failure through an implicit comparison of how merchants are, and how they could and should be.

Since Gower ultimately condemns merchants, how do we explain his movement from his initial conciliatory position to this final condemnation? We know that with the *Vox* in the next decade, he abandoned the conciliation with trade found in the trade section of the *Mirour*, and one can be reasonably sure that few merchants were equipped to tackle the *Vox*'s Latin. While most critics argue for a limited audience for the *Mirour*, with Fisher arguing that Gower mostly wrote it for himself,[60] and Yeager extending that potential audience to the Austin priory where Gower retired,[61] such a small audience might profitably be expanded by considering London merchants as a population which could have read the poem. With such a potential audience in mind, Gower's increasing condemnation of merchants in the *Mirour* may arise from the competing ideologies of trade at play in his text. On the one hand, he shows unusual sympathy with the promercantile position of balancing trade with charity, and his initial insistence that there can be good merchants suggest that he adopts at least in part the ideological position that there remains spiritual hope for those who make their living in trade. He also consistently manipulates rivalries between Londoners and aliens, basing much of his critique directly on merchants' own prejudices. His objections to the Staple policy, his attack on the Lombards, and his descriptions of sins that both the goldsmiths and the grocers took institutional care to avoid all argue that Gower shared merchants' understanding of the flaws within their estate. On the other hand, Gower uses traditional antimercantile material right along with that mercantile discourse. The grouping of usury, exchange, and chevisance, and the repetitive use of false measure and violation of the just price are entirely conventional, as is the general association of avarice with trade. The contrast with the *Vox* is instructive here, in that the *Vox* lacks the conciliatory elements of the promercantile ideology that abound in the *Mirour*. With the conventional focus on fraud and usury shared by the *Mirour* no longer balanced by the earlier poem's references to the Staple or to aliens, the critique of trade in the *Vox* seems more purely satirical. That being the case, the possibility of a mercantile audience for the *Mirour* shows why he might use traces of promercantile ideology to bring merchant readers into his analysis of trade. By coopting promercantile ideology, Gower can show merchant readers how their own prejudices and excuses deploy the deferral structure of the antimercantile position. Thus Gower both reveals limitations of antimercantile satire and reflects merchants' prejudices right back onto merchant readers. A clerical audience would have no need for such a ploy, but his attention to merchants' concerns renders his attacks potentially constructive, if they reach a receptive audience.

Gower thus shows himself early in his poetic career to be able to write a satire on the merchant estate that pulled no punches, but also cast itself in terms that its targets could understand. He certainly abandoned this approach in his later courtly poems. The *Vox* takes a much harder line with merchants and makes no effort to speak to their own concerns, and the *Confessio Amantis* abandons merchants altogether, except for a few appearances like the father of the steward's wife in "Tale of the King and his Steward's Wife," who is the victim rather than the perpetrator of avarice.[62] We cannot know why Gower abandoned this address of his satire to the merchant community, but the result is that Gower has not been remembered for his engagement with the estate of merchants, to the extent that they have not even occurred to scholars seeking Gower's probable audiences. Still, Gower shows an unheard-of sympathy for and understanding of the subjects of his satire of trade, even if he does abandon that conciliatory approach for more direct condemnation by the end of the *Mirour*. Rather than blaming merchants for the sins of the market, he suggests ways such as honesty and modestly scaled trade that merchants might compromise between the pressures of clerical antimercantilism and the lure of easy profits. That he did not continue in this vein could mean that his message fell on deaf ears or simply that he lost interest in mercantile sins, moving through them stereotypically in the *Vox* and avoiding them entirely in the *Confessio*. Certainly Gower's shifting approach to mercantile sins acts as a reminder that his work is not as unitary in its voice as we may assume.

CHAPTER 4

THE DELIBERATE AMBIGUITY OF CHAUCER'S ANXIOUS MERCHANTS

Geoffrey Chaucer's *General Prologue* Merchant reveals only indirectly the conflict between the residual antimercantile ideology developed in early response to an increasingly complex money economy, and the more conciliatory ideology emerging by Chaucer's time.[1] Indeed, this chapter will be in part an exploration of the Chaucerian critical tradition, as the poet himself avoids unequivocal adherence to either ideology, and generally refuses to be pinned down on his attitudes toward his birth-estate. His merchants do incorporate elements of the antimercantile ideology of his estates satire and penitential sources, but Chaucerian merchants also reflect the mercantile estate's own responses to fears and expectations of damnation. This adaptation of both pro- and antimercantile traditions in Chaucer's merchants suggests that the critical tradition of Chaucerian merchants has been so confused because Chaucer himself subtly negotiates between pro- and antimercantile treatments of merchants, thus supporting both readings. His deliberate ambiguity concerning merchants, though by no means central to the overall movement of the *Canterbury Tales*, does provide some insight into Chaucer's much more central concern with the efficacy of satire, because he ultimately uses satiric material to charge merchants with discursive inadequacy. I focus initially on the site of the critical battleground of the *General Prologue*'s description of the Merchant, and will then briefly follow the trajectory of Chaucer's adaptation of antimercantile satire in the *Tales*, where Chaucer carefully structures his ambivalence toward merchants as a subtle criticism of their relations with texts.

I will not, however, propose the *General Prologue* as a key to all Chaucerian merchants, as there are important differences between Chaucer's approach to estates satire material in the *General Prologue* and his treatment of merchants elsewhere. Most obviously, he treats them as entirely unproblematic in the *Parson's Tale*, wherein the Parson simply distinguishes between good and bad merchandise (the latter being simony), and presents the familiar defense of trade that "there as God hath ordeyned that a regne or a contree is suffisaunt to hymself, thanne is it honest and leveful that of habundaunce of this countree, that men helpe another contree that is moore nedy. / And therfore ther moote been marchantz to brygen fro that o contree to that oother hire marchandises."[2] Still, the traditional practice of using the *General Prologue* as a key to the tales has encouraged close critical analysis of the *General Prologue* portraits. John Matthews Manly's search for historical antecedents for the pilgrims, Muriel Bowden's use of the *General Prologue* as a frame for a detailed treatment of the cultural milieux of the pilgrims, and Jill Mann's examination of estates satire in the *General Prologue* have all gone through it line by line.[3] These critics reflect the general acceptance of the dramatic principle first proposed by George Lyman Kittredge, which simply argues that the tales should not be read in isolation, but that they should be seen in a context both of teller and of sequence within the *Canterbury Tales* as a whole.[4] This approach has become so ingrained that nearly a century later it is difficult to imagine reading any other way. When critics then subordinate the tales to the tellers, however, scholarship on a single pilgrim can undermine subsequent scholarship on that pilgrim's tale; the *General Prologue* cannot bear the weight of an overly privileged position.

This critical problem of using the *General Prologue* applies especially to the Merchant, who remains the most-discussed merchant in medieval literature. Various theories of how to read both his portrait and his tale have dominated literary scholarship on medieval merchants, and the lack of consensus demonstrates Chaucer's deliberate ambiguity. Scholarly reluctance to view this portrait as ambiguous has also cast a shadow over most medieval literary merchants, despite the fact that many of the *General Prologue* portraits move between stereotyped satire and extra-satirical details, like the Wife's deafness or the Cook's mormel.[5] While critics do sometimes treat the Merchant neutrally, the Merchant has a long history of being found morally wanting, and as Wight Martindale suggests, "Chaucer's merchants do not normally receive a very good academic press."[6] When critics assumed that estates satire attacks were historically descriptive, the interpretation of Chaucerian merchants through a satirical reading of the *General Prologue* Merchant made sense, but Kenneth S. Cahn's exhaustive exposition of medieval currency exchange practices should have countered the traditional conclusion that the Merchant's financial practice requires a negative reading.[7] Lingering critical interest in the debt debate reminds us that the Merchant remains a slippery fellow, and his portrait needs a reexamination in light of the slippage between pro- and antimercantile ideologies, a reading that embraces the ambivalence of the text.

That Elusive *General Prologue* Merchant

Virtually every detail of the Merchant's portrait has been debated, if not in the light of the ideological conflict surrounding merchandise.[8] Also, the fact that critics still occasionally address the debt question suggests that a consensus on this *General Prologue* portrait has not been reached. For this purpose, I will divide the portrait of the Merchant into four sections: his appearance, his speech and desires, his trade practices, and the denial of his name, and I will rely upon the incoherence of the critical tradition to demonstrate the variety of interpretations available within the portrait's deliberate ambiguity. The portrait begins:

A Marchant was ther with a forked berd,
In mottelee, and hye on horse he sat;
Upon his heed a Flaundryssh bever hat,
His bootes clasped faire and fetisly. (I. 270–73)

From the beginning of the portrait, the Merchant's appearance itself seems significant. Reale suggests that the forked beard and motley indicate both duplicity and a mercantile livery,[9] while Bowden agrees that motley could be "customary...for members of every sort of company on state occasions."[10] Knott cites records concerning the Goldsmiths', Drapers', Grocers', Leathersellers', and Staplers' liveries, though he proves that guilds *had* liveries, not that liveries required motley cloth.[11] Some critics see the hat and boots as signs of overseas connections,[12] adding to the impression of a professional uniform. These details of dress do not necessarily indicate the Merchant's duplicity, though. That he wears livery, an expensive imported hat, and nicely buckled boots requires only that he be prosperous. Indeed, in a profession requiring guild membership, proper livery would not be optional. The critical leap from mercantile wealth to mercantile malpractice seems primarily grounded in the assumption that any merchant would be dishonest, thus presupposing that the Merchant's portrait will be satirical. A forked beard might indicate duplicity, like a forked tongue,[13] but since Chaucer himself seems to have worn his beard forked, we should not place much weight on that detail.[14] The forked beard supports several interpretations, ranging from a joke for a reader who knew both Chaucer's mercantile antecedents and his appearance, to a satire on merchants' susceptibility to style, to a reference

to a common beard style, to a suggestion of duplicity.[15] To assume that
the beard necessarily indicates the latter is to reason in a circle, from the
assumption that all merchants are duplicitous.

Similarly, the Merchant's motley, which certainly appears odd to a
modern audience accustomed to associate that pattern with jesters,[16]
might represent duplicity, just as his foreign hat can recall that merchants
cross borders, but it might also be a style shared by the Man of Law
in his "medlee" (I. 328). The motley pattern itself is ambiguous, as the
complicated dyeing of motley could either cover the flaws in poor cloth
or produce a popular visual effect in more expensive cloth.[17] Thus, the
cloth might mean that the Merchant properly adheres to his station by
wearing his guild livery, or that he advertises his wares by dressing in
expensive cloth, or that he uses his professional knowledge to choose
impressive but inexpensive cloth. Chaucer reveals here the ambiguity of
the language surrounding merchandise, a failure clearly to signify inherent to the ideological conflict around merchants. This moral ambiguity is characteristic of the *General Prologue* as a whole; as H. Marshall
Leicester, Jr., observes, "where we are never in doubt about what we are
to think of the monks or friars or townsmen in other estates satires, we
are almost always unsure of exactly how good or bad their counterparts
in the *General Prologue* are."[18]

The other details in the Merchant's appearance are similarly ambivalent. Rodney K. Delasanta interprets the Merchant's "hye" position on
his horse to signify the Merchant's pride, along with that of the Monk,
Pardoner, Reeve, and Wife of Bath, and Reale sees the boots as symbols of trade, possibly because of their expensive metal clasps (she does
not specify).[19] These details might suggest that the Merchant is a social
climber, but these details can also suggest that the merchant travels frequently, horseback and afoot. It would have been a rare medieval merchant who did not travel extensively, since even wool merchants had a
vast number of small producers from whom to buy wool, and thus at
some point in their careers traveled widely (see chapter 1). With every
detail of the Merchant's appearance, the portrait *can* conform to a reader's
expectation of an antimercantile critique of merchants, but without a
reader presupposing the Merchant's duplicity, his appearance shows him
simply to be a merchant. This reading might appear reductive, but it
reveals Chaucer's technique here. He borrows elements from the estates
satire which regularly condemned merchants, and he never directly contradicts a satirical view of merchants. On the other hand, he also refuses
to go into detail about potential mercantile malpractice, and the portrait of the Merchant is one of the least embellished (and shortest) in the
General Prologue. Most importantly, every potentially negative detail of

the Merchant's description can have, but need not have, a completely innocent explanation. Familiar with the estates satire tradition through Mann's analysis of Chaucer, critics continue either to assume the worst of the Merchant and then to use that assumption to read his tale, or to rise indignantly to his defense. The result is that the ambivalence carefully retained in the portrait often disappears from criticism using that portrait as a guide to Chaucer's thoughts on merchants.

The portrait continues with the Merchant's speech:

His resons he spak ful solempnely,
Sownynge alwey th'encrees of his wynnyng.
He wolde the see were kept for any thyng
Bitwixe Middelburgh and Orewelle. (I. 274–77)

This section continues the portrait's deliberate ambiguity, as the Merchant speaks solemnly and worries aloud about sea routes to the Low Countries. Jill Mann argues from these lines and the portrait's description of mercantile practice that "the professional façade is the basis of our knowledge of the Merchant."[20] Paul Strohm, following Mann, also interprets the Merchant's solemnity as a business pose, meant to attract investors but lacking "the depth or resonance of the stances adopted by the Knight, the Parson, or the Plowman."[21] Loy D. Martin finds in this passage the Merchant's "mercenary system of values."[22] Mann interprets the Merchant's concern with the sea between England and the Continent as a sign of "a professional, not an individual consciousness,"[23] while Bowden reads such concern as "typical of his class," and points to Gilbert Maghfeld's tenure as "keeper of the sea."[24] Crane even argues that the Merchant was a smuggler, an embezzler, a usurer, and a pirate.[25] Crane's position is extreme, but his interpretation of the Merchant's concern with the sea shows the passage's potential to support a range of negative readings. Reale demonstrates how a presupposition of antimercantilism informs such an interpretation of the Merchant's speech, as she argues that "man's ability to use speech (a talent with which Chaucer is obviously intimately concerned) and the world itself are shown at one stroke to be—for the merchant—valuable primarily (if not exclusively) in the interest of profit."[26] While Reale recognizes the resonances between the Merchant's speech and the antimercantile position, and acknowledges that the Merchant seems to talk primarily about business, it is less clear that discussing business necessarily satirizes a merchant in the same way that it would satirize, say, a monk.

Part of this expectation of satire has a basis in the prologue to the *Merchant's Tale*, which leads critics to assume the solemnity of the *General*

Prologue Merchant is a pose, but given only two speeches from a character, it seems unsafe to assume one or the other is normative. Connotations of the terms "reson" and "sownynge" also influence whether one reads the passage positively or negatively. *The Riverside Chaucer* glosses "resons" as "remarks, opinions," but the Middle English Dictionary (MED) lists a wide range of meaning in the period, including "motive," "excuse," "principle," "account, a reckoning," "income," "discourse," "stated opinion," "joke," "motto," or "meaning." Chaucer has chosen a word here that can be damning, if "resons" means "excuses" (which presumes something to excuse) or "income," but can also be relatively morally neutral, just conversation.[27] "Sowning" also has some semantic range: *The Riverside Chaucer* glosses it as "concerned with, or, making known," and Strohm prefers "concerned with," as it allows the conclusion that the Merchant's solemnity represents a façade to increase his profit.[28] On the other hand, the Merchant's solemn conversation *making known* "th'encrees of his wynnyng" could be bragging, avoidance of uncomfortable moral topics, incessant shop-talk, or even the conversation expected between an exporter and the controller of the Customs. The Merchant may be a dull fellow, but the passage need not be antimercantile: "he was a bore" is not antimercantile as such. There also remains the question of how the punctuation here affects our reading. If we exchange the period and comma at the ends of lines 274 and 275, we can separate the Merchant's solemnity from his concern for his profits, and link those profits syntactically to the open sea:

> His resons he spak ful solempnely[.]
> Sownynge alwey th'encrees of his wynnyng[,]
> He wolde the see were kept for any thyng
> Bitwixe Middelburgh and Orewelle.

Such a slight change, simply shifting the entirely modern punctuation imposed on the manuscripts,[29] shifts the sense of the passage: now the Merchant speaks solemnly in general, and shows concern for his business in times of uncertain travel, a sentiment logically shared by any merchant or traveler. For a reader who finds trade itself morally objectionable, such a concern would be sinful, but such an interpretation requires the reader to presuppose an antimercantile position.

Such a reader would be highly gratified, however, by the lines immediately following the description of the Merchant's speech, the description of his trade practices:

> Wel koude he in eschaunge sheeldes selle.
> This worthy man ful wel his wit bisette:

Ther wiste no wight that he was in dette,
So estatly was he of his governaunce
With his bargaynes and with his chevyssaunce. (I. 278–82)

Mann argues convincingly that this wording is characteristic of antimercantile satire, particularly the collocation of "eschaunge," "bargayne,"
and "chevyssaunce."[30] As a result, partisans of the Merchant's culpability
have been able to use this passage as their primary evidence, supported by
these terms' satirical career. John Reidy, for example, uses the negative
satirical connotations of trade language to attack the Merchant's speech
on trade, arguing that the Merchant's "secretive" nature and his focus on
business contrasts specifically with the Clerk's sharing of "his treasure,"
so that the "nobility of the one's pursuit emphasizes the baseness of the
other's."[31] Reidy shows how Chaucer manipulates the satirical tradition
here, as only in that discursive tradition do the connotations of trade
language require that it relate ultimately to usury and avarice, so that a
reference to trade equals a reference to avarice.

To a reader expecting the conventions of the estates satire tradition, it
is indeed easy to read "chevyssaunce" as Mann's "simple euphemism for
usury,"[32] and to hear the echoes with *Piers Plowman* (B.V. 249) and the
Mirour de l'Omme (l. 25417). The Merchant's apologists counter this expectation primarily by arguing that trade language need not have negative
connotations for Chaucer's readers.[33] Cahn, for example, explains that
"selling shields" meant taking delivery of English currency in London
in exchange for a later payment of Flemish currency in Flanders, which
allowed merchants to borrow money to buy English merchandise, and
then to repay the loans in Flanders after selling that merchandise.[34] Since
a borrower might make money from these exchanges,[35] exchange was
not synonymous with usury, but was instead a licit alternative to charging interest as such. Similarly, "bargayne" was a legal term for the mercantile process,[36] and the MED attests that "chevyssaunce" had a wide
range of meaning both neutral and negative, including simply "profit"
or "acquisition" (3) and the more troubling "borrowing of money…at
interest" (6a), and "usury" (6b).[37] What needs to be clear from the contrast between this renovation of trade language and Mann's acceptance
of estates-satirical connotations of these terms is that the *General Prologue*
draws on both mercantile practice and antimercantile discourse. The
double life of words like "chevyssaunce" creates the ambiguity characteristic of Chaucer's treatment of his *General Prologue* Merchant; Chaucer
could easily enough have called his merchant a usurer outright. Cahn's
analysis of borrowing practices in terms of the Merchant confirms that
to a knowledgeable reader these details of the Merchant's practice, his

exchange, bargains, and chevisaunce, can represent either the Merchant's ability *qua* merchant, or the traditional condemnation.[38]

Just as Chaucer's trade terminology supports divergent readings, his description of mercantile debt is ambiguous. Oscar Johnson and Gardiner Stillwell point out the syntactical indeterminacy of the passage in their arguments for the Merchant's opulence, while Cahn normalizes mercantile debt.[39] The passage allows for three possibilities: the Merchant is in debt, he is not, or no one knows which. The hypothetical debt might be a guilty secret or a business expense, while a lack of debt might represent either mercantile success or usury, following the logic that any merchant not himself in debt must be a lender, and thus a usurer. Given the line's careful indeterminacy, the interpretation that no one knows the Merchant's debt status represents the best choice, representing the passage's most explicit moment of deliberate ambiguity. Thus the line's syntactic connection to the Merchant's "estatly...governaunce" demonstrates why many critics agree with Stillwell and Mann in reading the Merchant's entire portrait as a self-serving façade: Chaucer presents the reader's ignorance of the Merchant's debt as a direct result of the Merchant's solemn self-presentation.[40]

Where I part company with Mann is in her implication that such a façade must be fraudulent, as she associates hiddenness with hypothetical victims of trade.[41] Instead, I see "estatly governaunce" as potentially but not necessarily satirical, both in Mann's sense and through Reale's suggestion that the terms "seem to point not only to positive but indeed to noble qualities" inconsistent with satire on merchants.[42] Since the term "estatly" ranged in meaning from a simple positive term, "imposing" or "splendid," to "having the bearing or demeanor befitting high rank, courtly,"[43] it plays a double role in a satirical reading of this line, and also supports a nonsatirical reading. "Estatly" presents the Merchant as maintaining a manner above his station, and loosely invokes the model of the Three Estates: a suggestion of false nobility accuses the Merchant of social climbing. On the other hand, "estatly governaunce" can also function in a promercantile fashion: instead of a fraud, this sober, stately Merchant can be a credit to his estate, managing his affairs according to his station in life and avoiding the appearance of dishonesty. A merchant reading this description could interpret it as an indication of Chaucer's understanding of the complexities inherent in a merchant's public face.

Then there is the problem of the passage's conclusion:

> For sothe he was a worthy man with alle,
> But, sooth to seyn, I noot how men hym calle. (I. 283–84)

Few lines in Chaucer resist interpretation more effectively than this denial of the Merchant's name. J. Stephen Russell argues that opening the portraits with vocations rather than names forces the reader to read the portraits in terms of an individual "*fictum* or mental image associated with the noun" of the vocation, or in essence to read the portraits in terms of the estates satire images to which they relate.[44] Bowden suggests, following Rickert, that Chaucer might want to avoid offending influential model Gilbert Maghfeld.[45] Taylor reads the last line of the portrait as symbolic of the Merchant's hollowness, as "the truth of the Merchant is the absence of his name,"[46] while Gerald Morgan argues that there must be some good reason not to name the Merchant.[47] The absence of a name fits right into my model of how this portrait works, though. If a reader, following Russell, approaches the portrait expecting a type from estates satire, namelessness simply reinforces the Merchant's function as that familiar type, *Marchant* to Langland's *Coveitise* or Gower's *Triche*. This typical merchant is thus distinct from Harry Bailly or Hogge of Ware, both of whose names, at least, seem to be taken from life.[48] If, on the other hand, a reader recognizes that the Merchant's slipperiness reflects Chaucer's ambivalence toward that estate, shown in the care with which the Merchant avoids easy classification in his motley, solemnity, and stately governance, namelessness reinforces that slipperiness and Chaucer's refusal to be pinned down on the subject of merchants. Chaucer's resistance to unequivocal satire creates a rhetorical space for a mercantile reader or the Merchant to deny the wrongdoing implied by estates satire. The Merchant's clothing and mercantile practice necessarily indicate only his profession, and namelessness means both that he can represent *any* merchant, and that he can represent *no* merchant in particular. Hence, Chaucer calls attention to the Merchant's namelessness where he did not need to with the equally nameless Parson, because he is far less equivocal in his treatment of the Parson. This merchant's lack of a name bears within itself both the contempt of antimercantilism, the sense that merchants are all the same, and a response to that moral condemnation, so that hiding his name protects the Merchant just like his other features. Chaucer thus includes within this ambiguous portrait both sides of the debate surrounding merchandise in late fourteenth-century estates satire.

Before I move on to the tales, I must digress briefly on a point with which I have thus far been rather casual: Chaucer's audience, in which I have been imagining a mercantile reader to search out the promercantile elements of the Merchant's portrait. It seems appropriate here to invoke Paul Strohm's influential model for Chaucer's readers, which argues that while the *Canterbury Tales* omits any references to an actual historical audience, it features detailed descriptions of its fictional inscribed audience, and addresses to the future reading audience of posterity. It is into this last category that I place a hypothetical mercantile audience. It is not inscribed, in the sense that only one merchant witnesses the fictional performance of the *Canterbury Tales*, which lacks direct address like "oh, ye marchauntes!" Chaucer's provision for a promercantile reading of his portrayal of a merchant that largely fits the estates satire form suggests that he allowed for the possibility of later mercantile readers. Strohm warns against reading the pilgrims as a representation of the actual audience, and he describes an actual audience of the "esquire" class.[49] This specific audience does not, however, preclude a mercantile awareness on Chaucer's part, as Strohm also points out Chaucer's connections with grocers Sir Nicholas Brembre, and Sir John Philpot, and fishmonger Sir William Walworth (see chapter 1), all of whom were highly prominent collectors of customs during Chaucer's tenure as controller.[50] Elsewhere Strohm remarks that "while we have no particular evidence that Chaucer found a 'bourgeois' readership prior to the fifteenth century, this possibility must also be entertained."[51] Chaucer's own mercantile antecedents as a vintner's son and grandson[52] also suggest that he would have to have been uncharacteristically obtuse to lack a detailed awareness of the ideological challenges facing that estate. Finally, Linne R. Mooney's recent work on Chaucerian scribe Adam Pinkhurst makes it clear that Pinkhurst, the scribe of the Hengwrt and Ellesmere manuscripts of the *Canterbury Tales*, was a long-term scribe for the Mercers' Company;[53] any mercer, at least, interested in the work of Chaucer would not have required any great effort to acquire it.

The Merchant, Mercantile Ideologies, and His Unmercantile Tale

If, then, the *General Prologue* portrait lays out both pro- and antimercantile positions, it remains to be seen what Chaucer does with merchants later in the *Canterbury Tales*. The Merchant as a narrator seems the obvious next step, but there is a problem: the *Merchant's Tale* is not about merchants or merchandise, except for the tale's narrative persona and its prologue. Surprisingly, while the *Merchant's Tale* does to a considerable degree critique the Merchant narrator, it does not do so directly in terms of traditional estates satire antimercantilism. This disjunction of Chaucer's critique of the Merchant from the antimercantile tradition has not always been recognized, as Martin Stevens effectively describes two camps on the subject of the Merchant's persona: those who find the tale "embittered" and "poisonous" and those who find it "spirited" and "extravagantly ironic." The resulting interpretations of the tale then apply these two assessments to its narrator, particularly in terms of his own marriage and his business.[54] More recently, Lee Patterson and Rosalind Field present readings that link the tale's narrative discontinuities to the Merchant's problematic social position, and as I will explain later, their arguments contextualize the *Merchant's Tale*'s treatment of its narrator within the conflict between pro- and antimercantile ideologies, if not within estates satire. In particular, Patterson insists that the *Merchant's Tale*'s incoherent mix of clerical and aristocratic discourse reflects the incoherent mercantile ideology of the period, while Field focuses on the tale's use of aristocratic discourse to characterize the Merchant's class hostility toward January as a knight. An understanding of the "mercantility" of the *Merchant's Tale* thus requires an analysis of how Chaucer creates this narrator by combining a traditional satiric view of merchants with a suggestion of mercantile responses to that view.

The setting has been the element of the tale most linked to the narrator's mercantility, largely because Paul A. Olson influentially argues that the setting in Pavia invites resentment of the ubiquitous Italian merchants, though of course Lombardy was associated with tyranny as well as usury.[55] Olson assumes that a Lombard knight can be read simply as a Lombard merchant, though David Wallace complicates this reading with his analysis of Chaucer's knowledge of the historical tyrants of Pavia.[56] Field's response to Olson then provides a useful entry into the problem of the narrator's class antagonism in the tale. Olson argues for the Merchant's "animus toward Italians or, at least, toward Lombards from Pavia," and links January to the mercantile estate by asserting that a fourteenth-century English reader could not have conceived of a Lombard who was not a merchant-banker.[57] Given Gower's use of Lombards as targets of mercantile hostility in the *Mirour de l'Omme*, Olson is not entirely illogical, but he neglects January's explicit social rank in the tale. He also seems to miss other literary associations with Lombards, and his description of Lombard government by "commercial aristocracy" seems to reflect a Florentine (Tuscan) model.[58] Field responds that while January lacks the trappings of a young romance knight like Sir Thopas, he does have a knightly household displaying magnificence, including his "paleys" (l. 1712), the presence of a squire as marshal of the hall, January's knightly responsibility in sending his wife to visit his sick squire, and the elaborate garden attached to the house.[59] Field also argues that January is explicitly *non*mercantile in his aristocratic generosity to his wife and squire, and in his carelessness with money.[60]

Fields here links the tale to the subject of merchants through the identity of the narrator and his scorn for January. This scorn is characterized most clearly in the primary financial transaction of the tale, January's acquisition of May and in particular the passage concerning the mirror in the marketplace (IV. 1580–87). This passage blurs the languages of trade and matrimony in the tale, and responses to this blurring have in the past demonstrated the way in which antimercantile expectations might determine readings of the tale. The "mercantility" of the narrator expresses itself most directly in this metaphor, which describes January's thought processes choosing May for a wife:

> Many fair shap and many a fair visage
> Ther passeth thurgh his herte nyght by nyght,
> As whoso tooke a mirour, polisshed bright,
> And sette it in a commune market-place,
> Thanne sholde he se ful many a figure pace
> By his mirour. (IV. 1580–85)

This marketplace in the context of choosing a wife does make marriage sound mercantile, and it is difficult to imagine a merchant mentioning a marketplace without invoking mercantile values, even if the image suggests a crowd rather than commerce. Those critics who identify January with the Merchant have traditionally read this passage to show January's overcommodified approach to marriage, for which they blame the Merchant.[61] The Merchant's portrayal of January's marriage itself, however, undermines such a reading: part of the dubious humor of the tale is that May is "of smal degree" (IV. 1625), so January loses money by marrying her (IV. 1696–99). Commodification of marriage here represents the narrator's critique of the protagonist. Since January suffers a financial loss through marriage, the invocation of the market with the mirror suggests that January's fancy reads the market poorly. While Christian Sheridan suggests that the *Merchant's Tale* commodifies texts in general, and May more specifically,[62] the tale's incoherence and the critique of January's commodification make it hard to read the tale as a critique of trade. While the tale as a whole ultimately satirizes the merchant narrator's approach to tale-telling, the Merchant as narrative persona uses this image dubiously to critique January paying too much for his wife.

If, then, this economic failure tied to an image of a marketplace represents part of the Merchant narrator's attempt to satirize his knightly protagonist, it remains to determine how else Chaucer constructs this narrator's persona. Lee Patterson provides the most useful approach here, by arguing that "the merchant class of medieval London gives every evidence of having been a class in search of a legitimizing ideology."[63] This characterization suggests the conflict I see between residual clerical antimercantilism and emergent promercantilism, though I differ with Patterson in that he points to Gower's and Langland's as bourgeois yet straightforwardly antimercantile texts without engaging with the conflict involved in their antimercantilism (see chapters 2 and 3).[64] Still, Patterson argues convincingly that the narrative confusion within the tale arises as the Merchant targets the "class-specific discourses" of "the two great cultural formations that dominated his world, the Church and the aristocracy."[65] According to Patterson, the Merchant remains in simultaneous conflict and affirmation with both courtly and clerical discourses in his tale. Thus, the narrative cancels itself out as the Merchant fails to find a coherent ideology around which to build his tale, and Chaucer here "explores this condition [of lacking an ideology] from the inside."[66] With this ideological confusion in mind, the question of January's relationship with the Merchant narrator shows how Chaucer layers our scorn for January with our scorn for the Merchant. The contrast between the mythographic and biblical elements and the sexually explicit denouement help to convert the Merchant's unstable discourse into particular antimercantilism, without deploying the full range of antimercantile satire. We dislike this *particular* merchant even while he successfully conveys his contempt for January, but a reader only connects distaste for this merchant to his estate by coming to Patterson's position, that the tale presents this kind of confused discourse as inherently mercantile. Almost any audience can find something offensive here; even the fabliau form takes somewhat of a beating in the *Merchant's Tale*.[67] Even if the Merchant is satirized as a bad narrator, though, his failings are only partially related to his estate, and his prologue's imperfect connection to the material of the tale helps explain how his grotesque narrative fits into this idiosyncratic satirical context.

We see this satire on the Merchant from the beginning of his prologue, when he echoes the envoy concluding the *Clerk's Tale*. Where the Clerk advised Wife-of-Bath-like "archewyves" (IV. 1195) to "lat hym [the husband] care, and wepe, and wrynge, and waille" (IV. 1212), the Merchant reports that "Wepyng and waylyng, care and oother sorwe / I knowe ynogh, on even and a-morwe" (IV. 1213). The absence of traditional antimercantile material here has frustrated critics expecting the *Merchant's Prologue* to continue in the satiric vein seen in the *General Prologue*. Instead, the Merchant places himself within the envoy's satire on marriage through the story of his own wife, an anti-Grisilde. Despite this marriage narrative's lack of surface antimercantilism, though, it supports Patterson's model of the Merchant caught between the discourses of the clerical and noble estates. Following a description by a member of the clerical estate of marriage within a noble setting, the Merchant cannot but contrast himself with the Clerk's idealization of Walter and Grisilde's marriage, but seems unaware that the Clerk's epilogue and envoy shift tone drastically from the atmosphere of most of the *Clerk's Tale*. Specifically, the end of the *Clerk's Tale* states that "It were ful hard to fynde now-a-dayes / In al a toun Grisildis thre or two" (IV. 1164–65) and then invokes the Wife of Bath (IV. 1170). With this ending and the subsequent envoy, the *Clerk's Tale* contrasts its idealized if troubling marriage between representatives of the manorial estates, the nobility and peasantry, with a misogynist counter-ideal of marriage. Specifying towns which lack Grisilde-figures in favor of the intimidating and urban Wife of Bath, the Clerk's satire on marriage here is not precisely antimercantile. The Merchant makes the Clerk's choice of words indirectly antimercantile, however, in the sense that he immediately sees his own marriage as fitting that counter-ideal, without realizing that such a recognition makes him the butt of the Clerk's satire.

The Merchant's reaction to the Clerk thus represents an ironically wrong-headed move to link himself with what he sees as the Clerk's successful mix of clerical and noble discourse, as does the Merchant's later use of the Wife of Bath to conjure a fear of marriage (IV. 1685). As he places himself within the envoy's satire, his ambitions of clerkly discourse prevent him from noticing the Clerk's ridicule of men who marry those "archewyves," so that the Merchant's attempted social climbing ultimately puts him back into his place. The Host's solidarity with the Merchant's miserable marriage then solidifies the satiric effect of the Merchant's narrative persona. Harry Bailly addresses the Merchant as an expert on marriage (IV. 1240–41), and in the *Merchant's Tale*'s epilogue the Host asserts that "wommen konnen outen swiche chaffare" (IV. 2438). Both men compare marriage to a financial transaction where women do the cheating, a conjunction of misogyny and commodified marriage that associates the Clerk's satire on modern marriage with the urban classes that included both the Merchant and the Host.[68] Bailly's acceptance of the Merchant's expertise on marriage, like the misogyny of the tale, distracts the reader from the Merchant's fragmented performance of clerical and aristocratic discourses. A reader must see past the Merchant's attack on marriage to see the tale's lack of a unifying discourse: we may dislike the Merchant as both husband and narrator, but if Patterson is right it is his narrative flaws that relate to his estate. Chaucer here does use traditional antimercantile material in terms of the Merchant's resentment of January's estate and his critique of January's unprofitable marriage, and the characterization of the Merchant here does critique some of his estate's failings, but that material is consistently redeployed to focus not on mercantile malpractice, but on other issues like ideological confusion and the question of marriage. The *Merchant's Tale* thus represents a major departure from the antimercantile tradition, despite its partial use of that tradition.

The Merchant of Seint-Denys and His "Mercantile Ethos"

Although the *Merchant's Tale* critiques mercantile discourse rather than their socioeconomic role, Chaucer does address the latter in the *Shipman's Tale*. Here Chaucer directly addresses the estate of merchants with a mercantile character defending his trade. Through this defense of merchandise in the mouth of another nameless merchant, this tale extends the deliberate ambiguity that characterized the *General Prologue* portrait to the ambivalence of narrative itself. Just as reader expectations in the *General Prologue* determined whether one saw the merchant portrait as satirical, the choice of which characters, if any, to identify with determines whether readers of the *Shipman's Tale* sympathize with trade. The passages where the merchant explains his trade to his wife and Daun John and in which the wife slanders the merchant to Daun John succinctly present the positions on trade available to a reader of the *Shipman's Tale*, while the details of trade and the commodifications of the tale provide ample material for an antimercantile reading to counter the merchant's self-justification. As with the *Merchant's Tale*, antimercantile critics allow a window into the potential thought processes of a medieval antimercantile reader, while less popular promercantile readings continue to provide a much-needed corrective.[69]

The most problematic characteristic of an easy antimercantile reading of the tale derives from a persistent misreading: Albert H. Silverman and those who cite him have read the wife's criticisms of the merchant, of his treatment of her, and his "niggardliness" as reliable information, despite the context of a wife speaking to a potential lover.[70] She labels her husband as "the worste man" (VII. 161), not worth "the value of a flye" in his "nygardye" (VII. 171–72); she then wishes for a husband who would be "Hardy and wise, and riche, and therto free, / And buxom unto his wyf and fressh abedde" (VII. 176–77). She clearly implies that her husband lacks the latter qualities, but in the same speech she also claims to feel suicidally depressed (VII. 122), swears faith to the monk "verraily for love and affiance" (VII. 140), and implies that she is in physical danger from her husband if caught without the hundred francs (VII. 181). Given the affection of the merchant's return (VII. 377–78), his nonviolent reaction when she reveals the loss of the money (VII. 427), and his acceptance of her spending the hundred francs on "array" (VII. 418), her claims to the monk are unsupported by the subsequent action of the tale. At the same time, her energy and the extent to which her interaction with the monk fits into a fabliau ethos encourage a reader to identify with her, and thus oppose her husband the merchant, as a reader accustomed to Chaucer's fabliaux expects a flawed husband like John the Carpenter or January. Certainly in the world of Chaucerian fabliau this unfaithful wife rates as highly successful, and is the only wife in all the analogues to the tale who keeps the money.[71] That critics have identified with her can be seen in Silverman's argument that the merchant is miserly,[72] and Thomas Hahn's suggestion that the merchant is unfaithful by spending (sexual) energy on money that he should on her.[73]

Aside from the wife's testimony about her husband, the tale is more effectively opposed to the money economy in its overall movement, particularly as a reader focuses on Daun John. The tale ultimately challenges the commodification of marriage inherent in the business transaction between the wife and the monk (sex for money), and by comparison that between the merchant and his wife (sex canceling monetary debt). According to such a reading of the tale, the similarity between the two transactions associates infidelity and marital sex for money to degrade the sacrament of marriage, thus impugning the morality of both characters and their estates. Similarly, the damning charge that the monk out-trades the merchant within the realm of marriage retains its appeal.[74] As Thomas Hahn describes the link of sex and money in the tale, the wife uses sex to get money, the monk uses money to get sex, and the merchant can only have sex when he has money.[75] This interpretation requires Hahn to accept the wife's dubious claim of her husband's sexual inattention, but he points out tangible links within the tale between money and sex. If we accept the monkish position that money is unequivocally negative, we would logically conclude that the tale's commodification of this merchant's marriage reveals how the merchant estate itself is tainted by its involvement in the material economy. This flaw would be easier to see when extended to the monk as an inappropriately effective merchant.

Hahn's extremity is instructive, in that he must conjecture about the merchant's business to make his case that money is unequivocally negative. He argues that the merchant must be involved solely in monetary exchange, and that such involvement would be invariably bear the taint of finance.[76] Thus, he condemns the merchant on the basis of this link between sin, exchange, and sexuality, so that "we view the Merchant as—we might say—screwing society and from this deriving a deep sexual excitement."[77] Just as an expectation of antimercantile satire coded the terms of the merchant's portrait as satirical in the *General Prologue*, an expectation of moral condemnation finds adequate support in the (vague) details of the merchant's business, in his wife's attack on him, and even in his role as wronged husband in a fabliau lust triangle. On the other hand, if a reader lacks such an expectation of antimercantile satire, the merchant's primarily failing is his apparent blindness to his wife's behavior, whether culpable or pitiable. That blindness does link the merchant and January in their modes of responding to infidelity, but the *Shipman's Tale* merchant never makes the apparent choice to be duped that made January ultimately complicit in May and Damian's fornication. Despite its potential to condemn trade, the *Shipman's Tale* only presents its merchant as deserving cuckoldry in the same way as January if a reader accepts the wife's dubious claims. Where January believes May's story over his own restored sight, the *Shipman's Tale* merchant's acceptance remains bound up in his obliviousness to the puns at the end of the tale.

It is these puns which help us to navigate between the positions on trade represented by the different characters and their points of view. Robert Adams sees the puns, on "taille," "wedde," and "good," as encoding the subtle moral of the tale, in the sense that they imply the "missing metaphorical referent" of "a sense of sin and the need for penance."[78] Adams here expects to see the language of debt playing a similar role for Langland and Chaucer, and if a reader naturally associates debt language with penance, penance might well be a silent third referent between the debt and sexuality embedded in the tail/tally, wedding/wed (collateral), and good/goods surrounding the wife's speech at the tale's conclusion. If so, such a moment in the tale demonstrates the power of reader expectations in providing the satiric content of antimercantilism: if debt implies penance, it would be almost impossible to discuss mercantile business without invoking penance. According to Gerhard Joseph's Derridean reading of the tale, though, these discursive puns replicate in their significatory indeterminacy the movement of money itself, so that the puns implicate discourse itself. He ties them to Derrida's metaphor of signification as the engraving on a coin, which wears off after much circulation.[79] Joseph's point that abundant circulation multiplies both the hundred francs and the meanings of financial language in the conclusion of the tale shows how the tale's ending relies on that multiplicity of meaning just as much as its plot relies on the confusing circulation of the hundred francs.[80] Karla Taylor then argues from the instability of the puns that Chaucer models the instability of mercantile language, as she observes that a full understanding of many of the puns in the text require a multilingual understanding of the slippage between Middle English and Anglo-French in the period (see chapter 3). Her observation that "cosyn" is only a pun with the later English "cozen" (to deceive) through French "*coçonage* (commercial dealings, often shady) [and]...*cosinage* (kinship)" effectively demonstrates this principle.[81] The result of these multilingual puns, according to Taylor, is "a parody of community defined by a linguistic social agreement that will not bear scrutiny."[82]

While these puns accentuate the circulatory nature of money and the complexity of financial language, they also call attention to the merchant's own point of view, in his steadfast surface reading of them. Certainly within the context of his own world, the merchant is a positive character, with no idea that he is in a fabliau. Kenneth S. Cahn normalizes the merchant's financial practice, for example, and John M. Ganim shows how the merchant's counting of money matches standard practice for northern France in Chaucer's time.[83] The counting-house scene establishes the merchant's financial status (VII. 77–84), while his loan to Daun John interest-free out of petty cash (VII. 293–94) demonstrates that he obeys the ban on usury. His business reveals that he is adept at complex financial practice, and his discomfort with the monk's suggestion that he is dunning the monk for money (VII. 351) suggests that he is not obsessed with money. V. J. Scattergood shares Cahn's assessment of the merchant's financial dealings as licit,[84] and also points out that "though the reader is nowhere told what kind of goods are involved in the merchant's transactions, practically everything else about his business is made clear."[85] Thus the merchant's business itself presents him to a knowledgeable reader as a positive figure.

If, then, these financial transactions need not be morally culpable, the merchant's own speeches in defense of his profession further articulate a mercantile point of view. As he responds to his wife's powerful assertion that "ye have ynough, pardee, of Goddes sonde" (VII. 219), he presents the defense of trade through risk that the Man of Law had earlier satirized through comparison to gambling. Where the Man of Law ironically praised merchants' good fortune with the lines "Youre bagges been nat fild with ambes as, / But with sys cynk, that renneth for youre chaunce" (II. 124–25), the *Shipman's Tale* merchant has a more sober understanding of his "curious bisynesse" (VII. 225), pointing out that "Scarsly amonges twelve tweye shul thryve / Continuelly" (VII. 228–29). In the face of such risk of failure, merchants must put a good face on their business, "make chiere and good visage, / And dryve forth the world as it may be, / And kepen oure estaat in pryvetee, / Til we be deed" (VII. 230–33), because "everemoore we moote stonde in drede / Of hap and fortune in oure chapmanhede" (VII. 237–38). Gardiner Stillwell characterizes this speech and the merchant's others as signs of his "sadness," in the sense of seriousness. Stillwell goes on to see a similar seriousness in the tone of Toulmin Smith's volume of guild ordinances, in which "when the medieval English townsman wants a new guild-member of the right sort...he chooses someone who is trusty, true, well-behaved, lawful, discreet, good, wise, able, 'wittye,' 'konyng,' 'boxom,' 'sad,' sufficient, honourable, worshipful, or of good conversation."[86] The merchant in the *Shipman's Tale* shares this concern in his attention to his reputation (VII. 43–52), and in his actions in Bruges, where "He neither pleyeth at the dees ne daunceth" (VII. 304). Such behavior represents a clear alternative to the Man of Law's satire of mercantile risk as gambling, as in his prologue dancing was another characteristic of merchants: "At Cristemasse myrie may ye daunce!" (II. 126)

The *Shipman's Tale* merchant seems aware of the need to seem beyond reproach, and we see a similar concern for mercantile image in his warning to Daun John before the loan. He explains that chapmen's "moneie is hir plogh," and that "We may creaunce whil we have a name, / But goldlees for to be, it is no game" (VII. 288–90). This speech has satiric potential, in that the comparison of money to a plow recalls both the sexual innuendo of the tale and the concern with money's sterility behind the usury prohibition (see chapter 1), but it also recalls the instability of the merchant's profession: without funds, he could buy nothing to sell, and he relies on a sober reputation to "creaunce," or "attract capital by being creditworthy."[87] Similarly, as poverty "is no game," the merchant here further repudiates the Man of Law's suggestion that mercantile risk is morally equivalent to dicing.

If, then, this tale has much in it to speak to a mercantile point of view, how does this promercantile material balance with the tale's concern over commodification? None of this promercantile material applies to the fabliau plot directly: the wife's and monk's transactions lack the licit nature of the merchant's trade, so that there is a large thematic gap between identification with the merchant and identification with the wife and monk. Here, Chaucer combines the flawed discourse of the *Merchant's Tale* with the deliberate ambiguity of the *General Prologue* portrait. While the fabliau plot predictably reveals the follies of the characters in the story, reader identification with the merchant produces almost a different tale than identification with the typical fabliau characters of the wife and the monk. The tale read with a focus on the merchant defends his trade, but shows him to be unable to comprehend his wife's infidelity; the tale read through a fabliau ethos celebrating the wife's cleverness suggests the merchant to be a bad husband because of his business; the tale read with a focus on the misbehaving monk condemns the commodification of marriage and ultimately challenges monetary values.[88] All these points of view are not equal, however. The wife's betrayal of her husband and her punning escape from the consequences of her actions show the dangers of merchandise out of context, while this merchant, and with him any reader who identifies too much with his sober mien, is easily fooled; as Scattergood puts it, "his outlook…is too limited."[89] This merchant as an example of a reading/interpreting subject, as a model for a promercantile reader, on the one hand responds twice to the Man of Law's characterization of trade as gambling, but on the other hand misses out on the verbal play of his wife. His linguistic inability thus echoes the earlier association of merchants with failed discourse in the *Merchant's Tale*, since the position even of this ideal merchant denies comprehension of the duality of language, a duality inherent in the satiric incoherence of the *Merchant's Tale* and the layers of satire and trade vocabulary in the *General Prologue*.

Finally, though, there remains the question of the setting of the tale, because it allows Chaucer to undertake a similar displacement to Gower's in the *Mirour de l'Omme*. As a French merchant depicted in the English vernacular, *The Shipman's Tale* merchant encourages an English reader to consider what it means for an alien to cross borders and exchange currencies. This displacement of these issues to France thus adapts the model used in the *Mirour de l'Omme*, where *Triche* initially seems both dangerous and foreign, but then through detailed local references and Anglo-French business vocabulary Gower leaves no doubt that English merchants can also focus too much on their own profit rather than the common profit (see chapter 3). What makes it possible to believe that the setting matters is the thickness of *The Shipman's Tale*'s French references. While some of the *Canterbury Tales*' settings are vague, this tale consistently mentions its locale: the town of Saint-Denis is mentioned five times (VII. 1, VII. 59, VII. 67, VII. 308, VII. 326), while French patron Saint Denis himself is invoked once (VII. 151). To establish the larger context "in al the reawme of France" (VII.116), Paris is mentioned three times (VII. 57, 332, 336), French saints Martin of Tours (VII. 148) and Ivo of Chartres (VII. 227) are also invoked,[90] and "Genylon of France" is cited as an icon of betrayal (VII. 194). There is also a very brief snippet of French, when the merchant answers his door with "Quy la?" (VII. 214) J. A. Burrow and V. J. Scattergood observe in their note to Benson's *Riverside Chaucer* that "this is Chaucer's only use of foreign speech in a foreign setting as local color."[91] These details are not necessarily aimed at a mercantile reader, but then the "frank" is mentioned ten times (VII. 181, VII. 187, VII. 201, VII. 274, VII. 276, VII. 293, VII. 315, VII. 334, VII. 372, VII. 389), a currency not mentioned elsewhere in the *Canterbury Tales*, and one with an unmistakable connection to its kingdom. The merchant's destination is also mentioned seven times (Brugges: VII. 55, VII. 61, VII. 258, VII. 301; Flaundres: VII. 199, VII. 239, VII. 300). Chaucer works hard to keep the setting fresh in the readers' mind, and this density of name repetitions has led scholars unsuccessfully seek a possible French source.[92] Since Bruges was a popular destination for English merchants, and Paris was of course a major trade center, that aspect of the setting would also have felt familiar for any experienced travelers reading the tale.

These French details can also lead us to an important French intertext, while also invoking details of international trade. Lorraine Kochanske Stock argues that some aspects of the merchant's wife echo La Vieille from the *Roman de la Rose*, so that "it seems sounder to attribute the French flavor in the *Shipman's Tale* to the influence of the *Roman de la Rose*."[93] Stock's analysis helps point the way to the significance of the French references, because of its economic angle: she focuses on the issue of the wife soliciting a loan, rather than a gift per se, so that the *Shipman's Tale* wife follows the La Vieille's advice to "Fair Welcome."[94] While Stock does not pursue the financial issues of lending, Chaucer's borrowing of the loan motif effectively combines the gender satire of the *Roman de la Rose* with the tropes of antimercantile satire floating around in the *Shipman's Tale*. This intertext thus supplements the tale's deferral of most of the negative aspects of the antimercantile satiric tradition onto the wife and Daun John, by intensifying the satiric critique of the wife. The finance of the tale also seems to have some French elements. Aside from Daun John's "loan" of the much-repeated "hundred frankes" (VII. 181, VII. 187, VII. 201, VII. 315, VII. 389) to the wife, the merchant himself engages in international currency exchange. Helen Fulton points out a key detail of this financial practice, observing that bills of exchange were "only introduced into England at the very end of the fourteenth century as a direct result of another innovation, the growth of foreign trade conducted by English merchants and their contacts on the continent," so that the merchant's methods would be relatively new and suspicious to "an English urban audience."[95] Fulton thus recognizes how this tale's setting addresses an audience concerned with the merchant estate. Such readers would know Paris and Bruges as banking centers representing major northern extensions of the Italian banking network; London was part of this network, though Peter Spufford labels the Bruges-London courier route "ancillary."[96] In addition to these trade routes, the currency terms used in the *Shipman's Tale* would also have strong national connotations for English merchants, associating the *franc* with France and the shield or *ecu* with Flanders.[97] Chaucer here addresses the business practices of continental merchants, foregrounding areas where they were dominant, and thus invokes English readers' strong feelings about their cross-Channel rivals.

This association then raises the related question of why the tale was not set in Italy, if Chaucer were planning to critique alien merchants. Given that Chaucer set the *Merchant's Tale* in Pavia, that the best analogues of the *Shipman's Tale* are Italian, and that the sneakiest aspects of international finance were associated with the Lombards (VII. 367), Chaucer could have satirized an Italian merchant with an untrustworthy wife. One reason to avoid Italy as a setting is raised by John Ganim's analysis of bookkeeping methods in the tale, which suggests that double-entry bookkeeping has not made it to Saint-Denis yet. Thus this merchant has something in common with the English, who also lacked this valuable technique.[98] The setting thus allows for a merchant somewhat more sophisticated than many English merchants, but not one whose business practices preclude an English reader's identification with him. It is important to remember here also that while medieval literary merchants tend to be figures of avarice like Langland's Coveitise, this merchant is satirized primarily as a husband. The setting thus affects how the reader might react to the satire. The tale's structure dismembers traditional antimercantile satire, by moving the traditional satiric traits of avarice and dishonesty from the naive merchant to his mercenary wife and the sneaky monk. Since this merchant's main shortcoming seems to be his failure to understand his wife's duplicity or her punning confession, a mercantile reader could identify with this merchant to some extent, sharing with him regular trips to Bruges, unwieldy bookkeeping, and a need to do business with those hated Lombards. Since Chaucer creates only an imperfect identification of reader and character, a merchant-estate reader would share some subjectivity with the *Shipman's Tale* merchant, but would also develop enough rhetorical distance from the *Shipman's Tale* merchant to be able to notice Chaucer's critique of his limited perception.

This move thus resembles Gower's approach in the section on merchants in the *Mirour de l'Omme*, which starts with promercantile material, and then blames alien merchants for mercantile malpractice before targeting specific London mercantile practice. This technique allows Gower to draw English merchants into his satire, by playing to their prejudices against aliens, and helping them see what is wrong with *Triche* (see chapter 3). When Gower then shifts to a direct critique of specific mercantile malpractice in London through sophisticated use of the business register, he reflects the reader's disdain for the alien Other back onto the reader, who in a sense becomes the Other in the *Mirour*. Chaucer's setting of the *Shipman's Tale* shares these key elements, though the result is not localized to London. Chaucer's satire of merchants shares Gower's critique of traditional antimercantile material, but goes much farther in that the traditionally mercantile sins of greed and duplicity in this tale move to the wife and monk. Chaucer very carefully establishes the merchant of Saint-Denis as the same sort of Other that Gower depicted in *Triche*, and just as *Triche* invoked a potential merchant-estate reader's resentment of his alien rivals, the merchant of Saint-Denis reminds such a reader of his French rivals. Where Gower then rebounds his satire on such a reader in recognizable, if atypical antimercantile terms, Chaucer leaves the antimercantile material in his tale attached to the monk and the wife, and instead critiques his merchant's inability to perceive his wife's infidelity. Where the Anglo-French business register in Gower supported the reader's identification with Triche, in the *Shipman's Tale* it contributes to an understanding of the puns.[99] This different focus alters the rebounding effect of Gower's model: while the *Shipman's Tale* merchant might push some international rivalry buttons for English readers, limited identification with him would be encouraged by his familiar bookkeeping skills and mercantile practices, and his speech about the contingency of trade (VII. 224). Thus while a reader with negative associations with France may not initially identify with the merchant, the more positive links between merchant-character and reader put that reader in the position of first seeing the tale's merchant as an Other, and then identifying with that merchant. This doubleness of perception allows the tale to function as a lesson for the reader, by bringing that reader to identify with the critique of the *Shipman's Tale* merchant's limitations.

When this shifting identification is combined with the tale's satiric focus on the discursive obtuseness of the *Shipman's Tale* merchant, Chaucer moves beyond the satire tradition's superficial criticisms of trade practice to a critique of mercantile responses to that satire. By associating satire with the duality of language, at the same time that he presents merchants and discourse as an unreliable combination, Chaucer goes far beyond Gower's verbal trap in the *Mirour de l'Omme*. Instead of drawing a potential mercantile reader into an antimercantile position, Chaucer draws readers' attention to the failures of satire itself to reach an estate with so conflicted an ideological context. His critique of mercantile discourse is less savage than traditional antimercantilism, and remains balanced by his ambivalent inclusion of promercantile material in the *General Prologue* and *Shipman's Tale*. He does not imply that all merchants are damned, but he does associate merchants with the Merchant narrator's misreading of the Clerk's envoy and his own flawed narrative, as well as the *Shipman's Tale* merchant's inability to read beneath the surface of his wife's puns. Such discursive failure represents a devastating charge in a work elsewhere highly concerned with readers' and hearers' ability to separate fruit from chaff. Chaucer shows a detailed understanding of the concerns of the mercantile estate, and his idealized merchant in the *Shipman's Tale* is as sympathetic a merchant as one can expect to find anywhere in medieval literature, but Chaucer's ambivalent treatment of merchants ultimately reveals the danger of reading too much on the surface, and reading with too much of an agenda. Thus, while merchants are by no means the main focus of the *Canterbury Tales*, they do provide an opportunity for Chaucer to address an issue that does seem central to the large work: the nature and value of poetic narrative. Chaucer's treatment of merchants demonstrates the subtlety that Chaucer requires from his readers, and the extent to which he is willing to experiment with different ways of delivering narrative *sentence* and *solaas*.

Chaucer thus plays a far different corrective role with merchants as an estate-grouping than either Langland or Gower did, as he indirectly approaches a problem fundamental to estates satire: if the "problems" of the estates have been known to and pointed out by satirists for all these years, why are they still so sinful? The two answers to this question both appear in the *Canterbury Tales'* merchants: on the one hand, the estates tradition was mistaken about many of the details of medieval trade. On the other hand, Chaucer so consistently associates merchants with discursive failure that he effectively isolates merchants from corrective literature, a devastating charge in a larger work with a sustained interest in the limits of literature's potential. Supposing that a merchant did buy or borrow copies of those works from his guild's professional scribe, a merchant who was as obtuse as either the *Merchant's Tale* narrator or the *Shipman's Tale* merchant might not learn much from Gower or Langland, because of the very sort of promercantile responses to antimercantile satire anticipated by the ambiguity of the *General Prologue* and the *Shipman's Tale*. As Chaucer foregrounds mercantile discursive failures in these tales, a mercantile reader has a chance to see and perhaps correct that pattern of failure. Thus Chaucer embeds within the *Canterbury Tales* a key for those readers who most need one, and effectively transcends the estates satire tradition from which he borrows so much.

CHAPTER 5

MERCANTILE VOICES OF THE EARLY FIFTEENTH CENTURY

Though estates satire has been my main focus thus far, no analysis of antimercantilism would be complete without a corresponding look at the conflicting mercantile responses to that satire. Chaucer and Gower imaginatively model hypothetical merchant responses to satire by creating discursive spaces for those mercantile readers who would have had access to their scribes and manuscripts, but without more evidence of mercantile manuscript ownership, those poets cannot provide adequate evidence for a historical mercantile subject-position. Exploring such a subjectivity requires a move to a different sort of text; there are no merchant poets, but there is certainly one mystic, and a body of anonymous poetry with a more overtly mercantile perspective. Approaching a historical mercantile subjectivity as a counterpoint to the satiric poets' treatment of trade, this chapter traces a crooked path from the anxiety and fractured subjectivity of *The Book of Margery Kempe*, to the overt political activism of *The Libelle of Englyshe Polycye*, to the charity of "The Childe of Bristowe" and its analogue, to the redemptive power of merchandise in the pseudo-Chaucerian *Tale of Beryn*. These texts have on the surface little in common, but they all demonstrate mercantile responses to the problem of living righteously in a sinful physical world. Merchandise's materialist associations are familiar from poems like *Piers Plowman*, but these texts break with that tradition in different ways. Kempe seems to have taken the satires to heart, and her *Book* performs the subject-position of a satirized merchant. The anonymous poems, on the other hand, all attempt to divorce materialism from merchandise, in the sense that they seek remedies to the sins and problems of the material world without scapegoating or rejecting trade. While no one valorizes trade quite like *The Libelle of Englyshe Polycye*, all these poems suggest that English culture was beginning to catch up with the material economy, and to see the possibility of morally neutral trade.

The Book of Margery Kempe: Satire's Shadow

Although some of these works do see trade as morally neutral, we need to start with one of the few texts written by a member of the merchant estate: *The Book of Margery Kempe*. Critics have argued for some time that Margery Kempe and her *Book* are resolutely anti-"bourgeois," and such a view has adequate support within Kempe's text, as Anthony Goodman recognizes Kempe's "rejection of bourgeois norms of familial, parochial, and commercial life."[1] Unfortunately, not enough has been done with Kempe's estate-position beyond Goodman's unsophisticated sense of the "bourgeois."[2] Certainly Kempe was "bourgeois" in the sense that her father and husband were burgesses, members of the twelve-man committee that chose Bishop's Lynn's mayor and other civic officers. Kempe's father, John Brunham, was himself mayor in 1370–71, 1377–79, 1385–86, and 1391–92, and held a variety of lesser offices including Alderman of the Gild of Holy Trinity. John Kempe, her husband, was a chamberlain of Lynn in 1394–95. Both men were free of the city, acted as jurats to elect the mayor and aldermen, and were active in the city's guild life. There were John Brunhams in the Gild of St. Giles and St. Julian and in the Gild of Corpus Christi, and John Kempe seems to have been a member of the Corpus Christi Gild as well. Margery Kempe's own economic activities are outlined in her *Book*, and late in life she joined the "Gilde mercatorie sancte Trinitatis Lenne."[3] Having a family prominent in a town's economic and spiritual life is not equivalent, however, to being "bourgeois" in the Marxian sense or "middle class" in the modern sense.

Instead, properly to explain Kempe's highly localized estate-position we must understand the guild structure of Bishop's Lynn. Prior to Kempe's time, Lynn had been a major port, rivaling London in volume of trade if not in population or size.[4] Unlike London or York, Lynn's guild structure was not organized by craft; instead Lynn had a dominant mercantile guild which included members of various crafts, and a variety of less prominent and variously religious guilds. William Richards lists thirty-one guilds in Lynn, including Kempe's Trinity, though not all date back to Kempe's time, and he labels five of them mercantile in nature.[5] The "Gilde Mercatorie Sancte Trinitatis," the leading and most overtly mercantile guild, had an annual income as high as £400, and owned the Guildhall and other civic properties.[6] The Trinity guild did not govern Lynn, but its Alderman chose four of the twelve jurats who elected Lynn's mayor and other civic officers,[7] and from at least 1417 Trinity's Alderman was responsible to finish the term of a Mayor who died in mid-term.[8] The guild itself had a fairly typical ordinance, describing an idealized social world for its estate (see chapter 1); the ordinance included the usual provisions for joining the guild, choosing its leaders, assisting and holding funerals for impoverished members, helping members in lawsuits, governing behavior at guild functions, enforcing attendance at meetings specified in the ordinance, and resolving disputes among members.[9]

Trinity's appended "Uses and Customs" also included a few less typical provisions, some having to do with charity, which are relevant in the context of Kempe's spirituality. For example, the annual meeting of Trinity's Alderman and brethren on the first Friday of Lent was set aside "to settle and order their alms and other works of charity."[10] This document expands on the main ordinance's provisions for funerals by providing twelve torches, and requiring all available members to attend. Also, the Alderman and officers responsible for managing the guild's property and income were required to visit "all the infirm, all that are in want, need, or poverty, and to minister to, and relieve all such, out of the alms of the said gild."[11] That such charity was not entirely indiscriminate is suggested by the provision that a member joining the guild "that he may be partaker of the alms and benefactions thereof" must pay "a certain sum of money to the maintenance of the said alms and benefactions."[12] This provision either determines rules for joining the guild in order to participate in the giving of charity, or suggests that one could join the guild in order to receive charity, but not for free or necessarily for the minimum fee. Also, one might join the guild in a period of personal prosperity in order to share in its giving of alms, and take comfort in the expectation of receiving those alms in a subsequent time of need.

Margery Kempe's own guild membership late in life supports the existence of primarily charitable members, and Janet Wilson sees it as a sign of "public respect for her spiritual aid."[13] Kempe's membership fee was 20s., midway between the going membership rate for the legitimate son of a member at 4s., and for a "stranger" at 100s.[14] By 1438 Kempe seems to have long since abandoned trade, so only the charitable and convivial activities of the guild would be plausible incentives for her to join. As there is no clause concerning a special rate for a woman to join, it seems entirely likely that Kempe would qualify for membership under the "Uses and Customs," a practice which allows the guild some control over members' charity through the guild. By charging a discretionary fee for members joining in order to be charitable, the guild both emphasizes and controls access to its acts of charity. On a corporate level, the governing estate of Lynn thus created an idealized nexus of power balanced with charity. The ordinance of this "Gilde Mercatorie" omits clauses governing trade in general in favor of a framework for the financial activities of its managers, although Gross describes how its funds were also used for public works.[15] The guild never states the assumption that institutional alms represent an antidote to trade, but it hardly seems accidental for a trade organization to emphasize charitable activities in the documents that create its idealized self-image. This emphasis on charity reminds members that the guild's institutional structure accounts for and responds to traditional moral and ecclesiastical objections to trade at the same time it continues to reify them. Similarly, while the ordinance of the Gild of St. Giles and St. Julian does address the familiar trade concern for "false weights or measures,"[16] Richards suggests that "there was an Almshouse connected with the said Gild, or under its patronage, from the first."[17] On parchment, at least, Lynn seems to have been a charitable place.

Of course, there remains the possibility that the "Margery Kempe" who joined the Gild of the Trinity was not our author, but the Trinity guild's documents still help us reconstruct the estate positioning of Kempe and her *Book*, because such ordinances are the primary record of the ideology of her estate-grouping. Kempe herself immediately associates guild membership with estate in her own statement of her estate-position. She is very concerned for the "worschyp of hir kynred," and when fighting with her husband she charges that "hym semyd neuyr for to a weddyd hir, for hir fadyr was sum-tyme meyr of þe town N. and sythyn he was alderman of þe hey Gylde of þe Trinyte in N."[18] Several key details emerge here: that Kempe ultimately rejects her estate is clear from the context, as she opens this statement with a reference to her "pride," a transparently negative quality in an (auto)hagiography.[19] As that pride directly depends on her father's status, she presents her estate as an obstacle to her piety. At the same time, Kempe's choice of characteristics to be proud of does not define her family's status through wealth or profession. She is proud to be a mayor's daughter, and daughter of an alderman of the Gild of the Trinity. That she associates the guild with material prosperity can also be seen when the "gret fyer" burns "þe Gylde-halle of þe Trinite" (p. 162), while she prays for a snowstorm to save St. Margaret's parish church. She directly contrasts church and guildhall, and God punishes the material but saves the spiritual; Kempe establishes her preferred estate-affiliation by "roaring" not on behalf of the guildhall, but on behalf of the church. In the earlier scene relating her youthful pride, Kempe similarly uses the guild to signify material success, directly contrasting to her divinely ordained material failure. As her mercantile pride represents a major obstacle to her piety later in her *Book*, she begins the text by addressing the anxieties of her estate-position with her rejection of merchandise and business. As Deborah S. Ellis observes, regular mercantile fears of the sins of business could be especially problematic for merchant women, so that "the need to balance business practices with the demands of spiritual righteousness...was automatically intensified for the merchant's wife, who had to pay in purgatory for not only her own but also her husband's sins of business."[20] Invoking the deadly sins of "envye" and "coveytyse" (p. 9), Kempe also reinforces her depiction of her own pride with an emphasis on her accompanying desire to be the best-dressed woman in the neighborhood. This impulse is familiar from Chaucer's Wife of Bath and the *Shipman's Tale* wife as a satiric characteristic of merchant women, so that here Kempe applies the satiric tradition to herself.

Kempe then reinforces this linkage of sin to the merchant estate she rejects, through her two ill-fated businesses. With her brewing business, she explains that "for pure coveytyse & for to maynten hir pride, sche...was on of þe grettest brewers in þe town N a iij ȝer or iiij tyl sche lost mech good" (p. 9), but the business ultimately failed, because "whan þe ale was as fayr standyng vndyr berm [*the yeast formed on brewing liquors*][21] as any man mygth se, sodenly þe berm wold fallyn down þat alle þe ale was lost euery brewyng aftyr oþer" (pp. 9–10). Reviled by her servants, she ultimately concludes that "hir pride and synne was cause of alle her punschyng and sche wold amend þat sche had trespasyd wyth good wyl" (p. 10). Then with her horse-mill enterprise, she describes a similar pattern: her healthy horses, like the ale's barm, simply refused to perform, and she follows that description with the usual rejection by her employees, and harsh criticism from her fellow townspeople (pp. 10–11). Concluding that God was punishing her again, "sche askyd God mercy & forsoke hir pride, hir coueytyse, & desyr þat sche had of þe worshepys of þe world, & dede grett bodyly penawnce, & gan to entyr þe way of euyrlestyng lyfe, as schal be seyd aftyr" (p. 11). These passages establish several characteristic patterns in the narrative: she emphasizes her rejection as her servants leave her, she confesses her exact sins so that her subsequent repentance is in no doubt, and she follows the description of her sins with an immediate explanation of her error and her correction thereof. With the brewing business, she also emphasizes her estate-position as an obstacle to her piety, by outlining her initial years of success, and discussing her abundant servants. Her choices of business are less tied to her estate, because while some women's occupations, such as regrating (street-vending victuals), were tied to lower status in the towns, the brewing industry in particular was "not a preserve of the privileged, nor was it abandoned to the poor."[22]

Kempe's servants also link her estate-position to her material failure, as the emotional power of the brewing passage comes partly from the servants ashamed of their mistress and refusing to live under her roof (an image she will use again in her rejection by her maid in Rome). Her material failures themselves act as an antidote to her pride in her status. Kempe's shifts of agency from her recalcitrant servants and animals to God then shows divine support for her rejection of her estate. She coopts her servants' and neighbors' scorn into her spiritual project by making them the instruments of God. In both passages, Kempe carefully inserts her use of the term "creatur" for herself into that shift of agency, as she goes from "sche" and "hir" to "þis creatur" (p. 10) at the very moment when she connects her material failure to God's punishment. This suggestion that her entrepreneurial failures were ordained by God makes both stories examples of God's protection from material temptation and mercantile sin, rather than stories of her ineptitude as a brewer or mill manager. The semi-miraculous failure of brewing chemistry also reminds the reader that her failure was not her fault, since the ale itself simply refused to brew. While the failure of the barm was overtly unnatural, the nature of the horse-mill incident requires her to outline her horseman's efforts to get the horses to cooperate. Since a balking horse would have been a familiar sight, the episode's sense of the miraculous relies on her repetition of the horseman's attempts, noticeable particularly in the recurring phrases "þis man" and "þis hors" in the passage (p. 10). The repetition takes on a folkloric or comic tone, as the horseman tries violence, kindness, a lead, and even riding with spurs to move the stubborn animal. While on the one hand this divine intervention helps to insulate her from the anxiety that she lacked either her father's business acumen or the basic skill to brew potable beer, it also emphasizes the pattern of direct interaction with God that characterizes her mystical life.

That this Langlandesque rejection of materialism takes place in the context of her business affairs then cements her linkage of her estate-position to materialism itself, so that she must escape her estate. This pattern had been established as a necessary part of merchant sanctity by Saint Homobonus, whose bull of canonization stresses his personal charity, and whose choral office "praises him for having given [trade] up."[23] Such an escape, however, remains problematic for Kempe, and much of her narrative relates her attempts to complete the escape begun with the businesses of Chapter 2. In particular she outlines her attempts at holy poverty, and to create a hybrid clerical/conventual estate-position within her urban context, what Caroline Walker Bynum calls her "escape from her normal role as 'married woman' into the role, two hundred years old at least, of the *mulier sancta*."[24] Perhaps the best examples of her attempts at holy poverty come through her constant giving and receiving of alms. In Chapter 24, for example, she advocates a merchant-estate charitable ideology when she presents her theory of alms to "a worshepful burgeys in Lenn, a meyrs pere & a mercyful man" and his wife, "a ful good woman": She encourages them to help their "powyr neybowrys whech þei knewyn wel a-now hadyn gred nede to ben holpyn & relevyd, & it was mor almes to helpyn hem þat þei knewyn wel for wel dysposyd folke & her owyn neybowrys þan oþer strawngerys whech þei knew not" (p. 56). This emphasis on local alms, rather than on donations to mendicants, church foundations, or the wandering priest she persuades the burgess not to support, reveals a kinship with the guild customs of the guilds, particularly of her own Trinity guild. The notion of giving to the local poor was hardly restricted to merchants, but it was idealized in the Trinity's requirements to visit "all the infirm, all that are in want, need, or poverty, and to minister to, and relieve all such, out of the alms of the said gild."[25]

Her adherence to her estate's approach to charity is not uniform, however, as she does not support the church endowment favored by many merchants. In an incident involving St. Margaret's parish church, she directly opposes a group seeking to upgrade the sacramental rights of a St. Nicholas's chapel within the church, a proposal that her father had also opposed decades earlier.[26] While we can expect this particular dispute to have been as personal and complex as any local politics, its closeness in Kempe's narrative to her description of righteous charity suggests her concern with the proper spending of charitable funds. The wealthy merchants here want to glorify their chapel to "makyn þe chapel eqwal to þe parysch cherch" (p. 59), and since adding a font and the accompanying lawsuit involve some expense, the controversy argues that what seem to be charitable expenses might actually glorify the giver in worldly terms, rather than demonstrate pure charity/caritas for the benefit of the recipient. The *Book* confirms Kempe's correctness in this rejection of the merchants' position by means of her successful prophecy that their project will fail (p. 60). Through this episode, Kempe tests the charitable positions available to a member of her estate, and her preference for alms over church endowment critiques her estate's involvement in the latter.

One can, however, overstate the extent to which she completely rejects her birth-estate; through much of her *Book*, Kempe's subjectivity balances her mercantile background and her spiritual ambitions. In the key scenes of Kempe's conversation with the Bishop of Worcester (p. 109), and her intercessory prayer for the parish church of St. Margaret (p. 162), Kempe struggles with this balance. The latter incident itself is fairly straightforward; on 23 January 1421, a great fire "brent up þe Gylde-halle of þe Trinite & in þe same town, an hydows fyer & greuows [was] ful lekely to a brent þe parysch cherch dedicate in þe honowr of Seynt Margarete, a solempne place & rychely honowryd, & also al þe town, ne had grace ne myracle ne ben" (p. 162). While she clearly privileges church over guild-hall, Kempe's presentation of her own actions also reveals an interesting point of fracture between different subject-positions, in terms both of her specific description, and of the larger context. The narrative even provides a necessary miracle for the perhaps-hoped-for sainthood that she never directly mentions. Her use of the term "miracle" seems hardly accidental; she also carefully supports her position of humility here, by carefully crediting God and the male church hierarchy: the first step to saving the church was when "hir confessowr, parisch preste of Seynt Margaretys Cherche, toke þe precyows Sacrament & went be-forn þe fyer as deuowtly as he cowde & sithyn browt it in a-geyn to þe Cherche" (p. 163). Her accompanying prayer, " 'Good Lorde, make it wel & sende down sum reyn er sum wedyr þat may thorw þi mercy qwenchyn þis fyer & esyn myn hert' " (p. 163), lays out the actual solution to the fire, an unexpected snowstorm, but the balance of "qwenchyn þis fyer & esyn myn hert" also emphasizes to the reader how Kempe's spirituality facili-tates the miraculous preservation of "al þe town." The townspeople's subsequent "slawndyr" (p. 164) of her reinforces the familiar trope of her suffering, as well. These details carefully align her self-fashioning directly with the subject-position created by the discourse of affective piety, and indeed in the following incident in Chapter 67 a parson defends her weeping as "a ryth gracyows ȝyft of God" (p. 165).

The fault-line in her subjectivity then comes through the episode's context, and the nonchronological, retrospective nature of the *Book*. While this incident takes place in 1421, and Kempe does not seem to have joined the Trinity Guild until 1438, her family's long-term association with the guildhall might well be known to a reader. More importantly, the reader knows about another event that took place after the fire but earlier in the *Book*, the 1432 squabble over the side chapel of St. Nicholas. This context thus aligns Kempe with her father and father-in-law's posi-tions on the same subject during her father's mayoralty in 1378.[27] When we look at the sequence of these episodes in the *Book*, however, with the 1432 church-enlargement squabble coming well before the miracle that had saved that very church, Kempe reinforces her persona as daughter of a mayor and guild Alderman (p. 9) who had a strong enough attachment to St. Margaret's parish church to name his daughter for its patron. While she names her father in Chapter 45, between these two incidents, the details about his high-status offices practically open the *Book* in Chapter 2. For Kempe, once she has established not only whose daughter she is, but that she "felt in hir sowle" (p. 59) that her father's support of St. Margaret's had been the correct choice, the saving of St. Margaret's from a fire in

Chapter 67 is not just about being a mystic. Through these associations established earlier in the *Book*, her miracle also aligns her with her father's faction among Lynn's merchants. The burning of the guildhall keeps this "miracle" from being too promercantile, but we should not ignore Kempe's merchant-estate background in this incident. The subtle interaction between Kempe's sense of identity as her father's daughter and her identity as a roaring mystic is what makes the miracle so important, as it reveals her deeply ambivalent connection to her community. The "slawndyr" that follows the miracle only cements that ambivalence.

We see this same interplay between her subject-position as "Iohn of Burnamys dowtyr of Lynne" (p. 109) and her persona as a mystic in an earlier scene in the *Book*, her conversation with Thomas Peverel, Bishop of Worcester. This scene, in which she defends herself before departing on pilgrimage "to-Seynt-Iamys-warde" (p. 109), brings her identities as mystic and mayor's daughter into direct conflict. The chapter primarily concerns her pilgrimage, but obstacles in her way include finding a man to accompany her, resisting the scorn of a "riche man of Bristowe" (p. 108) who objects to her use of a ship, her harassment by the Bishop's men, and her conversation with the Bishop. The important contrast here is between her scorn for the "riche man," and her conviviality with the Bishop. There is little reason given to object to her passage on the ship, except that the man of Bristol "held hir no good woman" (p. 108); perhaps her reputation preceded her. She quotes none of his words to her, but she responds with a threat of damnation: " 'Syr, yf ȝe put me owt of þe schip, my Lord Ihesu xal put ȝow owt of Heuyn, for I telle ȝow, ser, owr Lord Ihesu hath no deynte of a ryche man les þan he wil be a good man & a meke man' " (p. 108). While she does not clarify the source of this man's wealth, it seems reasonable enough to see this passage as a repudiation of her birth-estate, since she adopts the disdain for wealth so characteristic of the clerical ideology she adopts as a mystic. Certainly the image of Kempe threatening a wealthy man with damnation unless he is more "meke" and "good" recalls *Piers Plowman*.

If Kempe's interaction with the Bishop were as tense as, say, her brief imprisonment for Lollardy in Leicester in the following chapter, there would be no question that Chapter 45 would reinforce her identity as a mystic, tribulations and all. The actual conversation with the Bishop is actually one of the funniest moments in the *Book*, though, as it turns out that he was not summoning her for an ecclesiastical interrogation, but for dinner. He explains to her, "Margery, I haue not somownd þe, for I knowe wel j-now þu art Iohn of Burnamys dowtyr of Lynne. I pray þe be not wroth, but far fayr wyth me, & I xal far fayr wyth the, for þu xalt etyn wyth me þis day" (p. 109). The relevant details are the identity of the

Bishop, his politeness and deference, and the reason that he is not summoning her for an interrogation. His identity matters because, as Meech and Allen observe, in 1410 Peverel had convicted a Lollard of a capital charge of heresy.[28] This detail creates the anticlimax of the dinner invitation, because a reader who recognizes the Bishop of Worcester might expect the fuss over Lollardy that will not come until the next chapter. His politeness, asking that she "be not wroth," further supports the anticlimax, as it renders this powerful man as nonthreatening as a fifteenth-century bishop might be. The Bishop's immediate identification of her as her father's daughter further complicates the chapter: it seems less her reputation as a mystic behind this friendliness, than her reputation as a daughter of the merchant estate. He does not initially commend her spirituality, and although he goes on to ask for her intercessory prayers on his behalf (p. 110), his recognition of her invokes her identity as her father's daughter. Coming so soon after her repudiation of an individual wealthy man, this scene thus reveals another moment of fracture between her two identities as merchant and mystic. At one moment, she sharply rejects her birth-estate, and at the next, she happily acknowledges it. This scene presents some resolution, though, as she moves seamlessly from her recognition as a Brunham to her prayers for the Bishop. That move will not work in the next chapter, where the mayor of Leicester is not at all impressed by her identity as daughter of a mayor of Lynn (p. 111). For now, though, Kempe seems to have reached a working accommodation between these contradictory subject-positions. If a bishop can imagine a mayor's daughter as a mystic, after all, how dare a reader question her?

Despite this balance of subjectivities in parts of the *Book*, Kempe ultimately engages with the problem of holy poverty; she finds a way to be almost simultaneously on both the giving and receiving end of alms, thus neatly avoiding the pride that she shows to be behind the merchants of Lynn's patronage of their chapel. When she was in Rome, "owr Lord bad hir ʒeuyn a-wey al hir good & makyn hir bar for hys lofe" (p. 92), and she distributes everything in a thorough rejection of material goods. This episode's proximity to her visit to Assisi draws comparison to St. Francis of Assisi, who was himself a member of the merchant estate prior to dedicating himself to poverty with a somewhat similar and far more thorough rejection of worldly goods.[29] Like a mendicant, Kempe immediately must become the recipient of alms, and just in Chapter 38 she receives support from Dame Margarete Florentyn, who had brought her to Rome from Assisi, a man in the street, and Marcelle the Roman. Where the material world in *Piers Plowman* interfered with idealized holy poverty, Kempe makes it work, although her success requires divine intervention. She clarifies her vision of this holy poverty as an escape from her estate when labels herself a "partynyr...in meryte" (p. 94) with the poor. Such poverty is not without its fears, and it evokes another mercantile anxiety aside from fear of sin, that of economic failure, and Sheila Delany argues that Kempe is "deeply frightened" by her poverty.[30]

What this reliance on holy poverty reflects in Kempe's narrative is that she cannot cast off the anxieties of her estate-position as easily as she casts off her business failures. Some Marxian analyses have addressed those anxieties, and David Aers sees Kempe as thoroughly and inescapably interpellated by the ideology of the merchant elite, reading her rejection of the material in her failed trade enterprises as nevertheless working within that mercantile ideology. He argues in particular that her critiques of sins like avarice and pride attack "the individual sinner without bringing into question the system of relationships which organizes social life in a way that demands the behaviour judged as sinful if the existing order is to be maintained."[31] Aers sees many aspects of Kempe's persona as mercantile; he notes her drive to accumulate more pardons, for example.[32] Deborah S. Ellis similarly argues that Kempe's use of trade language "so conflates marital, religious, and commercial ideas of trade and partnership that each is explicable only in terms of the others."[33] Aers's observation that Kempe buys her way free from the "legalized, sacralized rape" of marriage by paying off her husband's loans[34] links her mercantile background to her resolution of the conflict between her pious ambitions and her gender, as well. Traces of her birth-estate's ideology thus continue to construct her subject position, with her emphasis on costs and her expression of acquisitive desires, but through her overt rejections of the material and her engagement with antimaterial strains of clerical discourse like Franciscanism, she repudiates at least part of the subject-position we would expect of a member of her estate to fashion herself as a mystic.

This is not to say, however, that she manages such a repudiation without cost. *The Book of Margery Kempe* tells a story of conflict, and while the *Book* foregrounds the conflict between materialism (which she associates with mercantilism) and spirituality, this is not meant to be a totalizing reading of the *Book*. Still, Kempe reinforces the centrality of her conflict with her birth-estate with her much shorter Book II, which introduces the narrative of Kempe's son, "whom sche desyryd to a drawyn owt of þe perellys of þis wretchyd & vnstabyl worlde ȝyf hir power myth a teynyd þerto" (p. 221). Karen A. Winstead outlines the parallels between Kempe's own conversion and that of her son: he starts as a merchant, has trouble with lechery, wears fancy clothes, and "like his mother, the young man loses everything—his health, his good looks, his livelihood, and his friends—before he resolves to mend his ways, and his transformation, like hers, is marked by a dramatic change in appearance as well as in temperament."[35] There is one major difference, however, in that the son has Kempe's intervention, and her "account emphasizes her agency both in his affliction and his deliverance: her son and his acquaintances blame her, rather than God, for his misfortunes, and, once converted, the son credits the mother for his good fortune."[36] This conversion of Kempe's son then provides an unexpected compromise between her own rejection of the material and her son's merchant business. While at first she counsels him to "leeuyn þe worlde & folwyn Crist" (p. 221), she later reduces her advice to "he xulde fle þe perellys of þis worlde & not settyn hys stody ne hys besynes so mech þerup-on as he dede" (p. 221). After the son recovers his health, he marries and has a child (p. 223), and given that he marries "in Pruce in Dewchelonde" (p. 223) it seems unlikely that he has left his trade, which is the most likely reason for an Englishman of his estate to be in Germany. Winstead argues that the purpose of Kempe's apparent moderation is "to assure readers that she is not the anti-family radical that so many of her detractors in Book I accuse her of being,"[37] but the converted son also fits the model of merchant piety suggested by the *Shipman's Tale* (see chapter 4), with his "sadde" mien and "pil-grimagys...to purchasyn hym pardon" (p. 224).

Were this episode the end of the *Book*, it might suggest a softening of Kempe's position on trade and materialism, but she immediately follows her advocacy of a compromise position for her son with her last trip. Her visit to Germany recapitulates her mystical antimercantile values, requir-ing divine intervention because of her poverty (p. 227), and she travels as a mendicant through those very areas with which Lynn's trade had historically been conducted, the coast of Norway and coastal Germany, and overland to Calais on her way home (p. 230–39).[38] This particular trip foregrounds alms-giving and holy poverty, when she offers to sup-port a friar (p. 239) and when she arrives in Calais needing a new smock. Although she does not present it as an antithesis to her son's compro-mise, the trip's position in the *Book* ensures that piety closes the narrative. While she seems to have reconciled herself enough with merchant piety to be willing to join her estate's Trinity guild, she takes care that this relative softening of her rejection of material values is not her last word. While the middle way she presents to her son is better than his earlier state of sin, she leaves no doubt for the reader that poverty presents the better path: Kempe is no apologist for trade.

The Libelle of Englyshe Polycye and Promercantilism

While Kempe shows effectively how even a successful member of the mercantile estate could embrace an antimercantile ideology, hers was by no means the only voice on the subject. While it certainly represents a significant divergence in tone and form from Kempe's *Book*, *The Libelle of Englyshe Polycye* embodies the other side of a coin from the *Book*, in the sense that the two texts both address the economic crisis of the late 1430s and the role of trade in society. Where Margery Kempe rejects trade, *The Libelle of Englyshe Polycye* is one of very few Middle English poems to valorize trade as such. Kempe associates trade with moral weakness and sin, but for the anonymous poet of the *Libelle*, trade enables politics, and the poet studiously restricts discussion of the morality of trade to a critique of alien merchants similar to that of John Gower in the *Mirour de l'Omme*, only without any application of that criticism to the English. As it posits a mercantile subject-position without any concern for the morality of trade, it would be useful for my project to be able to say that the *Libelle* was written by a member of the merchant estate. Unfortunately, such seems not to have been the case, or at least not to be provable. The poet's third-person address to "Ye worthi marchauntes" (l. 260) certainly implies a nonmercantile authorial persona, and no one has yet named a possible merchant author.[39] Sir George Warner, the editor of the *Libelle*, argues that the author must have "had a genuine love for his country, sound political judgement, and an extensive knowledge of trade," but can find no evidence that the poet was a merchant.[40] G. A. Holmes insists that the poem was written under the patronage of Humphrey, Duke of Gloucester (Henry V's brother), since it expresses "the point of view of the duke of Gloucester, the Staplers and the cloth exporters against the opposite policy pursued by the council."[41] He also suggests the authorship of John Lydgate, though he finds the *Libelle* too "pithy and vulgar" for Lydgate's pen.[42]

Despite its anonymity, however, the poem belongs to a highly specific historical context, in its regular reference to the 1436 siege of Calais and the general embargo on English trade with the Low Countries, and thus can be firmly dated to that time. In its political agenda of using trade as a weapon and the merchant fleet for naval power, the *Libelle*-poet takes the unprecedented step of divorcing trade entirely from any moral concern with avarice or the sins of merchants. The poem focuses directly on the power inherent in trade relations, and suggests how England might capitalize on that power through a stronger navy and its own embargo or blockade. Some of this potential "mercantile" power is directly military, since the medieval English navy was composed primarily of merchant ships. There was almost never a standing, permanent medieval English navy composed of oared "galleys." Instead, the English "navy" consisted of a balance of merchant ships carrying troops, sometimes with "temporary castles fitted" to facilitate ship-to-ship combat.[43] As a result of this practice of using the merchant fleet for naval power, merchants interacted directly with the crown in this military context. Since few English wars could be carried on without naval transport, this ad hoc navy meant that the interests of the merchant estate were inextricably bound up in the vast majority of English military activities, even leaving aside the crown's reliance on merchants for loans and customs duties. It also meant that the merchants and their crews were exposed to the dangers of war, if less directly than knights in military service. Like the lack of a standing army, this practice of borrowing a navy when needed also meant that the crown could be caught out by suddenly changing alliances.

At the time of the poem, this had just happened. As Scattergood points out, in 1436–37 England had lacked a navy for a decade "when England and its allies controlled most of the western seaboard of northern France and Flanders, [but] with the defection of [Philip the Good, Duke of] Burgundy [to Charles VII of France] this situation had changed";[44] now England needed a navy all at once. John D. Fudge explains that the crown's solution was to issue licenses in 1436 for roughly thirty shipowners to work as privateers, attacking ships at their own expense and keeping the captured ships and cargoes. The crown also suspended statutes forbidding receipt of pirated goods, and unsurprisingly the Hanse was not happy with this unofficial licensure of piracy.[45] The *Libelle*-poet does carefully distance himself from piracy by recounting the nostalgic tale of Edward III's defeat of Breton pirates (ll. 178–239), but there is some kinship between the crown's privateering policy and the poet's acknowledgment of the potential power of the merchant fleet. *The Libelle of Englyshe Polycye* then suggests the value of using naval power to interfere with other nations' trade, and thus to compel their cooperation, and argues that rivals of England might be using their own merchants to England's detriment. His discussion of Italians, in particular, consists of a mixture of familiar antimercantile tropes fitted into the poet's basic argument to suggest that Italian merchants were both cheating the English and spying on them.

What seems to control the *Libelle* poet's appropriation of antimercantile tropes, though, is less his interest in trade as such than his nostalgic nationalism, expressed most clearly in terms of a highly mercantile image: the gold noble. The poet opens his discussion of sea power controlling the English Channel with the story of "Sigesmonde the grete Emperoure" (l. 8), who advised Henry V that Dover and Calais were necessary to the security of his realm: " 'Kepe these too townes sure to youre mageste / As youre tweyne eyne to kepe the narowe see' " (ll. 20–21). While this image of the king's eyes describes how those two cities allow the English to survey every ship that passes through the Channel, the image also fits concern with the English channel into a body metaphor of the state and

invokes nostalgia for the idealized reign of Henry V.[46] The poem's next
symbol ties trade directly to this vision of English nationalism: "For iiij
thynges oure noble sheueth to me, / Kyng, shype and swerde and pouer
of the see" (ll. 34–35). Warner identifies this "noble" as "the gold noble
first coined in 1344 and showing on the obverse the king with drawn
sword seated in a ship . . . This new type of impression is supposed to com-
memorate the great naval victory of Edward III over the French at Sluys
in 1340."[47] With its nostalgia, this image avoids the satirists' concern with
"loue of the cros"[48] on the coin, or "la crois de l'esterling."[49] Warner shows
three gold nobles, and the ship on the obverse of the nobles of Edward III,
Henry VI, and Philip the Good, Duke of Burgundy, is clearly a merchant
sailing ship with castles added fore and aft for naval service.[50]

   While like the penny the noble bore a cross on its reverse, the *Libelle*-
poet does not use that image to suggest idolatry of money. Instead, the
Libelle-poet uses the coin's obverse iconography as a reminder of past
victories and present treachery in Philip the Good's new alliance with
France. This image of the armed king dominating a ship unites iconography of royal power in the upheld sword with that of overseas trade in
the sailing ship. The poet directly challenges Philip, asking,

   Shall any prynce, what so be hys name,
   Wheche hathe nobles moche lyche to oures,
   Be lorde of see and Flemmynges to oure blame
   Stoppe us, take us and so make fade the floures
   Of Englysshe state and disteyne oure honnoures? (l. 43–47)

Warner's plate shows a 1427 Flemish noble to be identical to a Henry VI
noble, aside from the inscriptions and the arms on the sovereign's shield.
Such similarity underlines the traditional economic ties between England
and the Low Countries, ties that were severely restricted by Philip's "official ban on the entry of English merchants and merchandise" into the
Low Countries from 1436 to 1439, an embargo that blocked the wool
trade and generated "a virtual cessation of trade at the Staple."[51] Instead
of focusing on the effects on trade of such a conflict, the *Libelle*-poet
focuses on lost lordship and damage to "oure honnoures." His assimilation of trade into chivalric rhetoric, combined with his use of numismatic
iconography in the image of the noble and the play on words inherent
in the coin's name, rejects previous satirical imagery of money and trade.
The poet here takes the radical step of normalizing economic images to
aristocratic/chivalric discourse, and breaks directly from the estates satire
tradition. By using terms like "noble" and "honnoure," the poet rejects
both the satiric implications of the coin image so richly mined by Gower,

and Langland's argument for moral consequences to aristocratic interest in trade, and leaves no place for satire in this part of his poem.

While the *Libelle*-poet can deploy images used by the satiric tradition without engaging with their satiric potential, he is also not above applying familiar satiric opprobrium to alien merchants, though he carefully insulates that opprobrium from the now-familiar concern with merchants' sins. Most of his discussion of the trade of individual countries avoids satirical material. While in his discussions of Spanish and Flemish trade he focuses on Flemish dependence on English wool, the poet primarily describes which essential commodities are shipped by which country through the Channel so carefully watched by the eyes of Dover and Calais, and implies that a strong English navy could control that trade and thus the profits of those countries. The poet only attacks national sins in the case of Breton piracy (ll. 178–239) and in the shady practices of Italian merchants. While with the Genoese he lists commodities (ll. 330–43), as he had with the Flemish and the Scots, the poet heads into familiar satirical territory by characterizing the cargoes of the Venetians and Florentines as useless (and effete) luxuries. While there may be some implicit criticism of the powerful Grocers, the *Libelle*-poet primarily attacks useless Italian fripperies:

> The grete galees of Venees and Florence
> Be wel ladene wyth thynges of complacence,
> All spicerye and other grocers ware,
> Wyth swete wynes, all manere of chaffare,
> Apes and japes and marmusettes taylede,
> Nifles, trifles, that litell have availed,
> And thynges wyth whiche they fetely blere oure eye,
> Wyth thynges not endurynge that we bye. (ll. 343–51).

By using terms which suggest the extravagance of these luxury commodities, "complacence," "nifles," "trifles," and "not endurynge," the poet both implies that English commodities are more important to the Italians than vice versa, trifles being easier to live without than "Clothe, woll and tynne" (l. 376), and trivializes the powerful Italian merchants. This carefully limited satiric mode reveals the poet's awareness of the satire tradition, but he harnesses that tradition to his nationalist project by restricting antimercantile satire to the long-hated Italians.

The poet then further subordinates satire to his politics by accusing these Florentine and Venetian merchants of another role:

> What harme, what hurte and what hinderaunce
> Is done to us unto oure grete grevaunce

Of suche londes and of suche nacions....
By wretynge ar discured oure counsayles
And false coloured alwey the countertayles
Of oure enmyes, that dothe us hinderinge
Unto oure goodes, oure realme and to the kynge,
As wysse men have shewed well at eye,
And all this is colowred by marchaundye. (ll. 386–95)[52]

It is not at all clear that there was necessarily a specific market for military intelligence involving the Italians spying for the Burgundians, "our enmyes, that dothe us hinderinge / Unto oure goodes" with the 1436–39 embargo. The *Libelle*-poet here invokes a fear of boundary crossing and unclear loyalties inherited from the estates satire tradition, but applies it only to the Italians who spy for the Burgundians. As with its critique of Italian commodities, the poem applies satirical material carefully, within its specific politics of naval and mercantile power, and without the generality of estates satire. The poet thus rejects the implication that the satirized character represents an entire class or estate, as Gower's Triche and Langland's Coveitise represented all merchants.

The poem's subsequent critique of Italian business practice then deploys the familiar satiric assumption that complex business practice must be transgressive, but again it restricts that satirical material to a limited context. Describing Italian ships much larger than the northern variety,[53] access to distant markets, and a sophisticated understanding of bills of exchange and large-scale banking, the poem complains that Italians could profit "In the Englysshe pounde... iij. shyllinges" (ll. 423–24) on their exchanges. What is characteristic of mercantile satire in *The Libelle of Englyshe Polycye* is the sense that such practices were to be condemned, not because they were immoral, but because they involved merchants from other countries making a profit from English trade, and because such practices added to the problem of dwindling gold reserves in England, as "they bere the golde oute of thys londe / And souke the thryfte awey oute of oure honde" (ll. 396–97).[54] This particular critique thus deploys satiric material specifically to attack those merchant practices beyond the level of English finance. The Italians were more advanced, in their reliance on companies rather than individuals, in their more thorough penetration of European markets, and in their greater understanding of and ability to manipulate finance; for example, in this period the English had yet to learn the Italian innovation of double-entry bookkeeping.[55] Because of this gap between Italian and English merchants, the *Libelle*-poet is able to adapt satiric material in a context similar to its original one, as an attack on merchant practice that seemed too profitable to be honest, but he completely drops any focus on sin.

The mercantile subject-position imagined by the *Libelle*-poet seems concerned far more with advantage than with sin. The poet attempts to write the personal advantage of profit onto national advantage through policy, and he entirely normalizes merchant activity to political action, to be judged by its expediency.

There is a similarly satiric emphasis in the *Libelle*'s concern with Italians being involved in local trading:

> In Cotteswolde also they ryde aboute
> And al Englonde and bien wythouten doute
> What them liste wythe fredome and fraunchise,
> More than we Englisshe may getyn in any wyse. (ll. 456–59)

Presumably, since the *Libelle* sees the Italians as part of the specie-exporting problem as "they bere the golde oute of thys londe" (l. 396), these Italians have more ready cash with which to buy up commodities, such as the wool their great ships could export directly to the Mediterranean. The *Libelle*-poet's suggested solution to this "problem" of being outmaneuvered is to reinstate hosting (ll. 460–64), which had required that alien merchants arrange for a franchised local host who would agree to restrict their activities, in order to limit alien merchants to urban areas. Hosting has the added advantage of providing another moment of nostalgia for Edward III, who

> ...made a statute for Lumbardes in thys londe,
> That they shulde in no wysse take on honde
> Here to enhabite, to charge and dyscharge,
> But xl. dayes, no more tyme had they large.
> Thys goode kynge be wytt of such appreffe
> Kepte hys marchauntes and the see from myscheffe. (ll. 240–45)

Of course, Edward III also regularly favored Italian merchants over his own because they would loan him large sums of money; the *Libelle* clearly has some rhetorical blind spots in its advocacy of a return to Edwardian glory days. Still, the author points out that other countries require hosting of English merchants. Such overt protectionism thus represents both a nostalgic return to Edward III and a matter of competition with economic rivals. The *Libelle*-poet has applied negative qualities of traditional satiric merchants, such as dangerous border-crossing, shady monetary deals, and grasping of gold, to the Italian merchants, but at the same time he has assimilated trade to politics, the territory of the aristocracy, by shifting the terms of his discussion of trade to political and economic expediency rather than sin. While the poem considers it a bad thing that

Italian merchants profit from English commodities, "bad" in this context means not "immoral" but "contrary to English interests." The poem never implies merchandise itself is sinful, and never raises the subject of avarice.

The significance of *The Libelle of Englyshe Polycye*'s treatment of merchandise then comes from the poet's matter-of-fact description of trade as a potential international weapon, and in his radical refusal to discuss trade in terms of sin. The poet uses some of the familiar apparatus of the estates satiric tradition, but he confines it to his discussion of the Italians, and he carefully strips reference to sin from such material. While he does not exactly make a case that merchandise is morally positive, he firmly aligns trade with the less universally condemned aristocratic estate in passages concerned with honor and worship:

> Put to gode wylle for to kepe the see,
> Furste for worshyp and for profite also,
> And to rebuke of eche evyl-wylled foo.
> Thus shall richesse and worship to us longe,
> Than to the noble shall wee do no wronge,
> To bere that coigne in figure and in dede,
> To our corage and to oure enmyes drede. (ll. 1069–75)

With the return of the image of the noble embodying the crown and profit together, the *Libelle* consistently presents trade as positive and deserving of high estate. Through the overlap of the merchant fleet and the navy, and the use of trade as an avenue for conflict between nations, the poem places merchants in a similar role to those knights and other soldiers who took part in international conflict. In this sense, the poem puts an entirely new face on the notion that danger justifies trade. Scattergood has no trouble finding contemporary texts far less accepting of merchants,[56] so the *Libelle*'s enthusiastic descriptions of England's potential power over international trade networks do not imply that the satirists' concerns had been laid to rest, but the *Libelle*'s polemical merger of mercantile and political discourses reminds us that it was possible in the fifteenth century to be familiar enough with the satire tradition to borrow from it without sharing its argument, and to present English merchants deserving "worship" (l. 486) and representing England in international conflicts, without recalling their historical association with avarice.

"The Childe of Bristowe" and Restitution

We see this borrowing of decontextualized satiric material in another pro-mercantile poem of the early fifteenth century, "The Childe of Bristowe," and its contemporary analogue "The Merchant and His Son." What Barbara A. Hanawalt characterizes as "fifteenth-century version of Horatio Alger stories,"[57] however, do not assimilate trade to politics. Instead the poems present trade as a profession with positive moral potential, in contrast to the shady legal dealing of the squire/franklin father: "To lawe he went a gret while, / pore men he lerned to begile / all ageyns the right."[58] The poems incorporate satire, though, by retaining the traditional counterpoint to satirical antimercantilism: an emphasis on the dangers of trade, albeit not in the purely physical terms of *The Libelle of Englyshe Polycye*. As Scattergood explains, "the rich squire in *The Childe of Bristowe* advised his son against becoming a merchant because trading 'is but caswelté.'"[59] An even stronger trace of the estates satirical tradition in "The Childe of Bristowe" poems appears in their relentless insistence on the necessity of restitution of goods gained avariciously, a need familiar from Coveitise's despair in *Piers Plowman*. What signals the increasing acceptance of trade that differentiates these poems from previous literary discussions of merchants is the shift in the relative roles of the estates in terms of restitution. Where the merchant Coveitise's avarice and usury necessitated restitution in *Piers Plowman*, here it is the "squyer mykel of myght" (*CB* l. 15) who must be brought out of hell. In contrast, the Childe's master, a merchant of Bristol, unknowingly helps to enable the Childe's execution of his father's will and provides a virtuous father-surrogate. Although the mercantile subject-position envisioned by these poems retains the concern with sin so characteristic of the estates satires, it does so from a position of moral virtue unavailable in the estates-satire tradition.

Before analyzing the poems' treatment of charity, restitution, and merchants, though, it seems worthwhile to contextualize these relatively unknown works. Each version survives in a single mid-fifteenth-century manuscript, "The Childe of Bristowe" in British Library ms. Harley 2382 and "The Merchant and his Son" in Cambridge University Library ms. Ff. 2. 38.[60] Frances McSparrow and P. R. Robinson, in their facsimile edition of the latter manuscript, characterize its contents as "a good index to the religious and literary tastes and pre-occupations of the bourgeoisie in the late fifteenth century."[61] Indeed, "The Childe of Bristowe" was even attributed in the nineteenth century to Lydgate, that great attributee of miscellaneous fifteenth-century poetry of dubious quality.[62] Barbara A. Hanawalt characterizes the poems as addressing the anxieties of the rising "middle class," which "centered on such questions as the most prestigious way of earning their wealth (law, trade, or landed estates), the appropriate education for their sons and marriages for their daughters, the type of clothing they should wear, the manners they should display, and their personal salvation."[63]

The extent to which "The Childe of Bristowe" poems feature these anxieties suggests why a historian of Hanawalt's caliber was drawn to them, as they feature each of the anxieties she lists: Childe-William (Hanawalt's term), son of a landed squire or franklin, chooses between the professions of law and merchandise, by choosing the latter; he is educated when "his fader put hym unto lore / to lerne to be a clerke; / so long he lernyd in clergie, / til he was wise and wittye, / and drad al dedis derke" (*CB* ll. 38–42); we see Childe-William's clothing when he gives it away at the end of the poems; Childe-William's manners "wax so curteise and bolde, / al marchauntz loved hym...in that contré" (*CB* ll. 82–84), and the bulk of both narratives concerns the problem of the father's personal salvation. Given this close match between the poems' content and the courtesy manuals to which she compares them, Hanawalt makes a convincing case for them as didactic texts for the middle class, much like the growing genre of advice and courtesy books.[64] She then provides a useful outline of the poems' adherence to early fifteenth-century guild practice, in particular noting that "gentlemen and yeomen's sons, like Childe-William, were more likely to enter prestigious guilds, such as the guild of long-distance merchants, than were sons of husbandmen,"[65] and that apprenticeship had grown quite expensive by the time of the poem.[66] She also points out that in Bristol, particularly, it was common for masters only to train a single apprentice, and as child mortality left many families without surviving sons, a "master with only one apprentice in his lifetime could form a strong attachment to this surrogate son."[67] If these poems reflect an idealized version of a young man's relationship with his father and master, as Hanawalt argues, it then remains to be seen how that young merchant's career reflects general social concerns with merchandise, and how these poems shift the terms of mercantile morality away from merchandise itself, breaking with tradition by imagining highly moral merchants.

The profession-choosing scene gives the first indications of the poems' vision of the relationship between profession and morality, as Childe-William rejects his father's overtures to go into law, the source of his father's illicit profits. Childe-William replies firmly,

they fare ful wel that lerne no lawe,
and so y hope to do;
that lyve wil y never lede,
to put my soule in so gret drede,
to make God my foo;
To sle my soule it were routhe.
Any science that is trouthe

y shal amytte me therto;
for to forsake my soule helthe
for any wynnyng of worldes welthe,
that wille y never do.
Hit hath ever be myn avise
to lede my lyf by marchandise
to lerne to bye and selle;
that good getyn by marchantye
it is trouthe, as thenketh me,
therwith wille y melle. (*CB* ll. 50–66)

This discussion of the relative virtues of law and merchandise retains the
satirical tradition's negative view of the legal profession. Childe-William
also firmly repudiates avarice in his refusal to endanger his "soule helthe"
for "worldes welthe," but the notion that "that good getyn by marchantye / it is trouthe" rejects previous literary treatments of trade, and
establishes merchandise as a legitimate, "true" profession. These terms
themselves, the familiarly played-upon "good" and the highly multiva-
lent ideal of "trouthe," with its connotations of honor and reliability, act
to place "marchantye" on a high moral and social plane. Indeed, the MED
cites line 65 for the headword "treuth" in the meaning "of a way of life or
vocation: not entailing deceit or dishonesty, morally legitimate; of goods:
honestly obtained."[68] Elsewhere in the fairly long entry for "treuth," it
becomes clear that the term has significant range and is shared in overlapping usage by chivalric, devotional, and mercantile traditions.[69]

Where the *The Libelle of Englyshe Polycye* divorced merchandise from a
moral context, though, in its assimilation of merchandise to aristocratic
discourse of "honnoure," "The Childe of Bristowe" simply asserts the
morality of merchandise, and proceeds to show merchants being good
Christians, without the fractured subjectivities of Langland's Coveitise,
the narrator of Chaucer's *Merchant's Tale*, or Margery Kempe. The relative extremity of this position can be seen in that "The Merchant and His
Son" is significantly less strongly worded: in that version Childe-William
simply replies, "A man of lawe, seyde Wyllyam, that wyll y nevyr bee; /
Y wolde lerne of marchandyse, to passe ovyr the see!" (*M&S* ll. 43–44).
The father's response then emphasizes the familiar merchants' response to
the sins and uncertainties of merchandise, previously modeled for us by
the merchant in Chaucer's *Shipman's Tale*: "Yf thou be a marchand, my
sone Wyllyam, the sothe y can telle the, / I have seyn men bothe ryse and
falle; hyt ys but caswelté" (*M&S* ll. 45–46). While the versions thus vary
in the approbation substituted for the opprobrium of satirical treatments
of merchants, they share contempt for the legal profession, and apply the
negative moral qualities of greed and refusal to make restitution to the

squire/franklin in his legal maneuverings. This retention of the sins of avarice in another context then allows the poems not only to show the possibility of moral merchants, but specifically to characterize merchants as overcoming traditionally mercantile sins with their active virtue.

The real heart of the poems' normalization of merchandise then comes in Childe-William's actions as executor of his father's will, and his exemplary restitution. Both versions specify that the squire/franklin was unable to find anyone else to execute his will: "Ther was no man in that contré / That his executour wold be, / nor for no good ne ille; / they seid his good was geten so, / they wold not have therwith to do, / for drede of God in heven" (*CB* ll. 109–114). The consequences of this lack of willing friends are made clear when his ghost appears to Childe-William either a fortnight (*CB*) or three days (*M&S*) after his death. In the more emphatic "Childe of Bristowe" version, the extra eleven days allow the Childe to arrange for a hundred priests "the dirige for to say" (*CB* ll. 195), and to sell off all available moveable goods, "catel" and "tresour" (*CB* ll. 208, 221), to do alms (*CB* ll. 211–16). Despite these efforts, the father appears burning as "the devel bi the nekke gan hym lede / in a brennyng cheyne" (*CB* l. 245–46). "The Merchant and His Son" skips this first round of charity, but instead moves directly to the franklin's burning soul accompanied by "fendys blake, that wroght hym mooche payne" (*M&S* l. 88), but the result in both texts is that Childe-William sells his inherited lands to his master, claiming "me nedith a litel somme of gold" (*CB* l. 286) and that he would rather his master than a stranger profit from his emergency sale (*CB* ll. 304–6; *M&S* l. 118). Notably, in both versions the merchant master gives his apprentice more than his asking price, 300 pounds instead of 100 marks in "The Childe of Bristowe," and 1,000 pounds instead of 1,000 marks in "The Merchant and His Son" (*CB* ll. 308–10; *M&S* ll. 124–26). The latter represents a peculiarly mercantile form of largesse, in the sense that both merchants show their generosity, but the shift from marks to pounds (both monies of account) relies on some knowledge of accounting on the reader's part, as a mark was was two thirds of a pound, or 13s. 4d.

This particular sale sets the moral tone for the apprentice's subsequent sale of himself into servitude with his master in order to get more money to make restitution (*CB* ll. 407–19; *M&S* ll. 185–90), followed by use of his clothing to pay back his father's final claimant, so that "Off his clothes he gan take, / and putt hem on the pore manis bake, / chargyng [him] for hys fader to pray" (*CB* ll. 448–50). This sequential divestment of his patrimony, which takes up most of the poem, emphasizes for the reader the danger of ill-gotten gains to the soul of the owner or inheritor, but not for the purchaser. Apparently, there is nothing wrong with the lands themselves, merely with the manner in which they were acquired, and this divine money-laundering does not require the intercession of a bishop as it had in *Piers Plowman*. The purchase of that land by the Bristol merchant adequately cleans the taint of finance from the land itself, as does his purchase of Childe-William's service. It is imperative that Childe-William not profit from his father's sins, and only Childe-William's nakedness can transform the father's soul to "a naked child in angel hand" (*CB* l. 464) accompanied by "aungels withowten nowmbur, that come downe fro hevyn" (*M&S* l. 235). The poems' conclusion then ratifies the appropriateness of Childe-William's behavior, when he gains his reward. In "The Childe of Bristowe" the Bristol merchant warns his apprentice that "thi governaunce, sone is bad" (*CB* l. 405), which confirms the merchant's paternal concern for his apprentice, as well as the merchant estate's concern with "trouthe" in the world of the poems. Once Childe-William explains what he has been doing with the money, though, the merchant makes him a full partner: "here now make y the / myn owne felow in al wyse / of worldly good and marchandise / for thy trouthe so fre" (*CB* ll. 536–40). This language emphasizes the values of this transaction, since "felow" recalls the guild structure invisible here, and emphasizes that the merchant accepts Childe-William as a full member of his fellowship, and thus no longer an apprentice.

Similarly, the familiar play on "worldly good," meaning both material goods and virtue on earth, emphasizes that the world of these poems distinguishes merchandise from the greed and rapine embodied by the squire/franklin, and even presents it as an antidote to avarice. Childe-William's "trouthe so fre," in its reminder of his honor, virtue, and reliability, both recalls his earlier assertion that "good getyn by marchantye / it is trouthe" (*CB* ll. 64–65), and reinforces the poems' linkage between trade and virtue, a linkage reinforced by the statement in "The Merchant and His Son" that "He savydd hys fadurs soule, and broght hyt unto blys, / Hys maystyrs soule also, wyth hys trewe marchandys" (*M&S* ll. 287–88). Once Childe-William has been firmly linked to the father-surrogate, the Bristol merchant, his master finds him a wife and eventually he inherits "landes, catelle and place" (*CB* l. 552). In "The Merchant and His Son," the sense of a father-surrogate is further reinforced by the details that Wyllyam marries his master's daughter (*M&S* ll. 265–66), and gives filial alms and endows masses after his master's death (*M&S* ll. 281–84). Through this happy ending, to be expected in a didactic narrative meant to foster an idealized mercantile subject-position, Childe-William reaps the rewards of his piety and self-sacrifice. Since he has sold his patrimony to his master, he reinherits it, and his happy exemplary life remains free from the threat of damnation that afflicts our previous literary merchants.

We cannot, of course, take these poems at face value as representations of the life of a fifteenth-century apprentice, even an unusually fortunate one. For one thing, the tale elides the historical difficulties of finishing an extended apprenticeship, since merchant apprenticeships had crept up to a full ten years by the fifteenth century, and increasingly required better-educated and hence older apprentices like Childe-William with his clerical training. Hanawalt describes the newer social problems encountered by apprentices of Childe-William's time, with the age of apprenticeship completion creeping up to twenty-eight from twenty-one, so that "Guilds and masters were essentially extending adolescent status to men who were essentially adult except for their dependent position."[70] Certainly some of these problems are implicit in these poems, particularly in Childe-William's abruptly ended apprenticeship following his revelation of his deeds, and his subsequent marriage. Once Childe-William has proven himself, part of the wish-fulfillment of the tale comes from his exemption from the remainder of his time as an apprentice. Also, his sale of himself to the Bristol merchant recalls the careful distinction between servants and apprentices: a key element of apprenticeship contracts was the guarantee that an apprentice would not be required to do servile work or be held beyond his contracted time.[71] The threat of servitude constantly shadowed the realities of apprenticeship, and Childe-William's voluntary drop in status both stresses his self-sacrifice and reinforces the fear of "caswelté" both worldly and spiritual which underlies the poem. So while this poem presents an idealized version of apprenticeship and mercantile success, the conceptual power of that ideal, strong enough to foster a narrative tradition with two distinct surviving versions, shows that avarice was losing its automatic association with the estate of merchants. As the poem's attack on avarice applies only to the father, the possibility of innocent trade and moral traders becomes as fully realized as we can find in fifteenth century. The fact that the manuscript title "The Merchant and His Son" seems to confuse the sinful franklin's legal manipulations with merchandise indicates that at least the rubricator of Cambridge University Library ms. Ff. 2. 38 either continued to associate the sins of the father with the profession of the surrogate father, or more likely wanted to stress the filial relationship between William and the Bristol merchant who was a better role model to him than his actual father.[72]

The *Tale of Beryn* and Mercantile Redemption

We can see further evidence of a modest literary tradition endeavoring to create a morally positive mercantile subject-position in the pseudo-Chaucerian *Tale of Beryn*, which presents an initially bad and impious son who finds virtue and happiness through merchandise. As such, *The Tale of Beryn* represents a far more logical candidate for an intuitively mercantile tale than Chaucer's own *Merchant's Tale*. It exists as a second tale by the Merchant only in Northumberland ms. 455, a manuscript that also substitutes the *Franklin's Prologue* for the *Merchant's Prologue*. John M. Bowers argues this manuscript's presentation of "the Merchant, not as shrew-ridden husband but as a father upset by his son's misconduct, makes almost poignant his interest in young Beryn, a prodigal son who causes his father much grief until the trials of his mercantile adventures succeed in reforming his character."[73] Since Bowers also argues that the individual who interpolated *The Tale of Beryn* also arranged the manuscript,[74] apparently at least one fifteenth-century reader envisioned a Chaucerian Merchant with a point of view far closer to that of "The Childe of Bristowe" than to that of the troubled figure from *The Canterbury Tales*. Given dates ranging throughout the first part of the fifteenth century,[75] this tale is roughly contemporary to the other texts in this chapter, but its Chaucerian context has begged interpretation of the poem in the context of Chaucer's work. While there has been some limited debate on the tale's Chaucerian qualities, its kinship with "The Childe of Bristowe" and its interaction with the subject of merchandise have been largely ignored. Indeed, the only detailed discussion of estate in the tale has been by Richard Firth Green, who addresses the tale's construction of "caswelté."[76] Before we reach that portion of the tale, however, the nature of Beryn as a subject in need of mercantile redemption requires some explanation.

There are some fairly major differences between the opening situations in *The Tale of Beryn* and "The Childe of Bristowe," but the overall situations, of a father trying to guide his son, and the son finding a merchant mentor and thus happiness, are broadly similar. Beryn's father, Faunus, is "a worthy man and riche...in Rome was noon hym lych" (ll. 835–36). He outranks the squire/franklin in his "highe lynage" (l. 839), and resembles January in the *Merchant's Tale*. As with that tale, the wealth of the older Italian aristocrat encourages the reader to blur the lines between estates. Unlike the squire/franklin or January, Faunus seems to be a virtuous representative of his estate, and the Beryn-poet carefully differentiates Faunus from January through Faunus's marriage to Agea, "like to his parage" (l. 840), who almost immediately bears the child Beryn. Agea also represents a major difference from "The Childe of Bristowe" tradition, as Childe-William lacked a mother. With Beryn's character, though, the real differences from "The Childe of Bristowe" tradition become clear. Where Childe-William was a paragon educated in a clerical school, Beryn desperately needs the redemption that will occupy the bulk of the narrative. What will make the tale promercantile, though, is the performance of that redemption by the merchant on his own behalf, rather than on behalf of another. From the age of seven, Beryn "wroght ful many an evill chek, for such was his corage / That there he wist or myghte do eny evill dede, / He wold never sese for aught that men hym seyde" (ll. 914–16). His misdeeds ultimately include dicing (l. 923), ire with the messenger sent to bring him to his mother's deathbed (l. 1003), and public fighting (l. 1072). While both Beryn and Childe-William ignore their fathers' advice, as Beryn "counted at litill price al his faders tale" (l. 1081), for Beryn that advice was simply to reform.

Once the tale establishes Beryn's lack of virtue and self-control, and introduces Faunus's second wife Rame, a former mistress of the Emperor (ll. 1111–30) with evil with her "bagg of trechery" (l. 1182), it introduces the familiar folkloric subject of a wicked stepmother. Certainly a stepparent's relationship with a stepchild was a familiar challenge for urban dwellers in the period, and Rame's question, "For if it were so fall I had a child by yewe, / Lord, how shuld he lyve?" (ll. 1202–3), has no doubt been asked by many a step-parent, evil or otherwise.[77] Rame's solution to the problem, however, bears an odd kinship to "The Childe of Bristowe," in that Beryn's nakedness when his father and stepmother cut him off from their financial support (l. 1225) finally redirects him onto the path of merchandise and virtue, whereas Childe-William's nakedness finally saves his father's soul. Why a moment of unclothing would represent a transition in both stories remains unclear, though the parallel with St. Francis rejecting his patrimony is evocative. Also, in an age of sumptuary laws, personal display, and livery, nakedness might reflect a symbolic rejection of estate-position and patrimony. Jenny Adams suggests that Beryn's various scenes of nakedness refer back to loss of his clothes at dice,[78] reinforcing a running theme of merchandise as a dangerous game.

Once Beryn has his moment of realization at his mother's tomb, though (l. 1340), he chooses trade as a way out of his situation, and there follows a conversation between Beryn and Faunus very similar to that between Childe-William and the squire/franklin. Beryn rejects his father's estate, explaining that "order of knyghthode to take is nat my liking" (l. 1445), and presents his departure from Rome as a solution to both his problem and his stepmother's:

> Wherfor to plese al aboute, my purpose and my thought
> Is for to be a marchaunte and leve myne heritage,
> And relese it forever, for shippes fyve of stage

Ful of marchandise, the best of al this londe.
And yff ye wol so, Fader, quyk let make the bonde. (ll. 1462–66)

This argument in favor of entering trade lacks "The Childe of Bristowe"'s
suggestion that trade would be less sinful than knighthood, and *The Tale of
Beryn* does not argue as strongly that trade is in itself moral, but its descriptions of Beryn's merchandise also lack the echoes of antimercantile satire that
characterized Chaucer's merchants. Also, like the franklin in "The Merchant
and His Son," Faunus immediately responds to Beryn by pointing out the
dangers of trade: "Where haddest thow this counsell to leve thyne honoure /
And lyve in grete aventur and in grete labour?" (ll. 1469–70), though this
concern with danger overlooks the parallel implied in *The Libelle of Englyshe
Polycye* between mercantile and knightly risk. Jenny Adams links this willingness to undertake risk to Beryn's earlier propensity for gambling,[79] but
Beryn's willingness to engage in the "aventure" of merchandise only after his
conversion experience at his mother's tomb suggests a distinction between
the "bicched bones" of Chaucer's *Pardoner's Tale*[80] and Beryn's subsequent
mercantile adventures. By echoing the *Shipman's Tale* merchant in his anxiety, Faunus in *The Tale of Beryn* both argues his case for taking an inheritance,
by asking "What nedeth thee be marchant and shal have heritage?" (l. 1504),
and reminds the reader of the now-familiar justification of profit through
the risk of merchandise. Certainly there were professions both dangerous
and immoral, like piracy, but in this context of an individual moving freely
between the estates of the aristocracy and merchandise, Faunus's fear of danger comes across as unworthy of his own estate affiliation.

With Beryn's knightly fearlessness firmly established, and reinforced
by the "tempest" Beryn's ships encounter (l. 1573), the rest of the poem
dwells on the difficulties Beryn experiences when blown off course to a
strange town, where he spends the next 3,000 lines or so fending off spu-
rious lawsuits and bad mercantile contracts. Jenny Adams points out the
extent to which the loss of Beryn's initial cargo in a game of chess reflects
a general cultural anxiety over the element of chance in merchandise,[81]
but she does not fully engage with the larger satirical tradition on the
subject. Richard Firth Green explains that the peculiarities of legal practice in *The Tale of Beryn* match primarily "the 'law merchant' as it was
administered by local borough courts in England," particularly in the
Cinque Ports.[82] While Green argues that the tale outlines specific mercantile malpractice, such as using "the lex mercatoria to fleece visiting
merchants,"[83] he does not make much of the detail that the tale's town
contains both malpracticing merchants such as Hanybald the burgess and
an example of a good, moral merchant in the person of Geffrey. The tale
does contain the familiar antimercantile tropes of cheating and tricking

the victim, in particular in Hanybald's scheme to trade Beryn's shiploads of linen and wool for whatever merchandise can be found in his empty warehouse (ll. 1919–52). Still, the counterexample of Geffrey, who has been victimized but still goes out of his way to help Beryn, suggests if not that merchandise is the source of "trouthe," then at least that there can be highly virtuous merchants. Indeed, Geffrey plays an exemplary role to Beryn similar to that the Bristol merchant provided for Childe-William. More torn clothing, when Geffrey "hent hym by the scleve / Of his nether surcote..., [and] Therwith the scleve torent" (ll. 2429–32) marks the next transition in Beryn's fortunes. Where Beryn's earlier nakedness emphasized his own movement away both from his previous behavior and his estate, here his ripped clothes allow Geffrey to get his attention. Since the crippled beggar turns out to be another Roman merchant, we again see a violation of clothing norms during a moment when estate in the tale is unstable, and during a moment which shifts the direction of the narrative.

Geffrey's virtue and wit then become the focus of the poem, as the narrative shifts from "these fals marchandes that dwellen in this town" (l. 2407) to Geffrey's altruism, his estate solidarity with Beryn, and his clever manipulation of the townspeople's legal tricks. While Geffrey does ask what his reward will be (l. 2486) and request to be brought home to Rome (l. 2536, 2570), he does so after establishing his estate solidarity with Beryn as a fellow Roman merchant cheated twelve years previously by the same lex mercatoria: "For I had in valowe in trewe marchandise / A thousand pound—al have they take in such maner wise" (ll. 2501–2). When Beryn's crew cannot help him decide whether to trust Geffrey, Beryn asks for help "for His love that us bought, / Dying on the rood" (ll. 2550–51), and Geffrey strongly implies that helping Beryn is an act of Christian charity, that he "myght nat do a more synfull dede, / ...then fayll yew in this nede" (ll. 2557–58). Beryn himself also seems to have become virtuous, albeit a little dim, since his transition to merchandise, despite Jean Jost's argument that he "seems less malignant in the audience's eyes only because he is being persecuted by unjust thieves."[84] Cheating the locals in revenge for his own mistreatment does not seem to be his goal. This is not, however, to say that Beryn has become entirely reconciled to his new status as a merchant: when he realizes what trouble entangles him, he declares that going into business was a mistake and that he deserves no less for his behavior to his late mother: forsaking his heritage, "thcrfor sorow and shame / Is oppon me fall, and right wele deserved, / For I tooke noon maner hede when my moder sterved, / And disobeyed my fader and set hym at naught also." (ll. 2330–33) Despite this moment of despair, future events bear out the wisdom of his course of action, as his despair leads to Geffrey's service as a mentor, and ultimately to Beryn's success. It is Geffrey's "wise instruccioune" (l. 3995) which allows Beryn to impress the local lord Isope enough that Isope offers Beryn his daughter in marriage. Lest we think that this personal victory represents a movement entirely away from Beryn's temporary estate status as a merchant, the Beryn-poet specifies that Beryn's and Geffrey's ascendance in the town ameliorates the burgesses' dishonest practices:

> But they [the burgesses] were ever hold so lowe under foot
> That they myghte nat regne, but atte last were fawe
> To leve hir condicioune and hir fals lawe.
> Beryn and Geffrey made hem so tame
> That they amended ech day and gate a better name. (ll. 4014–18)

Jenny Adams suggests that this imposes order upon the dangers of trade and exchange, so that "rules are enforced by a single authority speaking from a position of centralized power."[85] She positions this endorsement of regulated trade within the larger debate over merchandise as a rejection of the antimercantile position, but a less "optimistic" one than Chaucer's.[86] She does not engage as much as she might with the moral and satiric questions surrounding trade.

This moral element matters, because in the end, the lessons of *The Tale of Beryn* are not quite as clear as those of "The Childe of Bristowe." Beryn does not find fulfillment in merchandise per se, and he makes no exchanges in the spiritual economy that can match Childe-William's laundering of his sinful patrimony and the resulting exchange of his charity for his father's soul. Mercantile subjectivity in *The Tale of Beryn* retains far more of the concerns of satire here than it did in "The Childe of Bristowe." Still, within the constraints of redeeming the son-character rather than the father-character, *The Tale of Beryn* bears striking similarities to "The Childe of Bristowe" in its use of merchandise and involvement in the material economy as a catalyst for moral change, and its characterization in Geffrey of a moral, wise merchant. It also bears strong similarity to *The Libelle of Englyshe Polycye*, a connection drawn by Adams.[87] Both connect merchants to aristocrats, as in Beryn's willingness to advance through danger and in his round trip between estate affiliations, so that the poem shares the *The Libelle of Englyshe Polycye*'s partial assimilation of merchants into the aristocracy. Thus it is the "caswelté" of merchandise that brings Beryn to a mercantile mentor to enable his aristocratic success. The antimercantilism of the burgesses' greed has strong counterpoints in Beryn's easy trust, in Geffrey's successful intervention, and in Beryn's ultimate reform of merchandise in the town. *The Tale of*

Beryn shares the sense in *The Libelle of Englyshe Polycye* and "The Childe of Bristowe" that merchandise need not be sinful, and in particular the latter poem's willingness to show a merchant-character as a positive moral force. Do these poems thus demonstrate that merchandise was entirely acceptable in the literature of the fifteenth century, and that there were merchants who did not at all think about the morality of their profession? Probably not. While these poems establish that it was possible to praise trade in moral terms in the early fifteenth century, it should be clear from Margery Kempe's earnest rejection of trade during the same decades that these poems show us examples of how poets could move beyond the satirical dismissal of trade, but the older satires could still convince readers like Kempe that merchandise could not but lead to avarice and sin. Thus, while these are the earliest promercantile examples that I have discussed, they do not indicate a sea-change in attitudes toward trade. Instead, they show that the promercantile ideology implicit in Gower's and Chaucer's careful treatments of merchants had found a voice in these relatively minor poems, and that a transition away from estates satire images of merchants had begun in the fifteenth century, but by no means finished. It is also worth noting that modern critical popularity does not reflect these texts' circulation in the fifteenth century—while Kempe's *Book* remains by far the best-known of these texts, the *Libelle of Englyshe Polycye* has far more surviving manuscripts—Warner mentions nine partial or complete manuscripts in his introduction.[88] We should not underestimate the growth in promercantile discourse over the century. The dramatic texts studied in my next chapter, later than these and still engaged with antimercantile ideology, show how that ideology retained some of its power a full century after Gower engaged with it in his estates satires. That Margery Kempe, the only author in this chapter known to be a member of the merchant estate, wrote the most antimercantile text of the four also reminds us that merchants themselves could not be assumed to have rejected the satirical tradition. The transfer of the sins of merchants to lawyers in "The Childe of Bristowe" and *The Tale of Beryn* suggests that by the early fifteenth century, the satirical tradition had begun to fragment, with complaints about some estates and not others retaining their rhetorical force, and with those complaints even being transferrable to transgressors of other, similar estates. At the same time, the estate of merchants was beginning to find a voice.

CHAPTER 6

THE MERCERS, CIVIC POWER, AND
CHARITY IN THE YORK CYCLE

Scholarship of the Corpus Christi cycle form remains productive for scholars interested in urban social history and cultural production, especially for the York cycle, where the city's own register of the plays shows the hand of the town clerk.[1] The same record-keeping also preserved city archives that allow scholars to understand the York cycle's urban milieu, enabling exploration of the ties between civic identity and the representation of faith. Since the merchants dominated the oligarchy sponsoring the cycle, the York cycle also represents one of those rare literary texts to have a direct link to that estate. For the influential mercers' guild in particular, a prime position in this collective production presented an opportunity to interpret biblical history in terms of their anxiety about trade's sinfulness, and to counter the estates satire tradition's vision of mercantile greed. With the York register, we can see how that response was formulated in the later fifteenth century, since as Richard Beadle observes, the current consensus dates the register to "the third quarter of the fifteenth century."[2] The mercers' "Last Judgement" reveals how, roughly a century after John Gower's *Mirour de l'Omme*, merchants could sponsor a performance that argued for their salvation; from the possibilities of scribal connections between mercantile readers and literary texts in the late fourteenth century, we have moved to the certainty of mercantile involvement in literary production. The mercers' ideological self-fashioning thus manifests itself in their play's assurance of a moral position commensurate with the mercers' social position in the city. As importers, exporters, and retailers of finished cloth, the York mercers held a powerful position in York's economy, and were able through the guild system to parlay that economic power directly into political power,[3] which allowed them some control over the cycle. While the authorship of the cycle remains unknown, and Beadle observes that the form and apparent dates of the individual plays range widely,[4] many of the plays, and not just those produced by powerful sponsors, show some rhetorical connection to those sponsors' ideological orientation.[5] Thus, especially for the plays of the powerful mercers and Mayor, a close reading of the play texts and recoverable details of production can show how those sponsors express their values within the city's collective pious enterprise. At the same time, a contrast of the Towneley "Judgment" to the mercers' "Last Judgement" will show how the mercers avoid the estates-satiric implications of the available Judgment story.

Who Saw It

That this play was a single collective enterprise is less than obvious, though, and before discussing the mercers' play we must address shifts in the dominant view of the cycle, both as a citywide experience and as a manifestation of the city oligarchy's ideological needs. For example, there remains doubt about the proportion of viewers who were able to see the plays up close, because of the narrow streets and the possibility that scaffolds occupied much of the available space. This material detail matters, because a limited audience would heavily curtail claims about the play's influence on the populace. Insisting on a relatively small audience for the play, David J. F. Crouch argues from the records of various craft-held stations along the route that since the first eleven stations occupied extremely narrow streets, only "the city élite, the master artisans, and their households" could have had a good view of the play because of the stationholders' scaffolding.[6] Crouch thus argues for the play as an elite production, which precludes the cycle's use as an instrument of oligarchic rhetoric. As far as his evidence goes, there can be little doubt that the elite were consistently part of the audience, as they did typically pay for good seats, and thus could consistently hear the words.[7] Still, Peter Meredith uses the same civic records to argue that those scaffolds were *only* placed in those years specified in the records, leaving far more room for a mobile street audience in other years.[8] Crouch also discounts the twelfth performance site, the Pavement, because the right to hold its station often went unsold. Crouch evocatively imagines "the poor auditors gathered on [the] Pavement, to watch tired actors in the fading light,"[9] but such a vision of the play assumes that the final site's performance would be sub-par, assumes successful control of the cycle by the elite itself, and assumes the address of the cycle's rhetoric to that elite.

Margaret Rogerson raises the possibility that the entire cycle was *not* performed every year, thus allowing for a performance time within daylight hours.[10] Since the Mayor was often a mercer, it seems unlikely that "The Last Judgement" and "The Coronation of the Virgin" were canceled very often.[11] Crouch's image of tired actors also fails to account for the number of professional actors in the production, including perhaps the performers of the Mayor's and mercers' plays, and assumes as well that amateur actors would have more energy to give in a performance for elite employers than for their family and friends.[12] Since each play had its own cast, Crouch overstates the extent to which the day would necessarily exhaust the actors, even with their considerable hike through the city. The city oligarchy would also probably have wanted a large audience: the cycle presented an unparalleled political and ideological opportunity for those in control of its text, because whatever ideology the drama might reinforce would potentially have behind it the weight of all of biblical history. Ruth Nissé argues, for example, that the plays support "the political desires of both the city's mercantile governors and the guild artisans or 'commonality' acting their parts in the invention of this new, dramatic public discourse."[13] This is not to say that the cycle's ideology was necessarily shared by the entire audience, however, because ideology does not work so simply. The cycle also had to keep the crowds coming. As John Coldewey characterizes the cycle's economic role, it brought in visitors from the city's hinterland, "attracted royalty," and was "an advertisement for a town's wealth, power, status, and stability" as well as providing moving "shop windows for a guild's wares and services."[14] This combination of politics and commerce would have driven the city to seek the largest possible audience for the cycle.

Who Controlled It

If, then, the cycle sought a large audience, there remains the question of how closely the city oligarchy controlled it, since each play had its own producing guild or other institution. In the last several decades, the dominant theory of the cycle's social function has moved from a vision of unity to one of conflict, and it is important to our understanding of the mercers' relationship to the cycle to understand this shift. Mervyn James argues that the Corpus Christi holiday as a whole reflects an ideal structure of urban society, both hierarchical and (in his vision) egalitarian, by invoking through the *corpus Christi* itself a body metaphor of society unified by the rituals of the day.[15] According to James's model, the city used the varied order of the guilds within the cycle's procession to counterbalance the strictly hierarchical procession of the Eucharistic host through the city followed by the guilds marching in ascending order.[16] Richard Homan similarly argues that the cycle mediated between hierarchical and egalitarian impulses within the city's social structure.[17] Homan's emphasis on that structure has meant, however, that recent debates about the unbalanced nature of the political reality of York in the later fifteenth century relate directly to our understanding of the cycle's rhetorical and ideological function, particularly Heather Swanson's reinterpretation of the guild structure itself (see below). Homan argues that the cycle functioned as a ritual that resolved the conflicts resulting from oligarchic government,[18] so that the yearly process of arguing with the Aldermen over the cycle production displaced any potential challenge to the merchant oligarchy's political power. In Homan's view, containment of interguild conflict within this arena of cultural production subverted more meaningful political interactions within the community, and distracted the populace from genuine reform of the city's government. That thorough political reform required stronger forces than argument before the councils became evident after election riots in 1516–17.[19]

Emphasizing the contingency of the cycle's ideological power, though, historian Heather Swanson and critics Sarah Beckwith and Christina M. Fitzgerald have all challenged the descriptive power of the guild structure, with the result that they portray a government system in York far too unstable for the cycle successfully to distract from its conflicts. They see the cycle, not as a spontaneous manifestation of the city's unity, but as an instrument by which the oligarchy attempted to consolidate its imposition of the guild structure onto the city's economy. This model agrees that the mercers and other merchants would have retained a great deal of power over the cycle, but suggests that such power would be significantly more difficult to exercise than Homan suggests. Swanson argues that "craft guilds can be seen as a deliberate and artificial construct of the medieval urban authorities," and that at least one guild was "conjured into existence" in order to provide a play for the cycle.[20] Beckwith argues that the oligarchy imposed both the cycle and the guild structure as forms of social and economic control, so that guild resistance to the cycle would challenge the merchants' political power, rather than containing the subverting artisans' rebellious impulses. Beckwith sees the battle for control over the cycle as reflecting rather than containing political conflict, as part of "intensified polarisation in the relations of merchant and artisan in the recession of the post 1450s."[21] This view tends to understate the guilds' fraternal activities and cohesion, but Swanson and Beckwith effectively complicate previous ideas of the cycle as a wholly unified and successful expression of the oligarchy's ideology, a challenge that Fitzgerald develops in her extensive application of Swanson's model to the York and Chester cycles. While Homan and James relied on ritual to link guilds' religious and professional functions, Beckwith challenges the unifying power of ritual, arguing that such unity cannot be performed even by such overdetermined rituals as Corpus Christi processions and plays.[22] Beckwith here makes a significant contribution to study of the cycle as a whole by moving us away from the problematic notion of the cycle as a performance of the city's unity, and into readings that embrace York's complexity and conflict.

Central to this understanding of a complex relationship between the guild structure and cycle is Swanson's approach to the city's guild structure. She argues that the guilds' ordinances, which described an idealized and highly compartmentalized economic structure, did not adequately describe the complex economy.[23] Her reminder that the world of guild ordinances is an idealized one is important to those of us who would use those ordinances as a window into the social world of the guilds. It would be a mistake, though, to conclude that those ordinances did not delimit at least part of the economic structure, even if in an idealized fashion. No doubt the urban power structure did impose artificial distinctions between similar trades,[24] but Swanson discounts the extent to which economic groupings were intertwined with fraternal religious groupings.[25] Swanson concedes that "it was the fraternity which was of the greatest concern to the artisans,"[26] but her theory that guilds were imposed from above understates the complex interplay between economic and religious practice represented by medieval "craft" guilds. Even the economically powerful mercers' guilds had arisen out of "a fraternity supported by merchants and dedicated to the Virgin Mary."[27] Swanson insists that the omission of fraternal concerns from the city's records of guild ordinances indicates those guilds' artificiality and the city's use of existing groupings to control the economy,[28] but the continuation of fraternal activities in these guilds suggests that they could be simultaneously manifestations of spiritual solidarity *and* instruments of economic organization. For example, since the carpenters dedicated their guild as the "Holy Fraternity of the Resurrection," their performance of "The Resurrection" could have a devotional function distinct from the city government's control of the guild.[29] Requiring them to fund and perform "The Resurrection" might have been a way to control the carpenters, but it also reinforced their fraternal devotion to the Resurrection itself, and thus to their guild's spiritual role. Historian Jenny Kermode provides a more nuanced position on the ideological function of the cycle, arguing that the plays' context "makes it difficult to see them as anything other than politicized rituals reflecting the interests of the ruling groups of both city government and craft guilds," but the "use of religion to express a political aspiration did not always work."[30] Ruling groups may have hoped to create unity and curtail dissent, but we should never assume that they succeeded in doing so.

Given that Beckwith and Swanson argue for a city government in constant conflict, and Kermode takes such conflict as an initial expectation, just how did that conflict work? The government structure of the city shows how much its government attempted to *seem* egalitarian, even while the mercers' guild predominated. York's government ostensibly included representatives of each craft through the Council of Forty-Eight, which was composed of "the searchers of all the city's craft guilds."[31] The higher councils of the Twenty-Four and the Twelve (or Aldermen) were chosen directly by their own number, however, and these councils chose the Forty-Eight after 1516–17.[32] None of these groups was limited to their eponymous number of members. A man chosen as Sheriff automatically joined the Twenty-Four upon conclusion of his term, and the Aldermen chose replacements for their own number from the Twenty-Four,[33] and the Mayor from among their number.[34] Merchants and especially mercers dominated the Twenty-Four and the Twelve, made up the majority of Mayors, and even used the threat of the ruinously expensive office of sheriff to extort money from poorer businessmen, through fines the latter paid to avoid office.[35] In effect, the city was controlled by an oligarchy that limited its own membership, even while trying to appear egalitarian.

This oligarchy's use of its power concerning the play then abounds throughout the city archives. Beckwith observes, for example, the contradiction inherent in renting the public space of the play-viewing stations for private individuals' profit.[36] In addition to the cycle's potential to reinforce the oligarchy's power, the plays themselves could be sites of major contention. The greatest conflict over content was probably the refusal of both the masons and the linenweavers to perform the "Funeral of the Virgin" (*Fergus*) play, apparently because of its raunchy subject matter.[37] As an example of how heated this debate could get, the York Memorandum Book A/Y describes the masons' attempt to be rid of it in 1431–32. The masons "murmurabant" [were accustomed to murmur] about their assigned play, because the beating of the character Fergus "in sacra non continetur scriptura & magis risum & clamorem causabat quam deuocionem" [is not contained in the sacred scripture and used to produce more noise and laughter than devotion]; they wanted to be "alteri assignari que conueniens est scripture sacre" [assigned to another which is in harmony with sacred scripture].[38] The fact that the masons saw the play's humorous content to contradict its devotional purpose argues both that the guilds themselves wanted plays with subjects "contained in the sacred scripture," and that they understood the rhetorical effect of their performances. Since the council released them from the play, the text of which was subsequently suppressed or lost, clearly the merchant oligarchy did not have the perfect control over the cycle that Homan suggests. Like the *Fergus* play broken up by a rowdy audience, the Corpus Christi procession was subject to disruption and conflict. The carpenters and cordwainers objected violently to the unsanctioned participation of the skinners in 1419, and again the cordwainers caused trouble in the 1480s and 1490s by refusing to march on the left of the weavers, and thus to allow the weavers equal status with them.[39] As a result of this contested control of the cycle and procession, the cycle as a whole balanced a variety of presentations of biblical history in the rest of the cycle with variously direct advocacy of merchants' or oligarchic ideology in the plays successfully within the mercers' control. The councils controlled the cycle, but they also had to resolve regular complaints and battles over guilds' relative status. While the act of constructing the register itself shows the city oligarchy exerting its power over the cycle, there is no evidence that the councils rewrote the guilds' texts to fit their own ideology. Fixing the text might have prevented later subversion of it, and by the sixteenth century the city clerk did note in the register any differences between text and performance,[40] but one could overstate the city's control of the plays' words. Richard Beadle dates the practice of checking the register only from 1501.[41] In a context where the perceptive masons could refuse to perform a play that fails to conform to their devotional expectations, it seems unlikely that the oligarchy in control of the text could insert material into the plays that would have overly offended the guilds performing them. Given Swanson and Beckwith's sense of the crafts in continuous conflict with the merchant oligarchy, we should not expect to find much promercantile material in the craft guilds' play texts. On the other hand, it is no great shock that the city council did not allow any of the guilds to argue in their plays for merchants' damnation. Unlike those out of direct mercer control, though, the plays potentially within the direct control of mercers, the Mayor's "Coronation of the Virgin" and the mercers' own "Last Judgement," have far more complex relationships to mercantile ideology.

Most plays' independence from the promercantile ideology of the oligarchy can be demonstrated adequately by a single brief example. Richard Beadle provides a helpful analysis of one of the more obvious of the cycle's guild-play links, the shipwrights and "The Building of the Ark."[42] In this play, on a subject traditionally associated with shipbuilding crafts,[43] the only speakers are God and Noah, and apparently the performance involved the construction of an ark in front of the audience. Beadle argues that the dramatist does "equal justice both to the grand symbolic trend of God's redemptive scheme, and to the skills employed by the guildsmen in their daily work," which gives the shipwrights' craft a "sacral significance through its ancient role in the divine ordering of things."[44] Beadle outlines the technical language of the play, including "burdes and wandes" cut with the grain, Noah's "june"-ing (joining) of the wood with a "gynn" (gin, or specialized device), caulking with "symonde" (cement), the "cleyngked" (clinker-built) hull, and the "revette" (rivet) and "rewe" (rove) with which the timbers are assembled.[45] Christina M. Fitzgerald adds to this reading the observation that the relationship between God and Noah here is very evocative of an artisan-apprentice relationship, with "Noah as [God's] apprentice."[46] Beadle then points out the repetition of the word "work," so that "the dramatist…has saturated his verse with words emphasizing the idea of God as a worker, a craftsman who makes tangible objects."[47] Sarah Beckwith suggests in her reading of this play that the "meaning of the word for 'work' then is densely encoded to mean at once humanity as the object of God's work, the work of making him, the work of restoring him, and Noah's work of ark-building and salvation."[48] With their stress on "work" and "craft," the Shipwrights present God as one of their own masters, positing for themselves a special connection to the divinity. Beadle affirms the multivalence of "craft," as simultaneously "skill, trade" and "vessel," and further affirms this word's centrality through the manuscript's capitalization of it in the final lines of the play (*BA* l. 150). The shipwrights and their "Crafte" show how complex the connections of play and guild could be, particularly in comparison to the more directly devotional emphasis of the carpenters' ownership of "The Resurrection," which shared their guild's dedication. The variety of ties between the plays and their sponsors shows the connections of plays to guilds may not always have been entirely obvious, and the disunity of the city's government and guild structure was directly reflected by limited ideological independence for the individual plays.

"The Coronation of the Virgin" and the Mayor

Even if one questions the ideological dominance of the city's merchant elite, the craft self-interest of the shipwrights' play suggests how devotional plays might still reflect sponsors' ideologies. If craftsmen like the shipwrights could imagine themselves as God's apprentices, the plays controlled directly by the elite could similarly serve their needs. Since we have thus far discussed that merchant elite entirely in terms of their governmental function, it makes sense to start with the only play sponsored directly by a city office, the Mayor's early fifteenth-century play of "The Coronation of the Virgin." This play was presumably spectacular, but the textual history of it is somewhat clouded; part of its text appears only as a fragment in a sixteenth-century hand, and so dates from long after the Mayor had turned the play over to the hostlers, whose social status was so much lower than the Mayor's that a hostler could not serve as an alderman.[49] The version of the play in the main section of the play register, however, dates from only slightly after the Mayor relinquished the play in the 1460s. Thus while we cannot quite link this play text directly to the Mayor, the earliest text we have is close enough to the Mayor's sponsorship of the play to consider its ties to the Mayor.

What the play does not do is represent mayoral power. It opens with Jesus exercising his divine authority, and angels jumping to obey, a demonstration of power nothing like the contentious city government described by Swanson and Beckwith. Perhaps such a speech as "Lorde jesu Criste, oure gouernoure, / We are all boune atte þi bidding, / With joie and blisse and grete honnoure," represents the Mayor's dreams of authority, but the nature of civic government ensures that it could only be a dream.[50] This play's performance of authority is all that the mayoral authority cannot be—permanent and unquestioned—but it does associate great power with the play's sponsor. Similarly, Mary's apotheosis at Jesus' command bears some idealized resemblance to the promotions members of the city oligarchy could expect from their peers, but where Mary's appointment as queen of heaven bears no challenge, Kermode show that the election of a Mayor or any other civic office was a constant source of conflict.[51] Thus the power relations in "The Coronation of the Virgin" represent not the Mayor's actual power, but instead an idealization of power then linked to the idea of the Mayor as sponsor. The play cannot suggest that the Mayor *has* divine power, but the Mayor can hope that a little divine authority will rub off on him as sponsor.

The remainder of the play focuses on Mary's unique role as the mother of God, and works through a series of "hail" lyrics and a list of Mary's Six Joys. The language itself is notably shared by civic discourse, though. In particular the terms "worship" and "honor" describe Mary, particularly in the lines "In blisse þat schall euere indowre / With all worshippe and all honnoure" (*CV* ll. 132–34) and "þou schalte be worshipped with honnoures" (*CV* l. 141). While both are appropriate terms for their semidivine subject, they are also common in civic contexts related to estate and civic power. For example, in the 1415 proclamation preceding the Corpus Christi procession, "sqwyers of wirship…haue swerdes borne efter þame,"[52] so that here *worship* is almost synonymous with high estate. Later, the 1476 *Ordinacio pro Ludi Corporis Christi* declares that searchers would be appointed annually by the Mayor to examine the play texts, players, and pageants for the cycle; the searchers had to be "sufficiant in personne and Connyng to þe honour of the Citie and Worship of þe saide Craftes."[53] Given these contexts of procession and cycle, "worship" and "honor" represent here a collocation that would have been familiar for expressing Mayoral power, and these terms clearly describe the self-promotion and relatively exalted estate-position that characterized the oligarchy's relationship to the town and guild structure. Indeed, civic government was one of few avenues for the increase of one's estate in this period, and one of the only ways for a person born into trade to have a sword carried ceremonially before him in the street. Mary's Coronation in such terms thus applies a familiar discourse of praise and status to the immutable heavenly history of the plays. Praising Mary in terms used for the city elite cannot suggest that the elite are as praiseworthy as Mary, but it does encourage the same rubbing-off by association implicit in the play's embodiment of idealized power.

The available details of the play's production support a model of Mayoral self-promotion, both in its position near the end of the cycle, and in its potential for expensive spectacle demonstrating the economic power of the sponsor. While we lack any direct description of the pageant itself, the cast of "The Coronation of the Virgin" includes exclusively heavenly characters (Jesus, six angels, and Mary), none of whom should wear less than the best of clothing. Probably at least Jesus wore a gilded mask as well, like that specified for "The Last Judgement" (see later discussion). Also like "The Last Judgement," enthronement of Jesus on a higher level than that of the basic pageant wagon could involve ironwork similar to that on the mercers' pageant. The heavenly setting also opens up the possibility of expensive back-cloths and other decorations. "The Coronation of the Virgin" as a visual spectacle could present a vision of divine authority and magnificence reflecting positively upon the individual who produced the play. The visible manifestation of the worship and honor of Mary, precisely because the play does *not* blasphemously say that they do, reflect right back onto the Mayor, who even after turning the play over to Hostlers continued a "token subsidy" of 2s. per year to continue his office's association with the pageant.[54] It certainly would not do for this particular play to look cheap.

Ideologically, the association of such a display with the Mayor could act in the same way that the display surrounding the Mayor's person would have. As "the only annually elected official to receive a substantial fee,"[55] the Mayor embodied the city's power structure, so that "great emphasis was placed on the 'worship'" of "officials and council members," including "the upturned sword and mace which the mayors of York were allowed to have carried before them in processions."[56] Given this emphasis on display, the ceremonial display of "The Coronation of the Virgin" cannot but invoke the pomp and ceremony surrounding the

Mayor. The play's visual impact, like the Mayor's symbolic authority, relies on spectacle. In those years when the Mayor was himself a cloth-merchant, the display of his finest wares upon the backs of Jesus, Mary, and the angels could only have reinforced his power and authority, while reinforcing the cult of Mary and displaying the Mayor's piety. While the text of "The Coronation of the Virgin" idealizes power beyond the aspirations of any Mayor, the probable display of the production, in its dual meanings of "Mary is great" and "the Mayor is generous," links divine glory to the "worship" of an office that increasingly claimed the title "Lord Mayor" by the later fifteenth century.[57] At the same time, because of the merely oblique comparison of the Mayor to the subject of his play, and the lack of any mercantile concerns besides public piety, we can see that with this play York's merchant elite knew its limits. One can only imagine the public outrage had the Mayor wedged himself into "The Coronation of the Virgin," after all.

The Mercers, Their Guild, and Their Pageant

We find a much richer connection between play and producer in the play immediately following "The Coronation of the Virgin." Shifting from their role as civic oligarchs to their professional role, the mercers took the prime position within the cycle. By choosing "The Last Judgement," the mercers could be sure that their play would remain in the memory of the viewer long after the end of the Corpus Christi holiday. While the final plays' position would subject the Mayor's and mercers' plays to the pragmatic problem of waning sunlight, the conclusion of the cycle and of the day gave the mercers the chance to use their economic power to create a thoroughly impressive and fortuitously well-documented spectacle. Beyond this spectacle shared with "The Coronation of the Virgin," however, the thematic content of the play creates a privileged moral position for the mercers within the play's community of salvation, a position that the antimercantile tradition denied them, and a position that would have helped them assuage any potential Margery Kempe–like anxieties concerning their own salvation. By focusing "The Last Judgement" specifically on the charitable Corporal Works of Mercy and the representation of the Judgment in Matthew 25, rather than the Judgment of Revelation, the mercers both preempted cultural expectations of their avarice and displayed their economic power, while subtly reassuring themselves that they were suited to salvation. The high moral ground claimed by their play would have reinforced their dominant social position in the community, by implying that social and moral power coincided in their guild.

A viewer of the cycle would have seen a representation of this social power upon first glimpse of the pageant itself, as its actors pushed it up the narrow streets. Fortunately for the modern scholar, the mercers left an excellent record of their wealth, in the form of a now well-known indenture that describes their play properties in detail. As Alexandra F. Johnston and Margaret Dorrell point out, this pageant was superlatively lavish, establishing the political and economic power of the mercers relative to other guilds.[58] When the cycle was canceled in favor of the Creed play in 1535, and the guilds all "surrender[ed] their pageant funds to the civic treasury," the mercers had the most money with 24s., more than ten times the Mayor's contribution to the "Coronation."[59] As Johnston and Dorrell conclude, such an investment shows that the guild highly valued the pageant and hence the production.[60] The presence of a gilt mask, or "Veserne gilted," for God, "sternes of gold," "sunne bemes of golde," a gilded "crosse of Iren," and four small gilded angels supports this conclusion, because the guild invested a substantial amount of gold in the pageant's decoration.[61] The angels for the pageant alone cost 20s. when replaced or repaired in 1449–50.[62]

The large pieces of fabric, particularly the "grete coster of rede damaske payntid for the bakke syde of þe pagent"[63] and the assorted clouds, further allowed the mercers to display their textile wares to best advantage in a context which would not thematically undermine their profession. Placed at the end of the cycle and loaded with this lavish cloth and gilding, the mercers' pageant must have reinforced a strong impression of their conspicuous wealth, regardless of the play performed upon it, just as an impressive display on the pageant for "The Coronation of the Virgin" would have emphasized the power, wealth, and worship of the Mayor. The pageant indenture's focus on various characters' clothing reinforces the play's display of fine cloth, as well. As the characters wear their "Sirkes" and "Aubes,"[64] they simultaneously represent the biblical description of the Doomsday and display the guild's products to potential customers. The pageant also included expensive suspended iron works to draw God up into heaven, so that the pageant wagon demonstrates the wealth behind the mercers' temporal power, at the same time it performs and glorifies divine power. This overlap of divine and temporal power through visual spectacle thus places the mercers in a similar position to that of the Mayor with "The Coronation of the Virgin." Both pageants represent God's glory to show their own piety, and both displays tie their sponsors' economic power to that ostentatious piety. Such display was risky, because of the religious context of Corpus Christi. Just as the Mayor could not imply with his play that he might deserve the same sort of worship as the Virgin Mary, the mercers could not afford to imply that they themselves might share Christ's glory sitting in Judgment. While on the one hand the lavish pageant glorifies God, on the other hand the biblical context potentially reminds the viewer of the satiric tradition that expected merchants to be damned for their avarice on Judgment Day.

Material Charity and the Guild

Given the longevity of antimercantilism, the mercers may well have felt some anxiety about the subject of their own salvation. Certainly merchants in general persistently performed works of charity in the hopes of redeeming themselves (see Chapter 1), and the York mercers integrated this practice into the ordinance and structure of their guild. Demonstrating the truism that the lines between religious and professional guilds were vague at best, the trade guild of the mercers coincided with a religious fraternity dedicated to the Holy Trinity,[65] which operated a hospital and allowed the mercers to make an institutional commitment to material charity. The records of the hospital are intimately intertwined with those of the guild as a professional dues-gathering organization, and as Alexandra F. Johnston observes, the hospital and the guild were a single corporate body by the time of the play register; Holy Trinity became what Johnston calls "the Mercers Guild at prayer."[66] Ties between the mercers and their hospital abound in the guild's records. For example, when in 1430 John Warthill gained by indenture the right to assign the next free bed in "the hospital of the Trinite, in Fossegate, in York" to "a pouere man or a pouer woman, after the cas falles," he made the indenture with "Robert Jarom, Thomas Aton, William Bedale and Richard Louth, mercers of York, in the name of all the mercers of York,"[67] rather than with the hospital per se. This indenture presents the mercers' guild as the corporate body that legally determines who may distribute the hospital's alms, although the hospital had its own Master distinct from the guild's Master. Clearly, the guild did not distinguish between the management of the hospital and of the craft, and they even shared a seal.[68]

A controversy over the hospital's management further illustrates the relationship between the hospital and the guild. In 1482, William Cleveland, the Master of Trinity Hospital, made an indenture with John Harper, Thomas Barker, and John Elwald, Master and Constables of the "company of mercers," which established that Cleveland as Master of the hospital was subordinate to the leadership of the mercers' guild. The indenture admonished him among other things to "make no gyftes of no maner of thyng that now pertenes or shall pertene to the said hospitall, nor no person to brother or sister to resceve into the said hospitall, without will and assent of the…master and constables" of the guild.[69]

The guild exercised this authority a decade later in 1493, when "maister of the felewship" John Stokdale ordered Cleveland to "make a trew accompte yeirly of all his resaitts, and his expenses" to the guild leadership.[70] This clear hierarchy of Masters gave the guild control over the hospital, though the need repeatedly to remind Cleveland of his subordinate status suggests some contention about that hierarchy. As far as the guild was concerned, though, managing the guild's collective charity was clearly worth the time of its Master and Constables.

The details of Warthill's indenture show how the mercers exercised this control. By allowing Warthill limited control over the disposition of the beds of the hospital, in that the indenture allowed him to fill half of the next six vacancies but not to pass on the right to his heirs, the indenture establishes the extent to which Warthill could be personally charitable in conjunction with the guild, that is, *as a mercer*. The ordinances of the guild further reified this institutional link to the virtue of charity. Brothers of the "craft of merchaund and mercery of York"[71] are presented in the midst of the 1495 ordinance with an oath binding them to

> be lele and trewe brother into the hospitale of the holy Trinite...and favorable and frendeley to all brether and sisters langing thereto. And rules and ordenances and rights therof to mayntene at your myght, and gudely power, and truly pay and afferme and fulfill, as lele and trewe brother sulde do, be your faith, ye sall ask this hospitall for charite, ye sall worship iij solempne festes.... Ye sall pay ij*d.* ilka quarter, that is to say viij*d.* in the year, and ilka day say v pater noster, v aves and a credo, and if ye faile of this to gyf half a pond wax to the saide hospitall.[72]

This integration of daily devotions and loyalty to the hospital into the oath of a guild member shows that the mercers took their function as a religious fraternity with a hospital entirely seriously, and did not administratively distinguish these pious matters from their financial affairs as a guild. The provision that members will "ask the hospitall for charite," like the similar clause in the ordinance of the guild of Holy Trinity in Bishop's Lynn (see Chapter 5), works both as a promise that brothers in need, like former master Robert de Yarom in 1444,[73] can ask the hospital for help, and as a promise that members will be charitable through the hospital. Either expectation would be appropriate, and the choice of a hospital as a charitable enterprise reminds us that guilds provided some security from the dangers of poverty and old age (see Chapter 1). The mercers' institutional commitment to their religious life unites the guild's function as a revenue-collecting body, with dues and fines, to its pious function, by making the forfeit for a spiritual lapse the donation of a half-pound of wax to the hospital. Where Swanson outlines how the city used work-related guild fines to fund the cycle, here we see that the guild similarly uses moral fines for the material support of the hospital. Wedging the oath to the hospital in between discussions of fair measure and the oath for a Master or Constable, the guild's ordinance leaves no doubt that the hospital was as much a part of the guild as the guild officers.

The mercers also extended the unity of their trade guild with the Trinity fraternity in the appearance of the pageant itself. Johnston and Rogerson observe that the indenture of the pageant had appended to it an endorsement listing "j Baner of rede bukeram bett with golde with þe Trinite & with ostret feders & With j lange Stremer Item iiij Smale baners with Trinite in þam & Roset."[74] They explain that "the banners are those of the Confraternity," and suggest that "they were also used in the formal Corpus Christi procession the next day and on any other occasion of celebration or display in which the Confraternity of the Holy Trinity and the Mercers' Guild took part."[75] Similarly, Clifford Davidson suggests that the positioning of Christ with the Trinity in the later, post-1501 version of the pageant closely resembles the central image in the guild's seal, which "illustrates the Father seated above the water with both hands raised (his right hand giving his blessing) while before him is the smaller figure of Christ on the cross," so that the very structure of the pageant replicated the guild's iconography.[76] If we accept that the image of "þe Trinite" refers to the guild, the mercers' pageant visually emphasizes the link between the mercers and their Trinity guild. The fact that the large image of the Trinity itself was of "rede bukeram bett with golde" would contribute to the effect of the gold on display in the pageant, while at the same time showing that the representation of the Trinity deserved the best materials available. Thus, while the lavish pageant projected the ostentatious success of the mercers, and fitly represented God's power, the pageant's use of the golden symbol of the Trinity stressed both the pageant's godliness and the guild's link to its charitable hospital.

Charity in "The Last Judgement"

The text of the mercers' play then reinforces this link between the mercers and Trinity hospital, and counters any expectations of the mercers' avarice. It makes sense that a guild that already linked charity and business in the idealized self-fashioning of its ordinance would assert its charitable piety through its Doomsday play. Such an emphasis could only reinforce the hope that the mercers were not damned, at least not for being mercers. The mercers' assertion of their corporate moral virtue could reinforce their position of power within the community, while reassuring the mercers themselves that they did not fit the satiric stereotype. Clifford Davidson effectively links the play's reliance on material charity to its producing guild, comparing the Corporal Works of Mercy in the play to a window in All Saints Church, North Street that features merchants performing charitable acts (see later in chapter).[77] Still, the details of the play's dependence on charity are worth exploring, because the play negotiates between competing visions of salvation and its relationship to works. The good and bad souls all assert that their salvation or damnation has been bought specifically by their deeds, but the good souls go on to suggest penance's role in salvation. The good souls ask upon their first appearance on stage that

> Of oure ill dedis, lorde þou not mene,
> That we haue wroght vppon sere wise,
> But graunte vs for thy grace bedene
> Þat we may wonne in paradise....
> Ofte haue we greued þe, grette and small,
> Þeraftir lorde þou deme vs noght,
> Ne suffer vs neuer to fendis to be thrall,
> Þat ofte in erþe with synne vs soght.[78]

In these first speeches, the two good souls combine stress on works with an emphasis on repentance; these souls specifically ask for "grace." These good souls follow orthodox rules for salvation, and the play does not present any improbably sinless souls. Instead the "good" lament their own sins, while asking for forgiveness. These early speeches present an economy of salvation which balances the appropriate use of the language of judgment, through "mene" and "deme," against the souls' hopes that they "may wonne in paradise" and not be "thrall" to "fendis."

The bad souls, in contrast, present an entirely different model of judgment through their despair, lamenting

> ...we wrecchis þat are forlorne,
> Þat never ȝitt scrued God to paye,...
> What schall we wrecchis do for drede,
> Or whedir for ferdnes may we flee,
> When we may bringe forthe no goode dede
> Before hym þat oure juge schall be?
> To aske mercy vs is no nede[.] (*LJY* ll. 117–25)

The first bad soul's assertion that "Oure dedis beis oure dampnacioune" (*LJY* l. 138) leaves the Judgment as a *fait accompli*, and presents no room for repentance. The second soul's assertion that "Oure wikked werkis may we not hide, / But on oure bakkis vs muste þem bere" (*LJY* ll. 154–55) reinforces the bad souls' despairing belief that they cannot be saved, and presents an economy of salvation which lacks repentance and focuses primarily on good deeds. Someone in control of the register recognized the importance of this condemnation as a result of their sinful acts, and placed a "nota" to the left of the line "Oure wikkid werkis þei will vs wreye" (*LJY* l. 129) in the manuscript.[79] Part of the sinfulness of the bad souls is that they limit salvation to works alone, without any real discussion of repentance or grace. This contrast between the repentance of the saved and the despair of the damned emphasizes the play's distinction between the two groups. The two groups also seem to have worn the same types of garments, shirts, hose, masks, and wigs,[80] which could very easily have contrasted between good and bad souls. Certainly masks and wigs would contribute to the audience's sense of these characters as icons of good and evil. The effect of, for example, dressing the souls in similar clothing of contrasting color would manage to stress both similarity and difference between the two groups.

Regardless of the souls' costumes, the angels further distinguish between the groups of souls and reinforce the despair of the bad souls. The third angel speaks immediately after the second bad soul's speech, and he asserts that "All sam schall ȝe noght be in blisse; / Our fadir of heuene woll it be soo, / For many of yowe has wroght amys" (*LJY* ll. 170–72). This assertion of divine authority moves from the good souls' penitential model of salvation to the bad souls' works-based model, which dominates the rest of the play. Significantly, this angel's emphasis on what the souls "wroght" matches more closely with the salvation economy assumed by the bad souls. While the good souls' opening speeches initially assert an orthodox reliance on repentance, the subsequent emphasis on charitable activities focuses primarily on works. The play never quite claims that works are sufficient for salvation, but it gives little attention to virtues other than good works. For example, while the good souls' speeches performed verbal penance, the angel does not mention penance at all. This downplaying of repentance then suggests a potential mercantile response to the antimercantile satiric tradition, particularly the classification of ill-gotten profits as theft requiring restitution for successful repentance. Given the difficulty of restitution, particularly when the categories of licit trade remained poorly defined, the mercers' argument for their own virtue could only benefit from a shift in the terms of salvation from the extremely problematic repentance of restitution (which reduced Coveitise to tears) to the far more secure and tangible (for them) penance of charity.

Helping to mask the play's de-emphasis of repentance, Deus supports the mercers' works-based salvation in his own speech in this part of the play, when he announces that he will sit "for to deme folke ferre and nere / Aftir þer werkyng, wronge or right" (*LJY* ll. 191–92). His speech retains some emphasis on repentance when he reminds the apostles that "All þo þat wolde þam right repente / Shulde with you wende and wynly wake" (*LJY* ll. 194–95). According to Deus, the difference between works and repentance is in the timing, the play being set at the actual Judgment when the time for repentance is past: those who "wolde...repente" (*LJY* l. 195) had the opportunity, but "Of mercy *nowe* may noȝt be mente, / But aftir wirkyng, welth or wrake" (*LJY* ll. 199–200, italics added). Or so it seems. When, after describing the Crucifixion, Deus announces to the good souls that they "Commes to þe kyngdome ay-lastand / Þat ȝou is dight for youre good dede" (*LJY* ll. 281–82), he echoes Matthew 25.34 and shifts the play's salvation discourse to more comfortable ground for the mercers. His emphasis on repentance has played its part in covering the play with a patina of orthodoxy and confirming that the good souls deserve grace, but now it drops out of the play so that the mercers can remind the audience just how charitable they have been.

Deus goes on at great length to describe the good works of the saved, as he outlines the six Corporal Works of Mercy:

Whenne I was hungery ȝe me fedde,
To slake my thirste your harte was free;
Whanne I was clothles ȝe me cledde,
Ȝe wolde no sorowe vppon me see.
In harde presse whan I was stedde,
Of my payns ȝe hadde pitee;
Full seke whan I was brought in bedde,
Kyndely ȝe come to coumforte me.
Whanne I was wille and werieste
Ȝe herbered me full hartefully;
Full gladde þanne were ȝe of youre geste,
And pleyned my pouerté piteuously.
Belyue ȝe brought me of þe beste
And made my bedde full esyly,
Þerfore in heuene schall be youre reste,
In joie and blisse to be me by. (*LJY* ll. 285–300)

York's merchants had a history of emphasizing this particular conception of eleemosynary charity, as Clifford Davidson points out in his analysis of the window of All Saints Church, on North Street "where many affluent merchants lived in the early fifteenth century."[81] The passage describing the Corporal Works in the play goes beyond that window's depiction of them, though, by expanding upon specific details of Christ's similar biblical speech. In particular, the expansion of "I was a stranger, and you took me in"[82] to six lines emphasizes the importance of caring for the poor and harboring the homeless, portions of the Corporal Works to which the owners of a hospital were particularly suited. As "sick, and you visited me"[83] becomes "Full seke whan I was brought in bedde, / Kyndely 3e come to coumforte me," the play adds the detail of a bed just as it will in reference to taking in strangers, reminiscent of the terms of the Trinity hospital's indentures controlling access to its beds. The play's subtle shifts in the terms of Matthew 25 and the Corporal Works of Mercy emphasize charity given as an individual, within the institutional context of beds and a roof, instead of the donations to churches, endowments, or monetary donations also common to merchants. We see the personal nature of this charity when the good souls ask when they had the opportunity to give charity to God. He stresses personal action in his reply that "When any þat nede hadde, nyght or day, Askid 3ou helpe and hadde it sone" (*LJY* ll. 311–12), a reassuring sentiment. Deus further stresses this need for direct charitable intervention when he explains to the bad souls that

> Clothles whanne I was ofte, and colde,
> At nede of you, 3ede I full naked;
> *House ne herborow*, helpe ne holde
> Hadde I none of you, þof I quaked. (ll. 341–44, italics added)

As Deus's words mix the biblical "I was a stranger, and you took me not in: naked, and you covered me not,"[84] the play again stresses the need for a physical place in which to perform charity. While this model of salvation encourages private works of charity, its emphasis on a house privileges the institutional charity in which the hospitals engaged daily, and which directed some of the mercers' personal charity. As successful mercers no doubt participated in the general eleemosynary charity characteristic of their estate, all of the Corporal Works would have corresponded to the practice of the mercers sponsoring the play.

So how does the mercers' apparently self-serving manipulation of their play to glorify their own charity relate to the cycle's position in the city's ideological network? After all, it seems that "The Last Judgement" works more to make the mercers look and feel good than to reinforce the city oligarchy, or to strengthen the mercers' political power. As the mercers' exercise of their oligarchic power over their own play was relatively straightforward, the play's connection to my overall conception of the cycle comes in the inexact nature of the link between the mercers and the city councils. The potential similarity in visual presentation between the Mayor's "Coronation of the Virgin" and the mercers' "Last Judgement" suggests that both plays performed similar ideological functions, except that the former worked exclusively through spectacle and idealized power relationships. Both plays allow their producers to display the worship due to the divinity, and to do so in terms that emphasize the power, wealth, and generosity of the producer. The Mayor gave up the chance for such a display when he turned over "The Coronation" to the Hostlers. The reasons for this shift remain unclear, and while it is possible that the Mayor did not think the display provided an ideological return worth the expense, it is also possible that the suggestion of any similarity between Mayoral power and divine power was too obvious. After all, for the Mayor directly to compare himself to God would be to out-Herod Herod, and the unreasonable exercise of power is every bit as central to the cycle form as the idealized power of God. The link between political power and cultural production made by having the Mayor produce a play might well have been too threatening to the fiction of shared power in a city where the Mayor was already the target of failed attempts by the citizens to reduce his sizeable £50 fee.[85] The mercers' guild, on the other hand, was only *unofficially* linked to the ruling body of the town. While the "mercantile plutocracy" of York privileged mercers as city leaders,[86] the link between guild and government was rooted in the fact that in a cloth-producing area the mercers were inevitably going to be economically powerful. Thus, it was much safer for the mercers to connect themselves *as mercers* to divine glory, because their representation of divinity was less likely to be interpreted as blasphemous self-representation. The mercers' and the Mayor's probable hiring of actors would also minimize this effect somewhat: one can only imagine the political effect of the Mayor personally playing God.

This concern with excessive display also clarifies the mercers' choice of details for their Doomsday. While the mercers' guild had a position to maintain, and thus could justify major expense on their pageant and play, the excess of the mercers' pageant surely invoked the deadly sin of pride, and since the markers of pride in the play were primarily visual, they would be available to a far wider audience than the specifics of the dialogue. There was no way to avoid this problem and still present a spectacle, and a public reminder that the city leaders were puffed up with pride presented real dangers to their contingent but very real political power. The mercers' choice of the Matthew 25 Judgment helps to direct viewers' attention away from the sin that the guild was probably committing on the spot to a virtue for which they could have a positive reputation in the town. This focus on their strengths could only reinforce the notion that at some level they deserved their power, and this reinforcement fits right into my model of how the cycle works: the lack of civic unity in the cycle, a lack that seems increasingly more probable, necessitates reinforcement of mercer power through their play. If the city oligarchy's power was *not* sufficient to dominate the entire cycle, and we know that guilds like the shipwrights used their plays to reinforce their own piety and social role, the oligarchs in their capacity as mercers had a clear need to reinforce their hold on power, by preempting moral challenges to their right to power. The cycle play provided a highly powerful forum for such reinforcement, by harnessing the mechanics of public display to a spiritual subject outside the direct control of the church.[87] The mercers' reliance on charity in general fulfilled their ideological needs by indirectly countering the cultural association of merchants with avarice, reassuring the mercers and their audience that finance need not result in damnation.

The Rhetorical Path Not Taken

That the mercers' choice of subject matter in their Doomsday was not accidental becomes clear from comparison to the Towneley cycle, which takes an entirely different approach despite its proximity to the York "Last Judgement." In general, representations of this biblical episode had a tendency toward satire that the York text eschews, and the Towneley version follows that tendency.[88] Though the texts are related, only 174 out of the Towneley "Judgment" play's 830 lines correspond closely to the York version, so that the Towneley "Judgment" provides a window into another view of this subject matter in Yorkshire. The Towneley version retains the bad souls' expression of their ill deeds, as "Oure wykyd warkys can we not hide...Oure dedys this day will do vs dere."[89] In direct contrast to the York Doomsday, though, the Towneley "Judgment" adds a long section concerned with the Seven Deadly Sins, starting with Pride and continuing in some detail with Tutivillus's long diatribe against sinners. The demons converse extensively with each other, going over their lists of sinners, and the second demon explains, "Here is a bagfull, lokys, / Of pride and of lust," (*LJT* ll. 207–8), and lists sinners "of al kyn astates / That go bi the gatys" (*LJT* ll. 218–19). The first demon asks, "Is oght ire in thy bill?" (*LJT* l. 224), and the other deadly sins are listed later and amplified by Tutivillus. The use of the Seven Deadly Sins makes sense here, as Pamela Sheingorn and David Bevington point out that opposing them to the Corporal Works of Mercy, adding burial of the dead to make seven, was standard in church paintings of the Judgment at this time.[90] The Towneley play also employs satire in this episode's catalogue form and its listing of women (*LJT* ll. 237) and clerks (*LJT* ll. 259). Tutivillus's clothing satire further recalls the estates-satire form, in a way unavailable to the mercers. He attacks the "poynte of the new gett... Of prankyd gownes and shulders vp-set, / Mos and flokkys sewyd wythin" (*LJT* ll. 417–20), and he ridicules "Thise laddys thai leven / As lordys riall, / At ee to be even, / Pu[r]turd in pall / as kyngys" (*LJT* ll. 447–51) along with the visual effects of short doublets, and "Nell with hir nyfyls / Of crisp and of sylke" (*LJT* ll. 469–70). These attacks on fashion and on the transgression of estate norms implicit in "laddys" (low born fellows, rascals) who dress as lords, represents a completely different approach to this material from the mercers' play. The mercers could not have afforded to call such attention to their own spectacle, to the fine cloth that they sold, to their violations of sumptuary laws, or to the pride of their guild; the "new gett" profited mercers, after all. Unlike the mercers' play, the Towneley "Judgment" could also use terms associated with avarice in the antimercantile tradition. For example, one group of sinners "ar a menee, / Of barganars and okerars / And lufars of symonee, / Of runkers and rowners [*whisperers* and *tattlers, tale-bearers*]/ God castys thaym out, trulee, / From his temple, all sich mysdoers" (*LJT* ll. 431–35). The "runkers" and "rowners" mixed in with these mercantile sinners reflect the history of Tutivillus, "a minor devil who wrote down on strips of parchments, which were then gathered up in sacks, the words mumbled or dropped by clerics and those spoken idly by parishioners during church services."[91] Still, while the terms *usury* and *simony* remain unequivocally references to sin, the play's use of "barganars" in this context recalls the double life for trade language that characterizes the gap between the antimercantile tradition, and promercantile writing. This play clearly follows the former, and coming in the same textual tradition as the York "Last Judgement," it gives us an idea of how persistently such material survived even in the context of cycle drama. One can only imagine how the York mercers might have responded to a performance of the Towneley version of their play. Also, the Towneley "Judgment" performance of the carnivalesque in its satire shows the extent to which "The Last Judgement" of York is *not* carnivalesque. Anthony Gash argues for extensive carnivalesque in the Towneley cycle, arguing that its clown figures provide "a temporary reprieve from Christian eschatology."[92] The humorous overstatement of Tutivillus' long speech fits Gash's model, particularly in such vulgarities as "His luddokkys [*buttocks*] thai lowke / Like walk-mylne cloggys [*fulling-mill clogs*]" (*LJT* ll. 456–57). Given this successful carnival performance in the Towneley "Judgment," the relative lack of it in the "The Last Judgement" of York is striking. Martin Stevens does see the

York cycle as a whole as carnivalesque,[93] but his application of carnival to the cycle relies on a far broader definition of it than Gash's, and might better be termed simply "irony." The mercers' staid "Last Judgement," at any rate, studiously avoids the outrageous humor and tension of carnivalesque, and like the "Coronation of the Virgin" instead relies on straightforward symbolic display.

Returning to York, another trade link of the mercers to their play besides their charity might then invoke a similar comparison to that between mayoral and divine power, with the ironic effect Stevens suggests for the cycle as a whole. Alan Justice points out that the weights that mercers would have used daily recall the "weighing of human souls against the standard established by Christ sitting in judgment."[94] This observation suggests the possibility of a gap between the mercers' fairness in weights and that of God, and it also represents the only direct interaction of the play with the antimercantile tradition, however oblique. That reference to the satire tradition need not undermine the mercers with irony, though, as it happens to be the antimercantile criticism most commonly addressed in guild ordinances, including the mercers' own.[95] Any hint of a concern with measurement, as in God's measurement of souls, might recall social concerns with mercers, but it would also potentially remind an audience of merchants' fairness through the very guild structure that produced the plays, and which was celebrated (and idealized) by the cycle as a whole. After all, a primary function of a guild *was* to regulate weights and measures. Sarah Beckwith's suggestion that the plays' route through the city carried "The Last Judgement" past city prisons and the punishment site of the Pavement perhaps further emphasizes this concern with measurement and judgment,[96] but it may also represent a coincidence. Whoever portrayed a Doomsday play, with whatever text, would have been forced to perform it on the Pavement as the best place in the medieval city for a large-scale performance. Beckwith is right, however, that the visual image of God judging where the city oligarchy's courts judged can only point out the distance between the two, at the same time it potentially celebrates the worship of the city's justice system.

If we bring together these different elements of the performance—the spectacle, the text's tension between orthodoxy and the celebration of the charity of the guild, the careful avoidance of satire and carnival, and the possible ironies of the trade link between the play, the producers' roles as city judges, and the weight standards of the guild—the end result is a composite view of the developing merchant subjectivity that shows early life in Chaucer's *Shipman's Tale*, and further elaboration in the didactic "Childe of Bristowe" and *Tale of Beryn*. Between Gower and the York Play, while merchandise has not become morally unassailable, it has become possible for members of the merchant estate to sponsor a cultural production lacking the overwhelming anxiety about trade that so occupied Margery Kempe. Even without that level of anxiety, though, there remains some tension between the ultimately antimercantile orthodoxy of restitution and the moral optimism of "The Last Judgement," and the conflicting possibilities of the spectacle and ironic link to measurement underline this tension. The mercers' focus on their moral strength of charity and the justice of judgment allows the play to stress their right to political power, at the same time that the play can alleviate their own moral anxieties. Indeed, the emphatic tone here represents the best evidence available that these merchants did feel some anxiety, and the production of the play can itself be construed as an act of charity glorifying God. In a society that looked askance at the taint of finance, the political power involved in their financial power could not help but be suspect and generate some insecurity.

The men who ran both the guild and the city had the power regardless, but by using the cultural production of the play to define sin and salvation in their own terms, the mercers present an ideology in which such power is both natural and morally defensible. The occasional ironic fault-lines in the play, such as the possible negative comparison between their worship and that of the God they represent, show us that such an ideology remained contingent, and conflicted with the remains of the antimercantile ideology that has run throughout the texts of this study. Given that the Aldermen and Mayor received worship by virtue of their social position in the city, it was imperative that they appear and perceive themselves as worthy of such symbolic power and the political power that went along with it, though no cultural production could do so perfectly. If in their capacity as guildsmen they were able to determine the local religious discourse even a little, they could use the moral authority inherent in representing God to reinforce their own social and religious position. Too strong a statement of their moral ascendancy would have been more damaging than no statement at all, but the presentation of material charity as the necessary virtue, with the flag of Trinity Hospital flying proudly above the pageant of heaven, is hardly subtle.

CONCLUSION

FROM FINCHALE TO YORK: ARE MERCHANTS RESPECTABLE BY 1500?

Having traveled this long path through a century of representations of medieval English merchants, it seems appropriate to reflect briefly on what conclusions can be drawn from this analysis. Most importantly, we should recall that while this book suggests a progression from the antimercantilism of William Langland's *Piers Plowman* to the promercantile charity of the York Mercers' "Last Judgement," it would be misleading to argue that antimercantile ideology was in full retreat from emergent mercantilism by the late fifteenth century. Like the static representations of avarice and its moneybags on churches throughout Europe, the literary texts of the late fourteenth century remained relevant cultural texts long after their authors had died. While Gower was primarily remembered for his *Confessio Amantis*, which avoids the debate over merchants, and Margery Kempe's *Book* may not have been widely read, the works of Geoffrey Chaucer and William Langland remained popular throughout the period of this study. Indeed, Northumberland Ms. 455, the manuscript in which the *Tale of Beryn* survives, presents some of Chaucer's ambivalence toward merchants alongside the *Beryn*-poet's redemptive vision of trade, all within a single reading of the *Canterbury Tales*. The longer texts are also not entirely about merchants; the debate over the taint of finance is a running theme here, and worth further study, but it certainly is not the only or even most important thing going on in late medieval English literature.

What the nature of the transmission of literary texts does tell us is that the texts in this book are not a sequence, but a conversation. While it would have been improbable for a single reader to encounter all of these texts, as the *Mirour de l'Omme*, *The Book of Margery Kempe*, "The Childe of Bristowe" and "The Merchant and His Son," the *Tale of Beryn*, and the York Cycle all survive in single manuscripts, it is also hard to imagine the later authors to have been ignorant of some version of the work of the earlier poets. Certainly Kempe's own feelings about trade internalize the lessons that the satires tried to convey, and the York Mercers' "Last Judgement" suggests a response to the satirists. While the fifteenth-century texts thus respond at some level to the discourse of the fourteenth-century ones, we should not assume that the residual antimercantile ideology embedded in those earlier discourses had lost its capacity to challenge the money economy. Given how many modern Chaucer scholars have accepted that ideology even as conveyed ambivalently in the *General Prologue*, that discursive formation retains some force even now, in our own commercial age. Indeed, one might view Marxism's opposition to capitalism itself as a resurgence of the initial resistance to the money economy.

While the emergent ideology of mercantilism was by no means hegemonic, then, and the residual ideology of the satires retained its discursive force, what does change over the period of this study is merchants' capacity to respond to antimercantilism. While the late fourteenth-century satires show a carefully limited awareness of merchants' potential response to satiric ideology, the triumph of charity in the fifteenth century "Childe of Bristowe" and York Mercers' "Last Judgement" gives a literary respectability to merchants' opposition of charity to the sinful taint of finance. Where the twelfth-century ascetic reformed merchant St. Godric would allow no excuse for the desire for money, even to support the poor, by the late fifteenth century the justification of profit through charity had migrated from guild ordinances to literary representations of merchants. At the same time, the political and economic pragmatism of the *Libelle of Englyshe Polycye* redeploys the trappings of antimercantilism in its nationalist project, and acknowledges the prominence of English merchants while showing another path to literary respectability. Such an increased voice reflects the development of a promercantile discursive formation, though none of the literary texts discussed here quite shows that ideology in full flower. While Max Weber's thesis linking mercantile capitalism with Protestantism is no longer convincing, because it overlooks the economic complexity of the late Middle Ages, it reminds us that commerce did continue its transition toward respectability beyond the end of this study.[1] Gower, Langland, and Chaucer all invoke defenses of trade, so a manuscript-owning medieval merchant encountering representations of his or her estate in the fifteenth century was not that much more likely to encounter a form of promercantile ideology than in the previous century. Still, a later merchant reader would be able to find less equivocal representations of merchants that did not subsequently undermine that promercantile ideology. On the other hand, the closeness in time of *The Book of Margery Kempe* and the *Libelle of Englyshe Polycye* reminds us that writers at almost the exact same moment could draw entirely contradictory conclusions about the moral valence of trade.

If, then, literary merchants had become a little more respectable in the century or so of this study, it remains to consider what this study tells us about medieval estate. What is most striking about these different representations of literary merchants is the extent to which such a loosely defined estate group could have so consistent a complex of literary associations, and one that has not been studied more. Gower's use of the guilds to frame his antimercantile material in the *Mirour de l'Omme* unusually reflects the variety within the estate of merchants. Most of these texts, however, share a pattern of referring to merchants as a larger group, rather than separating them into their individual crafts and guild affiliations. There are a few exceptions, as in Kempe's overt references to her own Gild of the Holy Trinity, but the guildlessness of most of these merchants, including Chaucer's *Shipman's Tale*, *General Prologue*, and *Man of Law's Tale* merchants, Langland's Coveitise and Haukyn, the Childe of Bristowe, and Beryn, reflects a persistent gap between medieval social practice and social analysis. While historical merchants almost always had some guild affiliation, such affiliations only rarely appear in literature. What this suggests about medieval notions of class is a gap between descriptions of it in different discourses. In literary discourse, the guilds only rarely appear, but in the social discourse of London or York, where guilds determined the political structure and limited access to the franchise, individuals' estate affiliations were expressed through those guilds, mercers instead of merchants. This gap suggests that these literary discussions of estate could be substantially more abstract than the actual practice of a stratified society. Merchants as a category were a convenient focus for concerns about the economy, and such concerns were more easily expressed without reference to the complexities of competing guilds and the full range of merchant products and activities. Even in the promercantile texts here, such as "The Childe of Bristowe" or the *Tale of Beryn*, we never really find out what Childe-William or Beryn sell, because those texts are as concerned with the moral valence of the economy itself as they are about the individual merchant subjects they portray.

These merchants without merchandise thus suggest that literary manifestations of the estate ideology of the late Middle Ages represented merchants as a somewhat larger social category than did those merchants themselves, and defined them through their work rather than through their commodities. This gap between merchant self-representation and literary representations argues as strongly as any other detail of this study that these texts were not for the most part written by merchants. Indeed, it seems no coincidence that our one definite merchant-estate writer, Margery Kempe, is also the most specific about her own guild affiliation, in her insistence that she is the daughter of an alderman of the Gild of the Holy Trinity. Gower is similarly unusual in the guild-related detail of the *Mirour de l'Omme*, and this tantalizingly suggests his own possible involvement in the discourse of the London guilds. Even the York Mercers, who like Kempe focus on the devotional side of their guild, feature the iconography of their Gild of the Holy Trinity on their pageant wagon. This extremely localized sense of merchants' own estate as members of specific guilds might explain why merchants' responses to satire lagged so far behind the satirists, as the latter had a far more abstract vocabulary for their social analysis. So long as English merchants did not present themselves as a single estate, which happened only rarely in the late Middle Ages with such institutions as the Merchants of the Staple or the Merchant Adventurers, they were not ideologically equipped to respond directly to the charges of the satirists. It fell therefore to writers who were not themselves merchants to give merchants a voice. This is not to say, however, that this voice immediately resulted in the victory of promercantile ideology, because it did not. The religious affiliations of the guilds were suppressed by the English Reformation, and guild discourse itself never really recovered. The sixteenth century did produce some promercantile texts, such as Thomas Deloney's *Thomas of Reading* and *Jacke of Newberie*, but Deloney's works share the fifteenth-century promercantile works' sense of guildlessness, though he does at least specify that his merchants are clothiers. Still, the economy continued to grow more complex, and carried with it social conceptions of merchants and emergent mercantilism.

Finally, behind this study lurk generations of historical merchants, shipping their wool, buying country estates, and fending off damnation with frantic charity. It is to them, and to St. Godric wearing his hairshirt in his hermitage, that this book is ultimately dedicated, because while medieval merchants were far from perfect, they have not been treated fairly by posterity, particularly literary studies. I hope that I have been able to bring current thinking in economic history to bear in explaining the context of these literary representations of merchants, and to show how these texts deploy competing ideological discourses of merchandise. While England never had merchant dynasties like those of Italian cities such as Florence, merchants still left their mark on English literature, as embodiments of the material world, as sponsors of early drama, and as a troublesome estate. It is to be hoped that this book will support further inquiry into the ideological and literary connections of English merchants.

NOTES

1 An Introduction to Late Medieval English Literary Merchants

1. The most influential work remains Sylvia L. Thrupp, *The Merchant Class of Medieval London 1300–1500* (1948; repr. Ann Arbor: University of Michigan Press, 1962); more recently, there have been updates or supplements to Thrupp, focusing either on a different region or on a particular guild. See Jenny Kermode, *Medieval Merchants: York, Beverly, and Hull in the Later Middle Ages* (Cambridge, UK: Cambridge University Press, 1998); Pamela Nightingale, *A Medieval Mercantile Community: The Grocers' Company & The Politics & Trade of London, 1000–1485* (New Haven: Yale University Press, 1995); and Anne F. Sutton, *The Mercery of London: Trade, Goods and People, 1130–1578* (Burlington, VT: Ashgate, 2005).
2. See Lianna Farber, *An Anatomy of Trade in Medieval Writing: Value, Consent, and Community* (Ithaca: Cornell University Press, 2006).
3. Georges Duby, *The Three Orders: Feudal Society Imagined*, trans. Arthur Goldhammer (Chicago: University of Chicago Press, 1980), p. 354.
4. E. Talbot Donaldson, "Patristic Exegesis in the Criticism of Medieval Literature: The Opposition," in *Speaking of Chaucer* (New York: W. W. Norton, 1970), p. 134 [134–53]; see also D. W. Robertson, Jr., *A Preface to Chaucer: Studies in Medieval Perspectives* (Princeton: Princeton University Press, 1962).
5. Robert P. Miller, *Chaucer: Sources and Backgrounds* (Oxford: Oxford University Press, 1977), pp. viii–xi.
6. Lee Patterson, "Chaucer's Pardoner on the Couch: Psyche and Clio in Medieval Literary Studies," *Speculum* 76 (2001): 638–80.
7. See Penn R. Szittya, *The Antifraternal Tradition in Medieval Literature* (Princeton: Princeton University Press, 1986); Wendy Scase, *Piers Plowman and the New Anti-Clericalism*, Cambridge Studies in Medieval Literature 4 (Cambridge, UK: Cambridge University Press, 1989); Janet Coleman, *Piers Plowman and the Moderni* (Rome: Edizioni di Storia e Letteratura, 1981).
8. David Aers, "The Good Shepherds of Medieval Criticism," *Southern Review* 20 (1987): 168–85; David Aers, "Reading *Piers Plowman*: Literature, History, and Criticism," *Literature and History* 1 (1990): 4–23; David Aers and Lynn Staley, *The Powers of the Holy: Religion, Politics, and Gender in Late*

Medieval English Culture (University Park: Pennsylvania State University Press, 1996).

9. E. Talbot Donaldson, "The Effect of the Merchant's Tale," in *Speaking of Chaucer*, pp. 30–45.

10. Richard Firth Green, *Poets and Princepleasers: Literature and the English Court in the Late Middle Ages* (Toronto: University of Toronto Press, 1980), pp. 9–10.

11. Green, *Poets and Princepleasers*, p. 128; my italics.

12. Paul Strohm, "Saving the Appearances: Chaucer's 'Purse' and the Fabrication of the Lancastrian Claim," in *Hochon's Arrow: The Social Imagination of Fourteenth-Century Texts* (Princeton: Princeton University Press, 1992), pp. 75–94; Paul Strohm, "Queens as Intercessors," in *Hochon's Arrow*, pp. 95–119; Paul Strohm, *England's Empty Throne: Usurpation and the Language of Legitimation, 1399–1422* (New Haven: Yale University Press, 1998). Strohm's work has also included some discussion of the third estate, however: "Hochon's Arrow," in *Hochon's Arrow*, pp. 11–31; "'A Revelle!': Chronicle Evidence and the Rebel Voice," in *Hochon's Arrow*, pp. 33–56; *Social Chaucer* (Cambridge, MA: Harvard University Press, 1989).

13. Larry Scanlon, *Narrative, Authority, and Power: The Medieval Exemplum and the Chaucerian Tradition* (Cambridge, UK: Cambridge University Press, 1994); Janet Coleman, *Medieval Readers and Writers, 1350–1400* (New York: Columbia University Press, 1981), pp. 43, 202.

14. Scanlon, *Narrative, Authority, and Power*, p. 144.

15. Christopher Dyer, *Standards of Living in the Later Middle Ages: Social Change in England c. 1200–1520*, Cambridge Medieval Textbooks (Cambridge, UK: Cambridge University Press, 1989), p. 20, Table 1; Coleman, *Medieval Readers and Writers*, pp. 58–62.

16. Steven Justice, *Writing and Rebellion: England in 1381* (Berkeley: University of California Press, 1994). See also *Chaucer's England: Literature in Historical Context*, ed. Barbara A. Hanawalt (Minneapolis: University of Minnesota Press, 1992), particularly the essays by Lawrence Clopper [pp. 110–29], Richard Firth Green [pp. 176–200], and Susan Crane [pp. 201–21].

17. Kellie Robertson, *The Laborer's Two Bodies: Literary and Legal Productions in Britain, 1350–1500* (New York: Palgrave Macmillan, 2006), pp. 103–14.

18. Paul Miller, "John Gower, Satiric Poet," in *Gower's* Confessio Amantis: *Responses and Reassessments*, ed. A. J. Minnis (Woodbridge, Suffolk: D. S. Brewer, 1983), p. 79 n3 [79–105]; Jill Mann, *Chaucer and Medieval Estates Satire: The Literature of Social Classes and the* General Prologue *of the* Canterbury Tales (Cambridge, UK: Cambridge University Press, 1973); S. M. Tucker, *Verse Satire in England Before the Renaissance* (New York: Columbia University Press, 1908); John Peter, *Complaint and Satire in Early English Literature* (Oxford: Clarendon Press, 1956).

19. Robert L. Kindrick, "The Unknightly Knight: Anti-Chivalric Satire in Fourteenth- and Fifteenth-Century English Literature" (Ph. D. diss., University of Texas-Austin, 1971); Henrik Specht, *Chaucer's Franklin*

in the Canterbury Tales: The Social and Literary Background of a Chaucerian Character (Copenhagen: Akademisk Forlag, 1981); Terry Jones, *Chaucer's Knight: The Portrait of a Medieval Mercenary*, rev. edn. (London: Methuen, 1994).

20. Farber discusses Chaucer's *Shipman's Tale, Franklin's Tale,* and *Physician's Tale* (*Anatomy of Trade*, pp. 68–83, 129–40); Henryson's "The Cock and the Jasp" (*Anatomy of Trade*, pp. 83–92); *St. Erkenwald* (*Anatomy of Trade*, pp. 152–61); and "London Lickpenny" (*Anatomy of Trade*, pp. 174–79). Most of Farber's insightful book focuses on philosophical and theological texts.

21. For a recent discussion of the role of avarice within early formations of the Seven Deadly Sins, the Capital Vices, and other sin paradigms, see Richard Newhauser, *The Early History of Greed: The Sin of Avarice in Early Medieval Thought and Literature* (Cambridge, UK: Cambridge University Press, 2000).

22. T. H. Lloyd, *The English Wool Trade in the Middle Ages* (Cambridge, UK: Cambridge University Press, 1977), pp. 144, 289.

23. Caroline M. Barron, *London in the Later Middle Ages: Government and People, 1200–1500* (Oxford: Oxford University Press, 2004), p. 99.

24. On residual and emergent ideology, see Raymond Williams, *Marxism and Literature* (Oxford: Oxford University Press, 1977), pp. 122–24.

25. H. Leith Spencer, *English Preaching in the Late Middle Ages* (Oxford: Clarendon Press, 1993), pp. 65–68.

26. *Medieval English Political Writings*, ed. James M. Dean, TEAMS Middle English Texts Series (Kalamazoo, MI: Medieval Institute Publications, 1996), pp. 183–84.

27. On vexed evidence for Gower's involvement in the wool trade, real estate, and law, see John H. Fisher, *John Gower: Moral Philosopher and Friend of Chaucer* (New York: New York University Press, 1964), pp. 55–57; see also John Hines, Nathalie Cohen, and Simon Roffey, "Iohannes Gower, Armiger, Poeta: Records and Memorials of his Life and Death," in *A Companion to Gower*, ed. Siân Echard (Woodbridge, Suffolk: D. S. Brewer, 2004), pp. 23–41.

28. Rodney Hilton, *Bond Men Made Free: Medieval Peasant Movements and the English Rising of 1381* (New York: Methuen, 1973), p. 11; Robertson, *Laborer's Two Bodies*, p. 87.

29. Louis Althusser, "Ideology and Ideological State Apparatuses (Notes towards an Investigation)," in *Lenin and Philosophy and Other Essays*, trans. Ben Brewster (New York: Monthly Review Press, 1971), pp. 134–37 [127–86].

30. Mann, *Chaucer and Medieval Estates Satire*, pp. 203–6.

31. Dyer, *Standards of Living*, pp. 20–21, Table 1.

32. A. F. Butcher, "English Urban Society and the Revolt of 1381," in *The English Rising of 1381*, ed. R. H. Hilton and T. H. Aston (Cambridge, UK: Cambridge University Press, 1984), pp. 84–111.

33. Justice, *Writing and Rebellion*, p. 147.

34. A. R. Myers, *London in the Age of Chaucer* (Norman, OK.: University of Oklahoma Press, 1972), pp. 92, 94.
35. Caroline M. Barron explains that "Such knighthoods were quite rare in the fourteenth century and no London alderman, not even [three-time Mayor] Richard Whittington, was knighted the fifty-year period following the Peasants' Revolt in 1381" (Barron, *London*, p. 144).
36. Nightingale, *Medieval Mercantile Community*, p. 256.
37. Thrupp, *Merchant Class*, p. 326; see also Michael A. Hicks, *Who's Who in Late Medieval England (1272–1485)* (London: Shepheard-Walwyn, 1991), p. 186.
38. Nightingale, *Medieval Mercantile Community*, p. 315.
39. Myers, *London*, p. 99.
40. Myers, *London*, p. 178. On the other hand, David Wallace argues that this entry and one naming "'Jankyn' Philpot" rather indicated Gaunt's scorn for merchant upstarts. *Chaucerian Polity: Absolutist Lineages and Associational Forms in England and Italy* (Stanford: Stanford University Press, 1997), p. 188.
41. Reginaldo monacho Dunelmensi [Reginald of Durham], *Libellus de vita et miraculis S. Godrici, Heremitæ de Finchale*, ed. Joseph Stevenson, Publications of the Surtees Society 20 (London: J. B. Nichols and Son, 1847), pp. 21–32.
42. *The Oxford Dictionary of Saints*, ed. David Hugh Farmer, 4th edn. (Oxford: Oxford University Press, 1997), pp. 214–15.
43. *Selections from Early Middle English 1130–1250*, ed. Joseph Hall, vol. 1 (Oxford: Clarendon Press, 1920), p. 5.
44. Richard Newhauser cites in particular Evagrius Ponticus as a major source of this tradition (*Early History of Greed*, pp. 48–50), expressed in increasingly eschatological terms by Godric's time (*Early History of Greed*, pp. 128–31).
45. Reginaldo, *Libellus de vita*, pp. 275; my translation.
46. André Vauchez, *Sainthood in the Later Middle Ages* [*La sainteté en Occident aux derniers siècles du Moyen Age*], trans. Jean Birrell (1988; Cambridge, UK: Cambridge University Press, 1997), pp. 357–58.
47. David Wallace, "Mystics and Followers in Siena and East Anglia: A Study in Taxonomy, Class and Cultural Mediation," in *The Medieval Mystical Tradition in England: Papers Read at Darlington Hall, July 1984*, ed. Marion Glasscoe (Woodbridge, Suffolk: D. S. Brewer, 1984), p. 173 [169–91].
48. *Oxford Dictionary of Saints*, p. 240.
49. Dyer, *Standards of Living*, p. 23.
50. D. Vance Smith, *Arts of Possession: The Middle English Household Imaginary*, Medieval Cultures 33 (Minneapolis: University of Minnesota Press, 2003), pp. 25–36.
51. Barron lists the "grocers, mercers, fishmongers, drapers, goldsmiths, skinners, vintners, and ironmongers" as "members of the 'mercantile' companies" from whom the London Aldermen were almost always chosen (*London*, p. 139).
52. Dyer, *Standards of Living*, p. 24.

53. Steven A. Epstein, *Wage Labor & Guilds in Medieval Europe* (Chapel Hill: University of North Carolina Press, 1991), p. 197.
54. Barron, *London*, pp. 205–6.
55. Thrupp, *Merchant Class*, p. 4.
56. Thrupp, *Merchant Class*, p. 5.
57. See Kermode, *Medieval Merchants*, pp. 15–21, 23–155 for details of northern merchants of York, Beverly, and Hull.
58. Dyer, *Standards of Living*, p. 14.
59. Edward Miller and John Hatcher, *Medieval England: Towns, Commerce and Crafts, 1086–1348* (London: Longman, 1995), pp. 135–254.
60. James Masschaele, *Peasants, Merchants, and Markets: Inland Trade in Medieval England, 1150–1350* (New York: St. Martin's Press, 1997), pp. 52–53.
61. Barron, *London*, pp. 76–83.
62. Thrupp, *Merchant Class*, pp. 210–11.
63. Thrupp, *Merchant Class*, p. 265.
64. Kermode, *Medieval Merchants*, p. 16.
65. Thrupp, *Merchant Class*, p. 249.
66. Thrupp, *Merchant Class*, p. 272.
67. Virginia Bainbridge, *Gilds in the Medieval Countryside: Social and Religious Change in Cambridgeshire c. 1350–1558*, Studies in the History of Medieval Religion 10 (Woodbridge: The Boydell Press, 1996), pp. 8–9.
68. Nightingale, *Medieval Mercantile Community*, pp. 237, 292.
69. Thrupp, *Merchant Class*, p. 30.
70. Maud Sellers, *The York Mercers and Merchant Adventurers 1356–1917*, Publications of the Surtees Society 129 (London: Bernard Quaritch, 1918), p. x.
71. William Richards, *The History of Lynn*, vol 1. (Lynn: W. G. Whittingham, 1812), pp. 417–18.
72. Barron, *London*, p. 207.
73. Heather Swanson, "The Illusion of Economic Structure: Craft Guilds in Late Medieval English Towns," *Past and Present* 121 (1988): 29 [29–48].
74. Thrupp, *Merchant Class*, p. 312.
75. Barbara A. Hanawalt, *Growing Up in Medieval London: The Experience of Childhood in History* (Oxford: Oxford University Press, 1993), p. 91.
76. Kermode, *Medieval Merchants*, pp. 78–80.
77. Thrupp, *Merchant Class*, p. 153.
78. Sellers, *York Mercers*, pp. 32, 50–51, 80–81, 84–85; see also Chapter 6.
79. Barron, *London*, pp. 290–93.
80. *Facsimile of First Volume of Ms. Archives of the Worshipful Company of Grocers of the City of London, A. D. 1345–1463, Transcribed and Translated with extracts from The Records of the City of London and Archives of St. Paul's Cathedral*, ed. and intro. John Abernethy Kingdon, Part 1 of 2 (London: Printed for the Company by Richard Clay and Sons, 1886), pp. 18–21; his translation.
81. Frances Consitt, *The London Weavers' Company*, vol. I. (Oxford: Clarendon Press, 1931), p. 194.

82. *English Towns and Gilds*, vol. 2, no. 1 of *Translations and Reprints from the Original Sources of European History* (Philadelphia: Dept. of History of the University of Pennsylvania, 1902), p. 23; Kingdon, *Facsimile*, pp. 18–21.

83. Sir John Watney, *An Account of the Mistery of Mercers of the City of London, otherwise the Mercers' Company* (London: Blades, East & Blades, 1914), p. 33; Arthur Henry Johnson, *The History of the Worshipful Company of the Drapers of London: Preceded by an Introduction on London and Her Gilds Up to the Close of the XVth Century*, vol. 1 (Oxford: Clarendon Press, 1914), pp. 199–200.

84. Epstein, *Wage Labor*, p. 165.

85. Toulmin Smith, ed., *English Gilds: The Original Ordinances of more than one hundred Early English Gilds*, Early English Text Society o.s. 40 (London: N. Trübner & Co, 1870), pp. 6–8.

86. Epstein, *Wage Labor*, p. 167.

87. Epstein, *Wage Labor*, p. 158.

88. Judith Bennett, "Conviviality and Charity in Medieval and Early Modern England," *Past and Present* 134 (1992): 23 [19–41].

89. Ben R. McRee, "Charity and Gild Solidarity in Late Medieval England," *Journal of British Studies* 32 (1993): 196–99 [195–225].

90. McRee, "Charity and Gild Solidarity," p. 200.

91. McRee, "Charity and Gild Solidarity," p. 201.

92. McRee, "Charity and Gild Solidarity," p. 203.

93. McRee, "Charity and Gild Solidarity," p. 201.

94. McRee, "Charity and Gild Solidarity," p. 224.

95. Carlo M. Cipolla, *Before the Industrial Revolution: European Society and the Economy, 1000–1700*, 2nd edn. (New York: W. W. Norton & Company, 1980), p. 57.

96. See, for example, the document "Contention About a Tithe," in *A Source Book for Medieval Economic History*, ed. Roy C. Cave and Herbert H. Coulson (New York: Biblo and Tannen, 1965), p. 386.

97. N. J. G. Pounds, *An Economic History of Medieval Europe* (New York: Longman, 1974), p. 409. See also Henri Pirenne, *Economic and Social History of Medieval Europe*, trans. I. E. Clegg (1933; repr. New York: Harcourt, Brace & World, 1937), p. 130. The basic principle of taxation leading to banking arises out of the difficulty of transporting money as specie, particularly with bulky silver currency.

98. Newhauser, *Early History of Greed*, pp. xii, 10–14.

99. Lester K. Little, *Religious Poverty and the Profit Economy in Medieval Europe* (Ithaca, NY: Cornell University Press, 1978), p. 35.

100. Little, *Religious Poverty*, p. 36.

101. Little, *Religious Poverty*, p. 37. Newhauser's appendix also shows the range of early depictions of avarice, with 116 different headings for individual symbols of the sin (*Early History of Greed*, pp. 132–42).

102. Little, *Religious Poverty*, p. 38.

103. Edwin S. Hunt and James M. Murray, *A History of Business in Medieval Europe 1200–1550*, Cambridge Medieval Textbooks (Cambridge, UK: Cambridge University Press, 1999), p. 70.
104. Pounds, *Economic History*, p. 408.
105. Farber, *Anatomy of Trade*, p. 40.
106. Hunt and Murray, *History of Business*, p. 70.
107. Mann, *Chaucer and Medieval Estates Satire*, pp. 99–100.
108. *Middle English Dictionary* [MED], online edn. (Ann Arbor: University of Michigan Press, 2001), s.v. "chevisaunce."
109. Kenneth S. Cahn, "Chaucer's Merchants and the Foreign Exchange: An Introduction to Medieval Finance," *Studies in the Age of Chaucer* 2 (1980): 83 [81–119]; Hunt and Murray, *History of Business*, pp. 63–7.
110. Cahn, "Chaucer's Merchants," p. 84.
111. Peter Spufford, *Money and Its Use in Medieval Europe* (Cambridge, UK: Cambridge University Press, 1988), p. 254.
112. Hunt and Murray, *History of Business*, p. 65.
113. Cahn, "Chaucer's Merchants," p. 104.
114. Hunt and Murray, *History of Business*, p. 66.
115. Cahn, "Chaucer's Merchants," pp. 98–99.
116. John T. Noonan, *The Scholastic Analysis of Usury* (Cambridge, MA: Harvard University Press, 1957), p. 39.
117. Noonan, *Scholastic Analysis*, p. 31.
118. Hunt and Murray, *History of Business*, p. 71.
119. Pounds, *Economic History*, pp. 406–7.
120. R. H. Helmholz, "Usury and the Medieval English Church Courts," *Speculum* 61 (1986): 365 [364–80].
121. Helmholz, "Usury," p. 370.
122. Nightingale, *Medieval Mercantile Community*, pp. 213–33.
123. Smith, *Arts of Possession*, p. 132.
124. Hunt and Murray, *History of Business*, pp. 31, 205–6.
125. Hicks, *Who's Who*, pp. 92–93, 174–75.
126. Strohm, *Social Chaucer*, pp. 64–68; Coleman, *Medieval Readers and Writers*, pp. 43–45, 52–57; Linne R. Mooney, "Chaucer's Scribe," *Speculum* 81 (2006): 97–138.
127. Sutton, *Mercery of London*, p. 168; on Fetiplace, see Mary C. Erler, "Fifteenth-Century Owners of Chaucer's Work: Cambridge, Magdalene College Ms. Pepys 2006," *Chaucer Review* 38.4 (2004): 406–8 [401–14].
128. Sutton, *Mercery of London*, p. 169.
129. Thrupp, *Merchant Class of Medieval London*, pp. 163–65.
130. Barbara A. Hanawalt, "'The Childe of Bristowe' and the Making of Middle-Class Adolescence," in *"Of Good and Ill Repute": Gender and Social Control in Medieval England* (Oxford: Oxford University Press, 1998), pp. 194–95 n3 [178–201].
131. Peter Meredith, "John Clerke's Hand in the York Register," *Leeds Studies in English* n.s. 12 (1981): 245 [245–71].

132. Elizabeth Solopova, ed., *The General Prologue on CD-ROM* (Cambridge, UK: Cambridge University Press, 2000).

133. John Gower, *The Complete Works*, ed. G. C. Macaulay, vol. 1 (Oxford: Clarendon Press, 1899–1902), pp. lxviii–lxix.

134. *The Book of Margery Kempe*, ed. Lynn Staley (Kalamazoo, MI: Western Michigan University for TEAMS, 1996), p. xxxii.

135. William Langland, *Piers Plowman: A Parallel-Text Edition of the A, B, C and Z Versions, Volume II: Introduction, Textual Notes, Commentary, Bibliography, and Indexical Glossary*, ed. A. V. C. Schmidt (Kalamazoo, MI: Medieval Institute Publications, 2008), pp. 2–9, 273–74.

136. Mooney, "Chaucer's Scribe," p. 98.

137. Mooney, "Chaucer's Scribe," pp. 98–99.

138. Mooney, "Chaucer's Scribe," p. 120; Kathryn Kerby-Fulton and Steven Justice, "Scribe D and the Marketing of Ricardian Literature," in *The Medieval Professional Reader at Work: Evidence from Manuscripts of Chaucer, Langland, Kempe, and Gower*, ed. Kathryn Kerby-Fulton and Maidie Hilmo (Victoria, British Columbia: English Literary Studies, University of Victoria, 2001), pp. 217–37; A. S. G. Edwards and Derek Pearsall, "The Manuscripts of the Major English Poetic Texts," in *Book Production and Publishing in Britain, 1375–1475*, ed. Jeremy Griffiths and Derek Pearsall (Cambridge, UK: Cambridge University Press, 1989), p. 262 [257–278].

139. Linne R. Mooney, "More Manuscripts Written by a Chaucer Scribe," *Chaucer Review* 30.4 (1996): 403–4 [401–7].

140. Marion Turner, "Usk and the Goldsmiths," *New Medieval Literatures* 9 (2007): 139 [139–77]; Caroline Barron, review of *Wardens' Accounts and Court Minute Books of the Goldsmiths' Mistery of London 1334–1446*, edited by Lisa Jefferson, *Urban History* 32 (2005): 175 [173–75]; Linne R. Mooney identifies Hoccleve's hand on two receipts naming the famous mercer Richard Whittington, in "Some New Light on Thomas Hoccleve," *Studies in the Age of Chaucer* 29 (2007): 329, 332 [293–340].

141. Marion Turner, "'Certaynly His Noble Sayenges Can I Not Amende': Thomas Usk and *Troilus and Criseyde*," *Chaucer Review* 37.1 (2002): 26 [26–39].

142. Edwards and Pearsall, "Manuscripts," p. 260.

2   Langland's Merchants and the Material and Spiritual Economies of *Piers Plowman B*

1. E. Talbot Donaldson, *Piers Plowman, the C Text and Its Poet* (1949; repr. New Haven: Yale University Press, 1966), pp. 128–29.

2. James Simpson, "Spirituality and Economics in Passūs 1–7 of the B Text," *Yearbook of Langland Studies* 1 (1987): 85 [83–103].

3. F. R. H. Du Boulay, *The England of Piers Plowman: William Langland and His Vision of the Fourteenth Century* (Cambridge, UK: D. S. Brewer, 1991), p. 6.

4. David Aers, "Reading *Piers Plowman*: Literature, History and Criticism," *Literature and History* 1 (1990): 8 (4–23). See also David Aers, "The Good Shepherds of Medieval Criticism," *Southern Review* 20 (1987): 179 [168–85], and Anne Middleton, "Acts of Vagrancy: The C Version 'Autobiography' and the Statute of 1388," in *Written Work: Langland, Labor, and Authorship*, ed. Steven Justice and Kathryn Kerby-Fulton, The Middle Ages Series (Philadelphia: University of Pennsylvania Press, 1997), pp. 208–317.

5. Ralph Hanna, *London Literature, 1300–1380* (Cambridge, UK: Cambridge University Press, 2005), p. 255.

6. All citations from *Piers Plowman* are from William Langland, *Piers Plowman: A Parallel-Text Edition of the A, B, C and Z Versions, Volume I: Text*, ed. A. V. C. Schmidt (London: Longman, 1995). See also William Langland, *Piers Plowman: The B Version. Will's Visions of Piers Plowman, Do-Well, Do-Better, and Do-Best*, ed. George Kane and E. Talbot Donaldson, rev. ed. (London: Athlone Press, 1988); William Langland, *Piers Plowman: The C Version. Will's Visions of Piers Plowman, Do-Well, Do-Better, and Do-Best*, ed. George Russell and George Kane (London: Athlone Press, 1997); and William Langland, *The Vision of Piers Plowman: A Critical Edition of the B-Text Based on Trinity College Cambridge Ms. B.15.17*, ed. A. V. C. Schmidt, 2nd ed. (Rutland, VT: Charles E. Tuttle-Everyman, 1995). Because Schmidt's square brackets for emendations conflicts with my own use of brackets for glosses and quote management, I have silently removed his bracketed emendation markings. Italicized glosses in brackets come from Schmidt's Everyman edition.

7. John T. Noonan, *The Scholastic Analysis of Usury* (Cambridge, MA: Harvard University Press, 1957), p. 78.

8. "Langland's London," in *Written Work: Langland, Labor, and Authorship*, ed. Steven Justice and Kathryn Kerby-Fulton (Philadelphia: University of Pennsylvania Press, 1997), p. 191 [185–207].

9. For a clear discussion of fraud per se, see Thomas Aquinas, *Summa Theologica: Latin Text and English Translation, Introductions, Notes, Appendices and Glossaries*, 60 vols. (New York: McGraw-Hill-Blackfriars, 1975), II.2.77; pp. 38:212–13. For Aquinas' relevance to Langland's economic theory, see Pearsall, "Langland's London," in *Written Work*, p. 193. On Olivi's cutting-edge economic theory, see Joel Kaye, *Economy and Nature in the Fourteenth Century: Money, Market Exchange, and the Emergence of Scientific Thought* (Cambridge, UK: Cambridge University Press, 1998), pp. 121–22.

10. Interestingly, as Andrew Cole points out in a discussion of the Prologue and half-acre scenes, this list form itself replicates formal characteristics associated with legal and economic writing, including guild ordinances. Andrew Cole, "Scribal Hermeneutics and the Genres of Social Organization in *Piers Plowman*," in *The Middle Ages at Work: Practicing Labor in Late Medieval England*, ed. Kellie Robertson and Michael Uebel (New York: Palgrave Macmillan, 2004), pp. 179–206.

11. Laying and losing a wed closely resembles the terms of a late medieval mnemonic on usury, which among other things defined the sin as when "a man leneþ mone or oþer good upon a wed of catel moeble to a certeyn day, and for hi is noght payed at þe day, wiþholdiþ the wed for euere. For it is more worth þan þe lone." R. H. Bowers, "A Middle English Mnemonic Poem on Usury," *Mediaeval Studies* 17 (1955): 229 [226–32].
12. Howard Kaminsky, "Estate, Nobility, and the Exhibition of Estate in the Later Middle Ages," *Speculum* 68 (1993): 689 [684–709].
13. Pamela Nightingale, *A Medieval Mercantile Community: The Grocers' Company & the Politics & Trade of London 1000–1485* (New Haven, CT: Yale University Press, 1995), p. 354.
14. Schmidt, ed. *The Vision of Piers Plowman*, pp. 426–27 n249.
15. *Middle English Dictionary* [MED], online ed. (Ann Arbor: University of Michigan Press, 2001), s.v. "maintenaunce."
16. Paul Strohm, *Hochon's Arrow: The Social Imagination of Fourteenth-Century Texts* (Princeton: Princeton University Press, 1992), pp. 57–60.
17. D. Vance Smith, *Arts of Possession: The Middle English Household Imaginary*, Medieval Cultures 33 (Minneapolis: University of Minnesota Press, 2003), pp. 127–28.
18. *Largenesse* (largesse) is Langland's term in B.V. 623 opposed to Avarice (Schmidt, *The Vision of Piers Plowman*, p. 431 n618–24), and presumably shares *charity*'s meaning as *alms-giving*. *Charite* in the same passage (B.V. 621) opposes Envy, so that word must at this point in the poem refer to *caritas* in the sense of love, rather than the action of alms-giving associated linguistically with that love. Langland avoids confusion here by splitting the word temporarily.
19. All translations of Latin lines in *Piers Plowman* come from Schmidt, ed., *The Vision of Piers Plowman*.
20. See, for example, Aquinas, *Summa Theologica*, II.2.77; pp. 38:212–13.
21. Simpson, "Spirituality and Economics," p. 91.
22. Simpson, "Spirituality and Economics," p. 92.
23. Stella Maguire, "The Significance of Haukyn, *Activa Vita*, in *Piers Plowman*," in *Style and Symbolism in Piers Plowman: A Modern Critical Anthology,* ed. Robert J. Blanch (Knoxville: University of Tennessee Press, 1969), p. 196 [194–208]; her italics.
24. John Alford, "Haukyn's Coat: Some Observations on *Piers Plowman* B XIV 22–7," *Medium Ævum* 43 (1974): 133 [133–38].
25. Maguire, "Significance," in *Style and Symbolism*, p. 199.
26. W. A. Pantin, *The English Church in the Fourteenth Century*, Medieval Academy Reprints for Teaching 5 (1955; repr. Toronto: University of Toronto Press for Medieval Academy, 1980), pp. 47–75.
27. Donaldson, *Piers Plowman*, pp. 128–29.
28. Steven A. Epstein describes, for example, two suits taken to court in London in 1299 over the issue of working at night. *Wage Labor & Guilds*

in *Medieval Europe* (Chapel Hill: University of North Carolina Press, 1991), p. 202.

29. Edwin Craun attributes this "wanhope" more to Haukyn's background as a "mynstrall" (B.XIII. 225), reading this passage in the very different context of the pastoral discourse of minstrels. Edwin D. Craun, *Lies, Slander and Obscenity in Medieval English Literature: Pastoral Rhetoric and the Deviant Speaker* (Cambridge, UK: Cambridge University Press, 1997), pp. 174–77.

30. David Aers, *Chaucer, Langland and the Creative Imagination* (Boston: Routledge & Kegan Paul, 1980), p. 28

31. Lawrence M. Clopper, *"Songes of Rechelesnesse:" Langland and the Franciscans* (Ann Arbor: University of Michigan Press, 1997), pp. 242–43.

32. Penn R. Szittya, *The Antifraternal Tradition in Medieval Literature* (Princeton: Princeton University Press, 1986), p. 247; Clopper, *Songes of Rechelesnesse*, p. 77. See also Lawrence M. Clopper, "Langland's Persona: An Anatomy of the Mendicant Orders," in *Written Work: Langland, Labor, and Authorship,* ed. Steven Justice and Kathryn Kerby-Fulton (Philadelphia: University of Pennsylvania Press, 1997), pp. 144–84.

33. Szittya, *Antifraternal Tradition*, p. 258.

34. Szittya, *Antifraternal Tradition*, pp. 259–61; see also Middleton, "Acts of Vagrancy," p. 241.

35. Szittya, *Antifraternal Tradition*, p. 259.

36. Clopper, *Songes of Rechelesnesse*, p. 84.

37. Clopper, *Songes of Rechelesnesse*, p. 75.

38. Schmidt, ed., *The Vision of Piers Plowman*, p. 463 n16–21a. The various Do's change too rapidly in the poem to point to any single definition of Dowel, Dobet, and Dobest, but for a variety of definitions in the poem, see Nevill K. Coghill, "The Pardon of Piers Plowman," in *Style and Symbolism in Piers Plowman: A Modern Critical Anthology*, ed. Robert J. Blanch (Knoxville: University of Tennessee Press, 1969), pp. 40–86.

39. Lester K. Little, *Religious Poverty and the Profit Economy in Medieval Europe* (Ithaca: Cornell University Press, 1978), p. 35. Joerg O. Fichte counts up the commercial words used in the Prologue, and finds "eighteen in B and two more in C." "'For couetise after cros; þe croune stant in gold': Money as Matter and Metaphor in *Piers Plowman*," in *Material Culture and Cultural Materialism in the Middle Ages and the Renaissance,* ed. Curtis Perry (Turnhout: Brepols, 2001), p. 62n [57–74].

40. For those urban references, see Pearsall, "Langland's London," in *Written Work*, p. 188. For different political analyses of the Meed sequence, see Nicole Lassahn, "Literary Representations of History in Fourteenth Century England: Shared Technique and Divergent Practice in Chaucer and Langland," *Essays in Medieval Studies* 17 (2001): 49–64; Matthew Giancarlo, "*Piers Plowman*, Parliament, and the Public Voice," *Yearbook of Langland Studies* 17 (2003): 135–74.

41. Simpson, "Spirituality and Economics," p. 86.

42. Martyn J. Miller, "Meed, Mercede, and Mercy: Langland's Grammatical Metaphor and Its Relation to *Piers Plowman* as a Whole," *Medieval Perspectives* 9 (1994): 74–75.

43. Robert Adams argues that the "more complex description of human economic relationships and their figurative connection to divine grace" will in part arise from the distinction between *medes* in the B-Text. "The Evolution of the Economics of Grace in the *Piers Plowman* B and C Versions," in *Medieval English Studies Presented to George Kane*, ed. Edward Donald Kennedy, Ronald Waldron, and Joseph S. Wittig (Cambridge, UK: D. S. Brewer, 1988), p. 218 [217–232]. On the temporal significance of rewarding before and after deeds, see D. Vance Smith, "The Labors of Reward: Meed, Mercede, and the Beginning of Salvation," *Yearbook of Langland Studies* 8 (1994): 127–54. A more detailed investigation of the differences between the B-text and C-text versions of Langland's financial theology would be worthwhile.

44. Robert Adams labels this focus on rewards as "semi-Pelagian" ("Evolution of the Economics of Grace," in *Medieval English Studies*, p. 219); see also his "Piers's Pardon and Langland's Semi-Pelagianism," *Traditio* 39 (1983): 367–418.

45. Little, *Religious Poverty*, p. 36. See Introduction.

46. David Aers, "Class, Gender, Medieval Criticism, and *Piers Plowman*," in *Class and Gender in Early English Literature: Intersections*, ed. Britton J. Harwood and Gillian R. Overing (Bloomington: Indiana University Press, 1994), pp. 68–69 [59–75].

47. Clare A. Lees, "Gender and Exchange in *Piers Plowman*," in *Class and Gender in Early English Literature: Intersections*, ed. Britton J. Harwood and Gillian R. Overing (Bloomington: Indiana University Press, 1994), p. 117 [112–30].

48. Noonan, *Scholastic Analysis*, p. 39.

49. Smith, *Arts of Possession*, p. 115.

50. Noonan, *Scholastic Analysis*, p. 87.

51. This specific focus on the penny is also interesting in the light of J. A. Burrow's argument that many of Meed's bribes were not actually described in terms of specie; he insists that as a result the poem here is critiquing not money as such, but bribery. "Lady Meed and the Power of Money," *Medium Ævum* 74.1 (2005): 113–18. See also Smith, *Arts of Possession*, pp. 113–16.

52. Schmidt, ed., *The Vision of Piers Plowman*, p. 420 n258; his italics.

53. William Langland, *Piers Plowman: A Parallel-Text Edition of the A, B, C and Z Versions, Volume II: Introduction, Textual Notes, Commentary, Bibliography, and Indexical Glossary*, ed. A. V. C. Schmidt (Kalamazoo, MI: Medieval Institute Publications, 2008), p. 504 n313.

54. For Duns Scotus, see Kaye, *Economy and Nature*, pp. 125–26 nn34–36, 38. For Aquinas's use of *commutatio*, see *Summa Theologica*, II.2.77, pp. 38:212–13.

55. J. A. Simpson and E. S. C. Weiner, eds., *The Oxford English Dictionary* [OED], 2nd ed. (Oxford: Clarendon Press, 1989), s.v. "permutation"; MED, s.v. "permutacioun." See also Charlton T. Lewis and Charles Short, *A Latin Dictionary* (Oxford: Clarendon Press, 1879), s.v. "permutatio;" P. G. W. Glare, *Oxford Latin Dictionary* (Oxford: Clarendon Press, 1982), s.v. "permutatio." The medieval evidence is less clear, as J. F. Niermeyer does not even list *permutatio* in his *Mediae Latinitatis Lexicon Minus*, and defines *commutatio* as "directly contractual, either an exchange contract, a record of one, or property gained by one." *Mediae Latinitatis Lexicon Minus* (Leiden: E. J. Brill, 1976). R. E. Latham in defining *commutatio* reflects the economic usages seen above in Aquinas and Duns Scotus, while his *Dictionary of Medieval Latin from British Sources* lacks a specifically financial definition for *permutatio*, defining it as "giving or receiving in exchange," "interchange," "substitution, replacement," or "(act of) making or becoming (completely) different." *Dictionary of Medieval Latin From British Sources* (London: Oxford University Press for the British Academy, 1975–), s.v. "permutatio." Latham's *Revised Medieval Latin Word-List from British and Irish Sources* gives a financial definition for *permutatio* only as a word for the exchange of benefices (London: Oxford University Press for the British Academy, 1965), s.v. "permutatio." Based on Niermeyer and Latham, a preliminary conclusion might be that Langland chooses a relatively unused word that had a history of some monetary connotations, and substitutes it for the medieval *commutatio*, which had expanded into *permutatio*'s older semantic range.

56. Mary Catherine Davidson praises Langland's use of English-Latin code-switching in Conscience's debate with Meed, which would support a high degree of Latinity on Langland's part. "Code-Switching and Authority in Late Medieval England," *Neophilologus* 87 (2003): 476–78.

57. Joan Baker and Susan Signe Morrison read the permutation line in a manner evocative of the initial objections to the sterility of usury: "where Mede is concerned, we are dealing with a pattern based on exchange not reproduction, in which the good succeed only in reproducing or replicating themselves." "The Luxury of Gender: *Piers Plowman* and *The Merchant's Tale*," *Yearbook of Langland Studies* 12 (1998): 39 [31–63].

58. Kaye, *Economy and Nature*, pp. 121–25.

59. Raymond de Roover, "The Concept of the Just Price: Theory and Economic Policy," *Journal of Economic History* 18 (1958): 424 [418–34]. De Roover points out that opposition to Duns Scotus lasted into the fifteenth century ("Concept," p. 425).

60. Kaye, *Economy and Nature*, pp. 125–26.

61. Kaye, *Economy and Nature*, p. 132.

62. David Aers, "John Wyclif: Poverty and the Poor," *Yearbook of Langland Studies* 17 (2003): 69 [55–72].

63. Adams, "Piers's Pardon," p. 369.

64. Adams, "Piers's Pardon," p. 417.

65. Malcolm Godden, "Plowmen and Hermits in Langland's *Piers Plowman*," *Review of English Studies* n.s. 35 (1981): 129–63; Denise Baker, "The Pardons of *Piers Plowman*," *Neuphilologische Mitteilungen* 85 (1984): 464 [462–72].

66. Traugott Lawler, "The Pardon Formula in *Piers Plowman*: Its Ubiquity, Its Binary Shape, Its Silent Middle Term," *Yearbook of Langland Studies* 14 (2000): 118 [117–52].

67. Lawler, "Pardon Formula," p. 135.

68. Pearsall, "Langland's London," in *Written Work*, p. 193.

69. Simpson, "Spirituality and Economics," p. 92.

70. All biblical citations in English come from the Douay-Rheims translation in *The Catholic Comparative New Testament* (Oxford: Oxford University Press, 2005).

71. Prisons and prisoners appear elsewhere in the poem in key moments relative to charity and its relation to money. Mede "leteþ passe prisoners and paieþ for hem ofte" (B.III. 137), invoking the prisoners as an example of the abuse of money, like Coveitise's lending to the poor, which superficially resembles charity. The relief of prisoners is elsewhere a marker of charity or the lack thereof, as Pacience brings up prisoners when discussing pity and comfort (B.XIV. 168–78), and Charite himself visits prisons (B.XV. 182–83). We can see the link between charity and grace when "charite wiþouten chalangynge unchargeþ the soule, / And many a prison fram purgatorie þoru3 hise preieres he deliuereth" (B.XV. 344–45).

72. Janet Coleman, *Piers Plowman and the Moderni* (Rome: Edizioni di Storia e Letteratura, 1981), p. 139.

73. Janet Coleman, *Piers Plowman*, p. 138.

74. Schmidt, *Parallel-Text*, Indexical Glossary, p. 772, s.v. "chaffaren".

75. Wendy Scase, *Piers Plowman and the New Anti-Clericalism*, Cambridge Studies in Medieval Literature 4 (Cambridge, UK: Cambridge University Press, 1989), p. 97.

76. Schmidt reverses the order of "buggynge" and "sellynge" from the manuscripts for metrical reasons. He also notes that one C manuscript does use his order, and does not mark "buggynge and sullyng" (C.XXI. 236) as an emendation. (Schmidt, *Parallel-Text*, 2:457 n236). Both Kane and Donaldson's B-Version and Russell and Kane's C-Version list selling before buying.

77. Daniel F. Pigg, "Apocalypse Then: The Ideology of Literary Form in *Piers Plowman*," *Religion and Literature* 31.1 (1999): 108 [103–16].

78. Kathryn Kerby-Fulton, *Reformist Apocalypticism and "Piers Plowman,"* Cambridge Studies in Medieval Literature 7 (Cambridge, UK: Cambridge University Press, 1990), pp. 160–61.

79. Clopper, *Songes of Rechelesnesse*, pp. 287–89.

3   The *Mirour de l'Omme* and Gower's
London Merchants

1. John Gower, *The Complete Works*, ed. G. C. Macaulay, vol. 1 (Oxford: Clarendon Press, 1899–1902), p. liv. All citations of the *Mirour de l'Omme* (*MO*) in French and the *Vox Clamantis* (*VC*) in Latin are from this edition; *MO* is in vol. 1, and *VC* in vol. 4.

2. Derek Pearsall, "The Gower Tradition," in *Gower's* Confessio Amantis: *Responses and Reassessments*, ed. A. J. Minnis (Woodbridge, Suffolk: D. S. Brewer, 1983), p. 184 [179–97].

3. John Gower, *The Major Latin Works of John Gower: The Voice of One Crying and the Tripartite Chronicle: An Annotated Translation into English With an Introductory Essay on the Author's Non-English Works*, ed. and trans. Eric Stockton (Seattle: University of Washington Press, 1962); John Gower, *Mirour de l'Omme (The Mirror of Mankind)*, trans. William Burton Wilson, rev. Nancy Wilson Van Baak, foreword R. F. Yeager (East Lansing: Colleagues Press, 1992). All bracketed translations in Roman text come from these editions, which share Macaulay's line numbers. My own translations appear in bracketed italics.

4. Janet Coleman, *Medieval Readers and Writers: 1350–1400* (New York: Columbia University Press, 1981), p. 127; Jill Mann, *Chaucer and Medieval Estates Satire: The Literature of Social Classes and the* General Prologue *to the* Canterbury Tales (Cambridge: Cambridge University Press, 1973), pp. 99–102.

5. John Gower, *The Complete Works*, ed. G. C. Macaulay, vol. 1 (Oxford: Clarendon Press, 1899–1902), pp. lxviii–lxix.

6. For a more detailed discussion of mercantile overlap with Gowerian manuscript production, see Roger A. Ladd, "The London Mercers' Company, London Textual Culture and John Gower's *Mirour de l'Omme*," *Medieval Clothing and Textiles* 6 (2010): 132–36 [127–50].

7. Gardiner Stillwell, "John Gower and the Last Years of Edward III," *Studies in Philology* 45 (1948): 469 [454–71].

8. Thomas Aquinas, *Summa Theologica: Latin Text and English Translation, Introductions, Notes, Appendices and Glossaries*, 60 vols. (New York: McGraw-Hill-Blackfriars, 1975), II.2.77.4; pp. 38:227–29.

9. E. M. Carus-Wilson explains that the Gascony dominated the English wine trade by the thirteenth century, with England exchanging grain, fish, dairy, and cloth for Gascon wine. "The Effects of the Acquisition and of the Loss of Gascony on the English Wine Trade," *Bulletin of the Institute of Historical Research* 21 (1947), reprint in *Medieval Merchant Venturers: Collected Studies*, 2nd edn. (London: Methuen, 1967), 266–70 [265–78].

10. Pamela Nightingale, *A Medieval Mercantile Community: The Grocers' Company & the Politics & Trade of London 1000–1485* (New Haven: Yale University Press, 1995), p. 232.

11. Lester K. Little, *Religious Poverty and the Profit Economy in Medieval Europe* (Ithaca, NY: Cornell University Press, 1978), p. 36.
12. Paul Miller, "John Gower, Satiric Poet," in *Gower's* Confessio Amantis: *Responses and Reassessments*, ed. A. J. Minnis (Woodbridge, Suffolk: D. S. Brewer, 1983), p. 81 [79–105].
13. Gervase Matthew, *The Court of Richard II* (New York: W. W. Norton, 1968), p. 79.
14. W. Rothwell, "The Trilingual England of Geoffrey Chaucer," *Studies in the Age of Chaucer* 16 (1994): 47–49, 54 [45–67]. See also Kathleen E. Kennedy, "Changes in Society and Language Acquisition: The French Language in England 1215–1480," *English Language Notes* 35 (1998): 8 [1–17]. Bruce Harbert attests to Gower's Ovidian borrowing, and the relative difficulty of reading Gower, in "Lessons from the Great Clerk: Ovid and John Gower," in *Ovid Renewed: Ovidian Influences on Literature and Art from the Middle Ages to the Twentieth Century,* ed. Charles Martindale (Cambridge: Cambridge University Press, 1988), pp. 83–97. See also R. F. Yeager, "Did Gower Write *Cento?*" in *John Gower: Recent Readings,* ed. R. F. Yeager (Kalamazoo: Medieval Institute Publications, 1989), pp. 113–32; R. F. Yeager, "Learning to Speak in Tongues: Writing Poetry for a Trilingual Culture," in *Chaucer and Gower: Difference, Mutuality, Exchange,* English Literary Studies Monograph Series (Victoria: University of Victoria Press, 1991), p. 115 [115–29]; Joyce Coleman, "Lay Readers and Hard Latin: How Gower May Have Intended the *Confessio Amantis* to Be Read," *Studies in the Age of Chaucer* 24 (2002): 209–35.
15. Rothwell, "Trilingual England," p. 53.
16. See Laura Wright, "Bills, Accounts, Inventories: Everyday Trilingual Activities in the Business World of Later Medieval England," in *Multilingualism in Later Medieval Britain,* ed. D. A. Trotter (Cambridge, UK: D. S. Brewer, 2000), pp. 149–56; Lisa Jefferson, "The Language and Vocabulary of the Fourteenth- and Early Fifteenth-Century Records of the Goldsmiths' Company," in *Multilingualism in Later Medieval Britain,* ed. D. A. Trotter (Cambridge, UK: D. S. Brewer, 2000), pp. 175–211; Lisa Jefferson and William Rothwell, "Society and Lexis: A Study of the Anglo-French Vocabulary in the Fifteenth-Century Accounts of the Merchant Taylors' Company," *Zeitschrift für franzözische Sprache und Literatur* 107 (1997): 273–301; W. Rothwell, "Anglo-Norman at the (Green)Grocer's," *French Studies* 52 (1998): 1–16; W. Rothwell, "The French Vocabulary in the Archive of the London Grocers' Company," *Zeitschrift für franzözische Sprache und Literatur* 102 (1992): 23–41.
17. R. F. Yeager, "Gower's French Audience: The *Mirour de l'Omme,*" *Chaucer Review* 41.2 (2006): 111–37.
18. Coleman, *Medieval Readers and Writers,* pp. 18–19.
19. Kennedy, "Changes in Society," pp. 4–6. See also W. Rothwell, "English and French in England after 1362," *English Studies* 6 (2001): 542–46 [539–59]; Rothwell in "Trilingual England" characterizes Anglo-French

as "a major language of record for the purposes of government, law, and business" (p. 59), and points out that "time and time again from the late twelfth century into the fourteenth the mixing of the languages can be readily observed" (p. 66).

20. William Rothwell, "Aspects of Lexical and Morphosyntactical Mixing in the Languages of Medieval England," in *Multilingualism in Later Medieval Britain*, ed. D. A. Trotter (Cambridge, UK: D. S. Brewer, 2000), p. 213 [213–33].

21. Rothwell, "Aspects," in *Multilingualism*, pp. 222–26.

22. W. Rothwell, "The Legacy of Anglo-French: *faux amis* in French and English," *Zeitschrift für romanische Philologie* 109 (1993): 16–46. David Trotter argues for greater continuity between continental and Anglo-French than is often assumed, however, in "Not as Eccentric as It Looks: Anglo-French and French French," *Forum for Modern Language Studies* 39 (2003): 427–36.

23. Laura Wright, "Social Context, Structural Categories and Medieval Business Writing," *Bilingualism: Language and Cognition* 3.2 (2000): 124–25. She argues that "medieval business writing contains English content words..., a romance grammar, somewhat reduced and fossilised over time..., and considerable hybridisation" (p. 125). See also her "Bills, Accounts, Inventories," which among other things lists her tireless work on London business language on p. 152 n5.

24. Jefferson, "Language and Vocabulary," in *Multilingualism*, pp. 197–98. She also points out that "the French 'coustumier' and Latin 'custumarius' have very different meanings, including that of a customary tenant, a meaning which also existed in AF and ME" (p. 198).

25. Nightingale, *Medieval Mercantile Community*, pp. 38, 100; Carus-Wilson, "Effects of the Acquisition," p. 266; T. H. Lloyd, *The English Wool Trade in the Middle Ages* (Cambridge, UK: Cambridge University Press, 1977), pp. 207, 214.

26. Macaulay demonstrates how common this structure is throughout Gower's English and French poetry (1:xli).

27. Here I follow the medieval usage of the term "alien" rather than the modern term "foreign," because in the fourteenth century, to be "foreign" meant to be from outside London and without the franchise.

28. David Aers, "Representations of the 'Third Estate': Social Conflict and Its Milieu around 1381," *Southern Review* 16 (1983): 345 [335–49].

29. William Langland, *Piers Plowman: A Parallel-Text Edition of the A, B, C and Z Versions, Volume I: Text*, ed. A. V. C. Schmidt (London: Longman, 1995), line B.V. 240.

30. Charles Johnson, ed., *The De Moneta of Nicholas Oresme and English Mint Documents* (London: Thomas Nelson and Sons, 1956), p. 56.

31. Nightingale, *Medieval Mercantile Community*, pp. 91, 302.

32. Rothwell, "French Vocabulary," pp. 30–31.

33. Larry D. Benson, ed., *The Riverside Chaucer*, 3rd edn. (Boston: Houghton Mifflin, 1987), lines I.100–1.

34. Jill Mann, *Chaucer and Medieval Estates Satire: The Literature of Social Classes and the* General Prologue *to the* Canterbury Tales (Cambridge: Cambridge University Press, 1973), p. 100.

35. John Abernethy Kingdon, ed., *Facsimile of First Volume of Ms. Archives of the Worshipful Company of Grocers of the City of London, A. D. 1345–1463, Transcribed and Translated with extracts from The Records of the City of London and Archives of St. Paul's Cathedral,* Part 1 of 2 (London: Printed for the Company by Richard Clay and Sons, 1886), p. 22. Abernethy's translation is placed in brackets.

36. Mann, *Chaucer and Medieval Estates Satire,* p. 86.

37. A. H. Johnson, *The History of the Worshipful Company of the Drapers of London: Preceded by an Introduction on London and her Gilds up to the close of the XVth Century,* vol. 1. (Oxford: Clarendon Press, 1914), p. 205.

38. For more on this section of the poem, see Ladd, "London Mercers' Company," pp. 137–46.

39. John H. Fisher, *John Gower: Moral Philosopher and Friend of Chaucer* (New York: New York University Press, 1964), pp. 97–98.

40. Lloyd, *English Wool Trade,* p. 112; Nightingale, *Medieval Mercantile Community,* p. 228.

41. Rothwell, "French Vocabulary," p. 32; Louise W. Stone, William Rothwell, and T. B. W. Reid, eds., *Anglo-Norman Dictionary* [AND] (London: The Modern Humanities Research Association, 1977–), s.v. "governer;" *Middle English Dictionary* [MED], online edn. (Ann Arbor: University of Michigan Press, 2001), s.v. "governen."

42. Eileen Power's translation of this passage is instructive: "in England art thou born, but it is said that thou art by ill governed, for Trick, who hath much money, is made regent of thy staple; at his will he taketh it to foreign lands, where he purchaseth his own gain to our harm." Eileen Power, *Medieval People* (1924; repr. New York: Doubleday, 1954), p. 129.

43. Lloyd, *English Wool Trade,* p. 211.

44. Nightingale, *Medieval Mercantile Community,* pp. 236–37.

45. Mann, *Chaucer and Medieval Estates Satire,* p. 100.

46. Mann, *Chaucer and Medieval Estates Satire,* p. 101.

47. W. Rothwell, "The Missing Link in English Etymology: Anglo-French," *Medium Ævum* 60 (1991): 175 n6 [173–96].

48. Nightingale, *Medieval Mercantile Community,* p. 233.

49. Sylvia L. Thrupp, *The Merchant Class of Medieval London 1300–1500* (1948; repr. Ann Arbor: University of Michigan Press, 1962), p. 148.

50. Mann, *Chaucer and Medieval Estates Satire,* p. 104.

51. Jefferson, "Language and Vocabulary," in *Multilingualism,* p. 187.

52. Jefferson, "Language and Vocabulary," in *Multilingualism,* p. 190.

53. Jefferson, "Language and Vocabulary," in *Multilingualism,* pp. 190–91.

54. The English coinage was famously resistant to devaluation: see Carlo Cipolla, "Currency Depreciation in Medieval Europe," in *Change in*

Medieval Society: Europe North of the Alps, 1050–1500, ed. Sylvia L. Thrupp (New York: Appleton-Century-Crofts, 1964), p. 230 [227–36].

55. See, for example, Thomas Aquinas, *Summa Theologica*, II.2.77.3; p. 38:221.

56. Lisa Jefferson, ed., *Wardens' Accounts and Court Minute Books of the Goldsmiths' Mistery of London, 1334–1446* (Cambridge, UK: Boydell Press, 2003), pp. 62–67.

57. Langland, *Piers Plowman: A Parallel-Text Edition*, lines B.II. 214–15. This is close enough to a paraphrase to suggest that Gower had read *Piers Plowman*; this passage is quite similar in the A-text.

58. Langland, *Piers Plowman: A Parallel-Text Edition*, line B.XIX.187.

59. All biblical citations in English come from the Douay-Rheims translation in *The Catholic Comparative New Testament* (Oxford: Oxford University Press, 2005); the Latin text is taken from Alberto Colunga and Laurentio Turrado, eds., *Biblia Sacra iuxta Vulgatam Clementinam*, 4th edn. (Madrid: Biblioteca de Autores Cristianos, 1965).

60. Fisher, *John Gower*, p. 92.

61. Yeager, "Gower's French Audience," pp. 119–21.

62. *Confessio Amantis*, lines V. 2689–2696. John Gower, *Confessio Amantis*, ed. Russell A. Peck, 3 vols. (Kalamazoo: Medieval Institute Publications, 2000–2006).

4   The Deliberate Ambiguity of Chaucer's Anxious Merchants

1. Lee Patterson addresses this conflict directly in *Chaucer and the Subject of History* (Madison: University of Wisconsin Press, 1991), pp. 322–66.

2. Lines X.777–78. All references to Chaucer's poetry come from Larry D. Benson, ed., *The Riverside Chaucer*, 3rd edn. (Boston: Houghton Mifflin, 1987). Parenthetical references indicate both fragment and line number.

3. John Matthews Manly, *Some New Light on Chaucer: Lectures Delivered at the Lowell Institute* (1926; repr. New York: Peter Smith, 1951); Muriel A. Bowden, *A Commentary on the General Prologue to the Canterbury Tales*, 2nd edn. (1948; repr. New York: Macmillan, 1967); Jill Mann, *Chaucer and Medieval Estates Satire* (Cambridge, UK: Cambridge University Press, 1973). See also Edith Rickert, "Extracts from a Fourteenth-Century Account Book," *Modern Philology* 24 (1926–27): 111–19; 249–56. Laura C. and Robert T. Lambdin update Bowden in *Chaucer's Pilgrims: An Historical Guide to the Pilgrims in* The Canterbury Tales (Westport, CT: Greenwood Press, 1996), p. xii.

4. George Lyman Kittredge, *Chaucer and His Poetry* (Cambridge, MA: Harvard University Press, 1915), p. 156.

5. J. Stephen Russell, *Chaucer and the Trivium: The Mindsong of the Canterbury Tales* (Gainesville: University Press of Florida, 1998), p. 64.

6. Wight Martindale, Jr., "Chaucer's Merchants: A Trade-Based Speculation on Their Activities," *Chaucer Review* 26 (1992): 309 [309–16].

7. Kenneth S. Cahn, "Chaucer's Merchants and the Foreign Exchange: An Introduction to Medieval Finance," *Studies in the Age of Chaucer* 2 (1980): 81 [81–119].

8. See especially Bowden, *Commentary*, pp. 146–54; Mann, *Chaucer and Medieval Estates Satire*, pp. 99–03; Nancy Reale, "A Marchant Was Ther With a Forked Berd," in *Chaucer's Pilgrims*, pp. 93–07; Malcolm Andrew, ed., *Variorum Edition of the Works of Geoffrey Chaucer: Vol. II, The Canterbury Tales, Pt. 1 B, The General Prologue Explanatory Notes* (Norman: University of Oklahoma Press, 1993), pp. 249–67.

9. Reale, "A Marchant," in *Chaucer's Pilgrims*, p. 95.

10. Bowden, *Commentary*, p. 150.

11. Thomas A. Knott, "Chaucer's Anonymous Merchant," *Philological Quarterly* 1 (1922): 9–10 [1–16].

12. Reale, "A Marchant," in *Chaucer's Pilgrims*, pp. 95–96; Bowden, *Commentary*, p.150.

13. John Kenny Crane "An Honest Debtor? A Note on Chaucer's Merchant, Line A276," *English Language Notes* 4 (1966): 84 [81–85].

14. Derek Pearsall, *The Life of Geoffrey Chaucer: A Critical Biography* (Oxford: Blackwell, 1992), pp. 285–305; plates 3, 6–21. On historical merchants with forked beards, see Laura F. Hodges, *Chaucer and Costume: The Secular Pilgrims in the General Prologue* (Cambridge, UK: D. S. Brewer, 2000), pp. 80–86; plate 7.

15. Derek Pearsall argues that Chaucer expected readers to know his biography in the *House of Fame* (*Life of Geoffrey Chaucer*, p. 116).

16. Knott, "Chaucer's Anonymous Merchant," p. 9.

17. Laura F. Hodges, personal conversation at the 33rd International Congress on Medieval Studies, Kalamazoo, Michigan, 9 May 1998. See also her *Chaucer and Costume*, pp. 86–88.

18. H. Marshall Leicester, Jr., "Structure as Deconstruction: 'Chaucer and Estates Satire' in the General Prologue, or Reading Chaucer as a Prologue to the History of Disenchantment," *Exemplaria* 2 (1990): 246 [241–61].

19. Rodney K. Delasanta, "The Horsemen of the *Canterbury Tales*," *Chaucer Review* 3 (1969): 30–31 [29–36]; Reale, "A Marchant," in *Chaucer's Pilgrims*, pp. 95–96.

20. Mann, *Chaucer and Medieval Estates Satire*, p. 102.

21. Paul Strohm, *Social Chaucer* (Cambridge, MA: Harvard University Press, 1989), p. 89.

22. Loy D. Martin, "History and Form in the *General Prologue* to the *Canterbury Tales*," *English Literary History* 45 (1978): 10 [1–17].

23. Mann, *Chaucer and Medieval Estates Satire*, p. 102.

24. Bowden, *Commentary*, pp. 147, 151.

25. Crane, "Honest Debtor," pp. 83–84.

NOTES 181

26. Reale, "A Marchant," in *Chaucer's Pilgrims*, p. 96.

27. *Middle English Dictionary* [MED], online edn. (Ann Arbor: University of Michigan Press, 2001), s.v. "resoun."

28. The MED cites this passage to support "To proclaim" or "declare" (4a), but other meanings such as "to express" (6a) or "to concern (sth.)" would work here (s.v. "sounen").

29. Of the forty-four fifteenth-century witnesses to these lines, only three feature a *puncto* after line 276 ("solempnely"), and only two feature one after line 277 ("wynnyng"). London, British Library ms. Harley 1758 (Ha²) and Oxford, Bodleian Library ms. Laud Misc. 39 (Ld²) both feature full stops after both lines 276 and 277; Ha² (f. 3v) has a *puncto* at the end of every line in this passage, and Ld² has them after most lines. The third manuscript featuring line-end punctuation here is Oxford, Bodleian Library, Trinity College ms. 49 (To¹); punctuation for this witness shifts the phrasing of this passage considerably from the usual editorial choices. The manuscript evidence mandates neither my punctuation nor Benson's, and To¹ slightly supports my punctuation. Manuscript transcriptions and images all come from Elizabeth Solopova, ed., *The General Prologue on CD-ROM* (Cambridge, UK: Cambridge University Press, 2000).

30. Mann, *Chaucer and Medieval Estates Satire*, pp. 100–101.

31. John Reidy, "Grouping of Pilgrims in the General Prologue to the *Canterbury Tales*," *Papers of the Michigan Academy of Sciences, Art and Letters* 47 (1962): 600 [595–603].

32. Mann, *Chaucer and Medieval Estates Satire*, p. 100.

33. B. A. Park, "The Character of Chaucer's Merchant," *English Language Notes* 2 (1964): 167 [167–75].

34. Cahn, "Chaucer's Merchants," pp. 85–90.

35. Martindale, "Chaucer's Merchants," p. 312.

36. Cahn, "Chaucer's Merchants," pp. 101–2.

37 MED, s.v. "chevisaunce."

38. See also Lorraine Kochanske Stock, "The Meaning of *Chevyssaunce*: Complicated Word Play in Chaucer's *Shipman's Tale*," *Studies in Short Fiction* 18 (1981): 245–49.

39. Oscar E. Johnson, "Was Chaucer's Merchant in Debt? A Study in Chaucerian Syntax and Rhetoric," *Journal of English and Germanic Philology* 52 (1953): 51 [50–57]; Gardiner Stillwell, "Chaucer's Merchant: No Debts?" *Journal of English and Germanic Philology* 57 (1958): 192 [192–96]; Cahn, "Chaucer's Merchants," pp. 81–119.

40. Mann, *Chaucer and Medieval Estates Satire*, p. 102; Stillwell, "No Debts?" p. 195.

41. Mann, *Chaucer and Medieval Estates Satire*, p. 101.

42. Reale, "A Marchant," in *Chaucer's Pilgrims*, p. 97.

43. MED, s.v. "estatli."

44. Russell, *Chaucer and the Trivium*, pp. 63–64.

45. Bowden, *Commentary*, p. 153; Rickert, "Extracts," p. 256.

46. Karla Taylor, "Chaucer's Reticent Merchant," in *The Idea of Medieval Literature: New Essays on Chaucer and Medieval Culture in Honor of Donald R. Howard* (Newark: University of Delaware Press, 1992), p. 192 [189–205].

47. Gerald Morgan, "The Universality of the Portraits in the *General Prologue* to the *Canterbury Tales*," *English Studies* 58 (1977): 482–83 [481–93].

48. Benson, ed., *Riverside Chaucer*, pp. 814, 825.

49. Strohm, *Social Chaucer*, pp. 64–68.

50. Strohm, *Social Chaucer*, p. 29.

51. Paul Strohm, "The Social and Literary Scene in England," in *The Cambridge Chaucer Companion*, ed. Piero Boitani and Jill Mann (Cambridge, UK: Cambridge University Press, 1986), p. 10 [1–18].

52. Donald R. Howard, *Chaucer: His Life, His Works, His World* (New York: E. P. Dutton, 1987), p. 5.

53. Linne R. Mooney, "Chaucer's Scribe," *Speculum* 81 (2006): 98 [97–138].

54. Martin Stevens, "'And Venus Laugheth': An Interpretation of the *Merchant's Tale*," *Chaucer Review* 7 (1972): 118 [188–231].

55. Paul A. Olson, "The Merchant's Lombard Knight," *Texas Studies in Literature and Language* 3 (1961): 259–63.

56. David Wallace, *Chaucerian Polity: Absolutist Lineages and Associational Forms in England and Italy* (Stanford: Stanford University Press, 1997), pp. 294–95.

57. Olson, "Merchant's Lombard Knight," p. 259.

58. Olson, "Merchant's Lombard Knight," p. 262. See also Phillipa Hardman, "Chaucer's Tyrants of Lombardy," *Review of English Studies* n.s. 31 (1980): 172–78.

59. Rosalind Field, "January's 'Honeste Thynges': Knighthood and Narrative in the *Merchant's Tale*," *Reading Medieval Studies* 20 (1994): 39–41 [37–49].

60. Field, "January's 'Honeste Thynges,'" p. 43.

61. Robin Grove, for example, points out that the qualities January seeks "are not to be bought in a market-place." "*The Merchant's Tale*: Seeing, Knowing and Believing," *Critical Review* 18 (1976): 31 [23–38].

62. Christian Sheridan, "May in the Marketplace: Commodification and Textuality in the *Merchant's Tale*," *Studies in Philology* 102 (2005): 29–33 [27–44].

63. Patterson, *Chaucer and the Subject of History*, p. 330.

64. Patterson, *Chaucer and the Subject of History*, p 332.

65. Patterson, *Chaucer and the Subject of History*, p. 334.

66. Patterson, *Chaucer and the Subject of History*, p. 337.

67. On the ethos of fabliau, see Charles Muscatine, *The Old French Fabliaux* (New Haven: Yale University Press, 1986), pp. 73–104, 152; see also Joerg O. Fichte, "Chaucer's *Shipman's Tale* Within the Context of the French Fabliaux Tradition," in *Chaucer's Frame Tales: The Physical and the Metaphysical*, ed. Joerg O. Fichte (Cambridge, UK: D. S. Brewer, 1987), pp. 51–66.

68. Mark Allen characterizes the Host as urban and "bourgeois" in "Mirth and Bourgeois Masculinity in Chaucer's Host," in *Masculinities in Chaucer:*

Approaches to Maleness in the Canterbury Tales *and* Troilus and Criseyde, ed. Peter G. Beidler (Rochester, New York: D. S. Brewer, 1998), pp. 9–21.

69. In addition to Cahn, "Chaucer's Merchants," see V. J. Scattergood, "The Originality of the *Shipman's Tale*," *Chaucer Review* 11.3 (1977): 210–31; John McGalliard, "Characterization in Chaucer's *Shipman's Tale*," *Philological Quarterly* 54 (1975): 1–18.

70. Albert H. Silverman, "Sex and Money in Chaucer's *Shipman's Tale*," *Philological Quarterly* 32 (1953): 331 [329–36].

71. Our identification with her is further complicated by the tantalizing possibility that the tale was originally written for the Wife of Bath, who shares the wife's energy, concern with having a "buxom" husband, and apparent interest in clerks. On analogues' endings, see Larry D. Benson and Theodore M. Andersson, eds., *The Literary Context of Chaucer's Fabliaux: Texts and Translations* (Indianapolis: Bobbs-Merrill, 1971), pp. 275–337.

72. Silverman, "Sex and Money," p. 330.

73. Thomas Hahn, "Money, Sexuality, Wordplay, and Context in the *Shipman's Tale*," in Julian N. Wasserman and Robert J. Blanch, eds., *Chaucer in the Eighties* (Syracuse: Syracuse University Press, 1986), 242–44.

74. Bernard S. Levy, "The Quaint World of The Shipman's Tale," *Studies in Short Fiction* 4 (1967): 117 [112–18]; Janette Richardson, "The Façade of Bawdry: Image Patterns in Chaucer's *Shipman's Tale*," *English Literary History* 32 (1965): 306–7 [303–13].

75. Hahn, "Money, Sexuality," in *Chaucer in the Eighties*, p. 235.

76. Hahn, "Money, Sexuality," in *Chaucer in the Eighties*, p. 240.

77. Hahn, "Money, Sexuality," in *Chaucer in the Eighties*, p. 243.

78. Robert Adams, "The Concept of Debt in *The Shipman's Tale*," *Studies in the Age of Chaucer* 6 (1984): 93 [85–102].

79. Gerhard Joseph, "Chaucer's Coinage: Foreign Exchange and the Puns of the *Shipman's Tale*," *Chaucer Review* 17 (1983): 343–44 [341–57].

80. Joseph, "Chaucer's Coinage," p. 344. See also R. A. Shoaf, *Dante, Chaucer, and the Currency of the Word: Money, Images, and Reference in Late Medieval Poetry* (Norman, OK: Pilgrim Books, 1983), p. 173.

81. Karla Taylor, "Social Aesthetics and the Emergence of Civic Discourse from the *Shipman's Tale* to *Melibee*," *Chaucer Review* 39.2 (2005): 308 [298–322].

82. Taylor, "Social Aesthetics," p. 310.

83. Cahn, "Chaucer's Merchants," p. 116; John M. Ganim, "Double Entry in Chaucer's *Shipman's Tale*: Chaucer and Bookkeeping before Pacioli," *Chaucer Review* 30 (1996): 294–305.

84. Scattergood, "Originality," pp. 218–219.

85. Scattergood, "Originality," p. 213.

86. Gardiner Stillwell, "Chaucer's 'Sad' Merchant," *Review of English Studies* 20 (1944): 14 [1–18]; he cites Toulmin Smith, ed. *English Gilds: The Original Ordinances of More Than One Hundred Early English Gilds,* Early English Text Society o.s. 40 (London: N. Trübner & Co, 1870).

87. Wallace, *Chaucerian Polity*, p. 186.
88. Michael W. McClintock, "Games and the Players of Games: Old French Fabliaux and the *Shipman's Tale*," *Chaucer Review* 5 (1970): 112–36.
89. Scattergood, "Originality," p. 226.
90. See Ruth Huff Cline, "Four Chaucer Saints," *Modern Language Notes* 60.7 (1945): 480–82, and William P. Keen, "Chaucer's Imaginable Audience and the Oaths of *The Shipman's Tale*," *Topic* 50 (2000): 91–103.
91. Benson, ed., *Riverside Chaucer*, p. 912 n214. The note also points out the use of French in the *Summoner's Tale*, III.1832, 1838.
92. On the sources of the tale, see John Finlayson, "Chaucer's *Shipman's Tale*, Boccaccio, and the 'Civilizing' of Fabliau," *Chaucer Review* 36 (2002): 336–51; Peter G. Beidler, "Chaucer's French Accent: Gardens and Sex-Talk in the *Shipman's Tale*," in *Comic Provocations: Exposing the Corpus of Old French Fabliaux*, ed. Holly A. Crocker (New York: Palgrave Macmillan, 2006), pp. 149–61.
93. Lorraine Kochanske Stock, "La Vieille and the Merchant's Wife in Chaucer's *Shipman's Tale*," *Southern Humanities Review* 16 (1982): 337 [333–39].
94. Stock, "La Vieille," p. 336.
95. Helen Fulton, "Mercantile Ideology in Chaucer's *Shipman's Tale*," *Chaucer Review* 36 (2002): 320 [311–28].
96. Peter Spufford, *Power and Profit: The Merchant in Medieval Europe* (New York: Thames & Hudson, 2002), pp. 26, 34; see also map p. 26.
97. Cahn, "Chaucer's Merchants," p. 85.
98. Ganim, "Double Entry," pp. 299–302.
99. Taylor, "Social Aesthetics," pp. 301–10.

5   Mercantile Voices of the Early Fifteenth Century

1. Anthony Goodman, "The Piety of John Brunham's Daughter, of Lynn," in *Medieval Women,* ed. Derek Baker (Oxford: Basil Blackwell for The Ecclesiastical History Society, 1978), p. 356 [347–58].
2. Brian W. Gastle represents a notable exception here, in his article "Breaking the Stained Glass Ceiling: Mercantile Authority, Margaret Paston, and Margery Kempe," *Studies in the Literary Imagination* 36 (2003): 123–47.
3. *The Book of Margery Kempe*, ed. Sanford Brown Meech, pref. note Hope Emily Allen, notes and app. Sanford Brown Meech and Hope Emily Allen, Early English Text Society o. s. 212 (Oxford: Oxford University Press, 1940), pp. xlviii–li, 358–69.
4. Eleanora Carus-Wilson, "The Medieval Trade of the Ports of the Wash," *Medieval Archaeology* 6–7 (1962–63): 182 [182–201].
5. William Richards, *The History of Lynn*, 2 vols. (Lynn: W. G. Whittingham, 1812), pp. 1:417–18.

6. Charles Gross, *The Gild Merchant*, 2 vols. (Oxford: Clarendon Press, 1890), p. 2:151. While historians no longer accept Gross's interpretation of the "Gild Merchant," his collection of transcribed guild records remains highly useful.
7. Gross, *Gild Merchant*, pp. 2:151, 2:154.
8. Gross, *Gild Merchant*, p. 2:379
9. Gross, *Gild Merchant*, pp. 2:160–62.
10. Richards, *History of Lynn*, p. 1:459, cited in Gross, *Gild Merchant*, p. 2:162. Richards cites an eighteenth-century compilation of records of the guild, hence the postmedieval language.
11. Richards, *History of Lynn*, p. 1:460; Gross, *Gild Merchant*, p. 2:163.
12. Richards, *History of Lynn*, p. 1:460; Gross, *Gild Merchant*, p. 2:164.
13. Janet Wilson, "Communities of Dissent: The Secular and Ecclesiastical Communities of Margery Kempe's *Book*," in *Medieval Women in Their Communities*, ed. Diane Watt (Toronto: University of Toronto Press, 1997), pp. 175–76 [155–85].
14. Richards, *History of Lynn*, pp. 1:454–55.
15. Gross, *Gild Merchant*, p. 2:151.
16. Richards, *History of Lynn*, p. 1:426.
17. Richards, *History of Lynn*, p. 1:428.
18. Kempe, *Book*, p. 9. All citations from *The Book of Margery Kempe* are by page number from Meech and Allen. Their use of italics for expanded abbreviations has been regularized to Roman text.
19. On *The Book of Margery Kempe* as "an autobiographical saint's life" (p. 47), see Gail McMurray Gibson, *The Theatre of Devotion: East Anglian Drama and Society in the Late Middle Ages* (Chicago: University of Chicago Press, 1989), pp. 47–65. For use of the term "autohagiography," see Raymond A. Powell, "Margery Kempe: An Exemplar of Late Medieval English Piety," *The Catholic Historical Review* 89 (2003): 22 [1–23].
20. Deborah S. Ellis, "The Merchant's Wife's Tale: Language, Sex, and Commerce in Margery Kempe and in Chaucer," *Exemplaria* 2 (1990): 596 [595–626].
21. All bracketed glosses are from *The Book of Margery Kempe*, ed. Lynn Staley (Kalamazoo, MI: Western Michigan University for TEAMS, 1996).
22. Judith M. Bennett, "The Village Ale-Wife: Women and Brewing in Fourteenth-Century England," in *Women and Work in Preindustrial Europe*, ed. Barbara A. Hanawalt (Bloomington: Indiana University Press, 1986), p. 24 [20–36]. See also Maryanne Kowaleski, "Women's Work in a Market Town: Exeter in the Late Fourteenth Century," in *Women and Work in Preindustrial Europe*, ed. Barbara A. Hanawalt (Bloomington: Indiana University Press, 1986), p. 146 [145–64]. On husbands' role in registering brewing businesses, see Rodney H. Hilton, "Women Traders in Medieval England," *Women's Studies* 11 (1984): 148–52 [139–155]. On urban servants, see Barbara A. Hanawalt, *Growing Up in Medieval London: The Experience of Childhood in History* (Oxford: Oxford University Press, 1993), p. 174.

23. André Vauchez, *Sainthood in the Later Middle Ages* (*La sainteté en Occident aux derniers siècles du Moyen Age*), trans. Jean Birrell (1988; Cambridge, UK: Cambridge University Press, 1997), pp. 357–58.

24. Carolyn Walker Bynum, "Women's Stories, Women's Symbols: A Critique of Victor Turner's Theory of Liminality," in *Fragmentation and Redemption: Essays on Gender and the Human Body in Medieval Religion* (New York: Zone Books, 1992), p. 40 [27–51].

25. Richards, *History of Lynn*, p. 1:460; Gross, *Gild Merchant*, p. 2:163.

26. Clarissa Atkinson, *Mystic and Pilgrim: The Book and the World of Margery Kempe* (Ithaca: Cornell University Press, 1983), pp. 114–15. See also Lynn Staley, *Margery Kempe's Dissenting Fictions* (University Park: The Pennsylvania State Press, 1994), p. 74.

27. Atkinson, *Mystic and Pilgrim*, pp. 114–15.

28. Kempe, *Book*, pp. 309–110 n109.

29. David Hugh Farmer, *The Oxford Dictionary of Saints*, 4th edn. (Oxford: Oxford University Press, 1997), pp. 191–94. On Kempe's Franciscanism, see Atkinson, *Mystic and Pilgrim*, p. 139; Staley, *Margery Kempe's Dissenting Fictions*, p. 74.

30. Sheila Delany, "Sexual Economics, Chaucer's Wife of Bath, and *The Book of Margery Kempe*," *Minnesota Review* n.s. 5 (1975): 111 [104–15].

31. David Aers, *Community, Gender, and Individual Identity: English Writing 1360–1430* (New York: Routledge, 1988), p. 77.

32. Aers, *Community, Gender*, p. 80.

33. Deborah S. Ellis, "Merchant's Wife's Tale," p. 609. See also Deborah S. Ellis, "Margery Kempe and King's Lynn," in *Margery Kempe: A Book of Essays*, ed. Sandra J. McEntyre (New York: Garland, 1992), p. 152 [139–63].

34. Aers, *Community, Gender*, p. 95.

35. Karen A. Winstead, "The Conversion of Margery Kempe's Son," *English Language Notes* 32 (1994): 9 [9–13].

36. Winstead, "Conversion," p. 10.

37. Winstead, "Conversion," p. 12.

38. See Carus-Wilson, "Medieval Trade," p. 196; Gibson, *Theatre of Devotion*, pp. 53–59; Julia Bolton Holloway, "Bride, Margery, Julian, and Alice: Bridget of Sweden's Textual Community in Medieval England," in *Margery Kempe: A Book of Essays*, ed. Sandra J. McEntyre (New York: Garland, 1992), p. 209 [203–22].

39. All citations of the *Libelle* from Sir George Warner, ed., *The Libelle of Englyshe Polycye: A Poem on the Use of Sea-Power, 1436* (Oxford: Clarendon Press, 1926); all subsequent citations will be by line number.

40. Warner, ed., *The Libelle of Englyshe Polycye*, p. xxxix.

41. G. A. Holmes, "The 'Libel of English Policy,'" *English Historical Review* 76 (1961): 211–12 [193–216]. See also D. McCulloch and E. D. Jones, "Lancastrian Politics, the French War, and the Rise of the Popular Element," *Speculum* 58 (1983): 109 [95–138].

42. Holmes, "Libel," p. 216.
43. N. A. M. Rodger, "The Naval Service of the Cinque Ports," *English Historical Review* 111 (1996): 637–38 [636–51].
44. V. J. Scattergood, *Politics and Poetry in the Fifteenth Century* (London: Blandford Press, 1971), p. 92.
45. John D. Fudge, *Cargoes, Embargoes, and Emissaries: The Commercial and Political Interaction of England and the German Hanse 1450–1510* (Toronto: University of Toronto Press, 1995), p. 13.
46. On body metaphors for the state, and their regular inclusion of the merchant estates, see Scattergood, *Politics and Poetry*, pp. 268–71.
47. Warner, ed., *The Libelle of Englyshe Polycye*, p. 61 n34. See also D. Vance Smith, *Arts of Possession: The Middle English Household Imaginary*, Medieval Cultures 33 (Minneapolis: University of Minnesota Press, 2003), pp. 122–24.
48. William Langland, *Piers Plowman: A Parallel-Text Edition of the A, B, C and Z Versions, Volume I: Text*, ed. A. V. C. Schmidt (London: Longman, 1995), line B.V. 240.
49. John Gower, *Mirour de l'Omme*, in *Complete Works*, ed. G. C. Macaulay, vol. 1 (Oxford: Clarendon Press, 1899–1902), ll. 25270–71.
50. Warner, ed., *The Libelle of Englyshe Polycye*, plate III, facing p. 1.
51. Holmes, "Libel," p. 194.
52. Warner suggests that a "countertayle" was either half of a split tally-stick, or simply a counter-tale, a retort or reply; the Middle English Dictionary agrees, citing this line for the meaning "a counter blow, reprisal; retribution." *Libelle of Englyshe Polycye*, p. 78 nn390–95; *Middle English Dictionary* [MED], online edn. (Ann Arbor: University of Michigan Press, 2001), s.v. "countretaille."
53. Holmes, "Libel," pp. 199–200.
54. See Scattergood, *Politics and Poetry*, p. 335; Pamela Nightingale, *A Medieval Mercantile Community: The Grocers' Company & the Politics & Trade of London, 1000–1485* (New Haven: Yale University Press, 1995), p. 568.
55. John M. Ganim, "Double Entry in Chaucer's Shipman's Tale: Chaucer and Bookkeeping Before Pacioli," *Chaucer Review* 30 (1996): 294–305.
56. Scattergood, *Politics and Poetry*, pp. 332–35.
57. Barbara A. Hanawalt, "'The Childe of Bristowe' and the Making of Middle-Class Adolescence," in *"Of Good and Ill Repute": Gender and Social Control in Medieval England* (Oxford: Oxford University Press, 1998), p. 178 [178–201].
58. "The Childe of Bristowe," *Remains of the Early Popular Poetry of England*, ed. W. Carew Hazlitt, vol. 1 (London: John Russell Smith, 1864–66), pp. 1:110–31, ll. 19–21. Subsequent citations will be by line number with the abbreviation *CB*. References to the analogue "The Merchant and His Son," (*Remains*, pp. 1:132–52), recognizable by that poem's much longer line, will be specified with the abbreviation *M&S*.
59. Scattergood, *Politics and Poetry*, p. 331.

60. Hanawalt, "Childe," in *"Of Good and Ill Repute,"* pp. 194–95 n3.
61. Frances McSparrow and P. R. Robinson, eds., *Cambridge University Library Ff. 2. 38* (London: Scolar Press, 1979), p. vii.
62. Hanawalt, "Childe," in *"Of Good and Ill Repute,"* p. 194 n3.
63. Hanawalt, "Childe," in *"Of Good and Ill Repute,"* p. 179.
64. Hanawalt, "Childe," in *"Of Good and Ill Repute,"* pp. 180–86.
65. Hanawalt, "Childe," in *"Of Good and Ill Repute,"* p. 180.
66. Hanawalt, "Childe," in *"Of Good and Ill Repute,"* p. 182.
67. Hanawalt, "Childe," in *"Of Good and Ill Repute,"* p. 183.
68. MED, s.v. "treuth."
69. See Richard Firth Green, *A Crisis of Truth: Literature and Law in Ricardian England* (Philadelphia: University of Pennsylvania Press, 1999), pp. 1–40.
70. Hanawalt, "Childe," in *"Of Good and Ill Repute,"* p. 192.
71. Hanawalt, "Childe," in *"Of Good and Ill Repute,"* p. 182.
72. Note that the line between merchant and gentry was not as clear-cut in Bristol as elsewhere. Pamela Nightingale, "Knights and Merchants: Trade, Politics and the Gentry in Late Medieval England," *Past and Present* 169 (2000): 36–62.
73. John M. Bowers, *"The Tale of Beryn* and *The Siege of Thebes*: Alternative Ideals of *The Canterbury Tales*," *Studies in the Age of Chaucer* 7 (1985): 31–32 [23–50].
74. Bowers, *"Tale of Beryn,"* p. 35.
75. Bowers dates the manuscript "after the middle of the fifteenth century" (*Canterbury Tales: Fifteenth-Century Continuations*, p. 55), but suggests 1420 as a rough composition date. *The Canterbury Tales: Fifteenth-Century Continuations and Additions*, ed. John M. Bowers, TEAMS Middle English Texts Series (Kalamazoo, MI: Medieval Institute Publications, 1992), pp. 55–57. Subsequent references to the poem from this edition will be by line number.
76. Richard Firth Green, "Legal Satire in *The Tale of Beryn*," *Studies in the Age of Chaucer* 11 (1989): 43–62.
77. On the ubiquity of actual stepparents, see Hanawalt, *Growing Up in Medieval London*, pp. 89–108.
78. Jenny Adams, "Exchequers and Balances: Anxieties of Exchange in *The Tale of Beryn*," *Studies in the Age of Chaucer* 26 (2004): 291–93 [267–97].
79. Adams, "Exchequers," pp. 289, 291.
80. Geoffrey Chaucer, *The Riverside Chaucer*, ed. Larry D. Benson, 3rd edn. (Boston: Houghton Mifflin, 1987), line VI.656.
81. Adams, "Exchequers," p. 290.
82. Green, "Legal Satire," pp. 54–56.
83. Green, "Legal Satire," p. 62.
84. Jean E. Jost, "From Southwark's Tabard Inn to Canterbury's Cheker-of-the-Hope: The Un-Chaucerian Tale of Beryn," *Fifteenth-Century Studies* 21 (1994): 136 [133–48].
85. Adams, "Exchequers," p. 296.

86. Adams, "Exchequers," p. 297.
87. Adams, "Exchequers," p. 297.
88. Warner, ed., *The Libelle of Englyshe Polycye*, pp. x–xi.

6 The Mercers, Civic Power, and Charity in the York Cycle

1. Peter Meredith, "John Clerke's Hand in the York Register," *Leeds Studies in English* n.s. 12 (1981): 245 [245–71]. To clarify terminology: I use the term *cycle* to refer to the entire dramatic production of scriptural history, *play* for the sections performed by individual guilds, and *pageant* for the processional wagon on which those play were performed.
2. "The York Cycle," in *The Cambridge Companion to Medieval English Theatre*, ed. Richard Beadle (Cambridge, UK: Cambridge University Press, 1994), p. 88 [85–108]. See also Margaret Rogerson, "External Evidence for Dating the York Register," *REED Newsletter* 1 (1976): 4–5, and Richard Beadle and Peter Meredith, "Further Evidence for Dating the York Register (BL Additional Ms. 35290)," *Leeds Studies in English* n.s. 11 (1980): 51–58.
3. Jenny Kermode, *Medieval Merchants: York, Beverley and Hull in the Later Middle Ages* (Cambridge, UK: Cambridge University Press), p. 321.
4. Beadle, "The York Cycle," in *Cambridge Companion*, pp. 88–89.
5. See Christina M. Fitzgerald, *The Drama of Masculinity and Medieval English Guild Culture* (New York: Palgrave Macmillan, 2007).
6. David J. F. Crouch, "Paying to See the Play: The Stationholders on the Route of the York Corpus Christi Play in the Fifteenth Century," *Medieval English Theatre* 13 (1991): 101 [64–111].
7. Eileen White, "The Tenements at the Common Hall Gates: The Mayor's Station for the Corpus Christi Play in York," *REED Newsletter* 7 (1982): 14–24.
8. Peter Meredith, "The Fifteenth-Century Audience of the York Corpus Christi Play: Records and Speculations," in *"Divers Toyes Mengled": Essays on Medieval and Renaissance Culture/Etudes sur la culture européenne au Moyen Age et à la Renaissance: en hommage à André Lascombes*, ed. Michel Bitot, Roberta Mullini, and Peter Happé (Tours: Publication de l'Université François Rabelais, 1996), pp. 103–6 [101–111].
9. Crouch, "Paying," p. 100.
10. Margaret Rogerson, "A Table of Contents for the York Corpus Christi Play," in *Words and Wordsmiths, a volume for H. L. Rogers*, ed. Geraldine Barnes, John Gunn, Sonya Jensen, and Lee Jobling (Sydney: Department of English, University of Sydney, 1989), pp. 85–86 [85–90].
11. Alexandra F. Johnston and Margaret Rogerson, eds., *Records of Early English Drama: York [REED: York]*, 2 vols. (Toronto: University of Toronto Press, 1979), p. 1:109.

12. Johnston and Rogerson, eds., *REED: York*, pp. 1:95, 2:737; Margaret Dorrell [Rogerson], "The Mayor of York and the Coronation Pageant," *Leeds Studies in English* n.s. 5 (1971): 35–45.
13. Ruth Nissé, "Staged Interpretations: Civic and Lollard Politics in the York Plays," *Journal of Medieval and Early Modern Studies* 28 (1998): 434 [427–52].
14. John C. Coldewey, "Some Economic Aspects of Late Medieval Drama," in *Contexts for Early English Drama,* ed. Marianne G. Briscoe and John C. Coldewey (Bloomington: Indiana University Press, 1989), p. 87 [77–101].
15. Mervyn James, "Ritual, Drama and Social Body in the Late Medieval English Town," *Past and Present* 98 (1983): 4 [3–29].
16. For the distinction between the procession and the play see Martin Stevens, "The York Cycle: From Procession to Play," *Leeds Studies in English* n.s. 6 (1972): 37–61; James F. Hoy, "On the Relationship of the Corpus Christi Plays to the Corpus Christi Procession at York," *Modern Philology* 71 (1973–74): 166–68; Alexandra F. Johnston, "The Procession and Play of Corpus Christi in York after 1426," *Leeds Studies in English* n.s. 7 (1974): 55–62.
17. Richard L. Homan, "Ritual Aspects of the York Cycle," *Theatre Journal* 33 (1981): 315 [303–15].
18. Homan, "Ritual Aspects," p. 313.
19. D. M. Palliser, *Tudor York* (Oxford: Oxford University Press, 1979), p. 68.
20. Heather Swanson, "The Illusion of Economic Structure: Craft Guilds in Late Medieval English Towns," *Past and Present* 121 (1988): 31, 44 [29–48]; Sarah Beckwith, "Making the World in York and the York Cycle," in *Framing Medieval Bodies*, ed. Sarah Kay and Miri Rubin (Manchester: Manchester University Press, 1994), pp. 254–76. See also Sarah Beckwith's *Signifying God: Social Relation and Symbolic Act in the York Corpus Christi Plays* (Chicago: University of Chicago Press, 2001).
21. Beckwith, "Making the World," in *Framing Medieval Bodies*, p. 264.
22. Sarah Beckwith, "Ritual, Theater, and Social Space in the York Corpus Christi Cycle," in *Bodies and Disciplines: Intersections of Literature and History in Fifteenth-Century England*, ed. Barbara A. Hanawalt and David Wallace, Medieval Cultures 9 (Minneapolis: University of Minnesota Press, 1996), p 69 [63–86].
23. Swanson, "Illusion," p. 31.
24. Fitzgerald, *Drama of Masculinity*, pp. 30–31.
25. Gervase Rosser emphasizes this point in his review of Swanson's *Medieval Artisans: An Urban Class in Late Medieval England, The Economic History Review* n.s. 43.4 (1990): 741 [740–41].
26. Swanson, "Illusion," p. 38.
27. Kermode, *Medieval Merchants*, pp. 18–19.
28. Swanson, "Illusion," pp. 38–39.

29. Alan D. Justice, "Trade Symbolism in the York Cycle," *Theatre Journal* 31 (1979): 47–58.
30. Kermode, *Medieval Merchants*, p. 65.
31. Palliser, *Tudor York*, p. 62.
32. Palliser, *Tudor York*, p. 68.
33. Kermode, *Medieval Merchants*, p. 325.
34. Jennifer Kermode, "Urban Decline? The Flight from Office in Late Medieval York," *Economic History Review* s.s. 35 (1982): 190 [179–98]. Kermode notes elsewhere that choosing the mayor varied considerably over the fifteenth and sixteenth centuries, as the city experimented (in response to "election riots") with allowing the guilds to nominate aldermen, or nominate mayoral candidates to be chosen by the aldermen (*Medieval Merchants*, pp. 323–25).
35. Kermode, "Urban Decline," pp. 190–95; Palliser, *Tudor York*, pp. 60, 160; Maud Sellers, ed., *The York Mercers and Merchant Adventurers 1356–1917*, Publications of the Surtees Society 129 (London: Bernard Quaritch, 1918); P. J. P. Goldberg, *Women, Work, and Life Cycle in a Medieval Economy: Women in York and Yorkshire c. 1300–1520* (Oxford: Clarendon Press, 1992), p. 61.
36. Beckwith, "Ritual Theatre, and Social Space," in *Bodies and Disciplines*, pp. 72–73.
37. Johnston and Rogerson, eds., *REED: York*, pp. 1:110, 1:136, 1:143, 1:215–17, 1:245. Beadle, in his edition of the cycle, points out that this play remains lost, and that the register has no space for it to be inserted later. *The York Plays* (London: Edward Arnold, 1982), p. 460.
38. Johnston and Rogerson, eds., *REED: York*, pp. 1:47–48, 2:732 (their translation).
39. Erik Paul Weissengruber, "The Corpus Christi Procession in Medieval York: A Symbolic Struggle in Public Space," *Theatre Survey* 38 (1997): 120–21 [117–38]; Zina Petersen, "'As Tuching the Beyring of Their Torchez': The Unwholesome Rebellion of York's Cordwainers at the Rite of Corpus Christi," *Fifteenth-Century Studies* 22 (1995): 97 [96–108].
40. Meredith, "John Clerke's Hand," p. 255
41. Richard Beadle, "The York Cycle: Performances and the Bases for Critical Enquiry," in *Medieval Literature: Texts and Interpretations*, ed. Tim William Machan, Medieval and Renaissance Texts and Studies 79 (Binghamton, NY: Medieval and Renaissance Texts and Studies, 1991), p. 106.
42. "The Shipwrights' Craft," in *Aspects of Early English Drama*, ed. Paula Neuss (Woodbridge, Suffolk: D. S. Brewer, 1983), pp. 50–61. All lines of the play itself are cited from Beadle's edition, *The York Plays*, and subsequent citations will be by line number with the abbreviation *BA*.
43. Beadle, "Shipwrights' Craft," in *Aspects of Early English Drama*, p. 51.
44. Beadle, "Shipwrights' Craft," in *Aspects of Early English Drama*, p. 50.
45. Beadle, "Shipwrights' Craft," in *Aspects of Early English Drama*, pp. 56–57.
46. Fitzgerald, *Drama of Masculinity*, p. 64.

47. Beadle, "Shipwrights' Craft," in *Aspects of Early English Drama*, p. 54.
48. Beckwith, "Making the World," in *Framing Medieval Bodies*, pp. 258–59.
49. Kermode, "Urban Decline," p. 194. For the dating of the play fragment, see Beadle, ed., *The York Plays*, pp. 461–62.
50. Beadle, ed., *The York Plays*, "The Coronation of the Virgin" ll. 33–35. Subsequent citations will be by line number with the abbreviation *CV*.
51. Kermode, *Medieval Merchants*, p. 56.
52. Johnston and Rogerson, eds., *REED: York*, p. 1:24.
53. Johnston and Rogerson, eds., *REED: York*, p. 1:109.
54. Dorrell, "Mayor," p. 43.
55. Kermode, "Urban Decline," p. 189.
56. Kermode, "Urban Decline," p. 193.
57. Palliser, *Tudor York*, p. 65.
58. Alexandra F. Johnston and Margaret Dorrell, "The York Mercers and Their Pageant of Doomsday, 1433–1526," *Leeds Studies in English* n.s. 6 (1972): 11 [10–35].
59. Rogerson, "Table of Contents," pp. 86–87. The only comparable investments are the Tanners with 20s. for "The Fall of the Angels," the Cordwainers with 20s. for "The Agony in the Garden and the Betrayal," the Millers and Tilemakers with 16s. 4d. for "Christ before Pilate 2: the Judgment," and the Drapers, Tailors, and Hosiers with 20s. for "The Death of the Virgin."
60. Alexandra F. Johnston and Margaret Dorrell, "The Doomsday Pageant of the York Mercers, 1433," *Leeds Studies in English* n.s. 5 (1971): 30 [29–34].
61. Beadle, "The York Plays," in *Cambridge Companion*, p. 94, following Johnston and Rogerson, eds., *REED: York*, pp. 1:55–56.
62. Johnston and Dorrell, "York Mercers," p. 17.
63. Beadle, "The York Plays," in *Cambridge Companion*, p. 94.
64. Beadle, "The York Plays," in *Cambridge Companion*, p. 94.
65. Sellers, ed., *York Mercers*, pp. iv–v.
66. Alexandra F. Johnston, "English Guilds and Municipal Authority," *Renaissance and Reformation* n.s. 13 (1989): 75–76 [69–88].
67. Sellers, ed., *York Mercers*, p. 32.
68. Sellers, ed., *York Mercers*, p. 51.
69. Sellers, ed., *York Mercers*, p. 80.
70. Sellers, ed., *York Mercers*, p. 84.
71. Sellers, ed., *York Mercers*, p. 89.
72. Sellers, ed., *York Mercers*, p. 90.
73. Kermode, *Medieval Merchants*, p. 307; she cites Sellers, ed., *York Mercers*, p. 45.
74. Johnston and Rogerson, eds., *REED: York*, p. 1:56.
75. Johnston and Dorrell, "Doomsday Pageant," p. 34.
76. Clifford Davidson, *From Creation to Doom: The York Cycle of Mystery Plays* (New York: AMS Press, 1984), p. 182.
77. Clifford Davidson, "Northern Spirituality and the Late Medieval Drama of York," in *The Spirituality of Western Christendom*, ed. E. Rozanne Elder

(Kalamazoo, MI: Cistercian Publications, 1976), pp. 128, 142 [125–51]. See also Davidson, *From Creation to Doom*, pp. 178–81.

78. Beadle, ed., *The York Plays*, "The Last Judgement" ll. 101–12. Subsequent citations will be by line number with the abbreviation *LJY*.

79. Beadle, ed., *The York Plays*, p. 409 n129.

80. Johnston and Rogerson, eds., *REED: York*, p. 1:55.

81. Davidson, *From Creation to Doom*, pp. 179–80.

82. Matthew 25.35. All biblical citations in English come from the Douay-Rheims translation in *The Catholic Comparative New Testament* (Oxford: Oxford University Press, 2005).

83. Matthew 25.36.

84. Matthew 25.43.

85. Kermode, "Urban Decline," p. 189.

86. Kermode, "Urban Decline," p. 181.

87. Nissé, "Staged Interpretations," p. 427.

88. Rosemary Woolf, *The English Mystery Plays* (Berkeley: University of California Press, 1972), pp. 298–99. Woolf points out that the Seven Deadly Sins were common tropes in Continental treatments of the Judgment, and featured in the *N-Town* version.

89. Martin Stevens and A. C. Cawley, eds., *The Towneley Plays*, 2 vols., Early English Text Society s.s. 13 (Oxford: Oxford University Press for EETS, 1994), ll. 16–39. Subsequent citations will be by line number with the abbreviation *LJT*; all glosses come from Stevens and Cawley's glossary.

90. David Bevington and Pamela Sheingorn, "'Alle This Was Token Domysday to Drede': Visual Signs of Last Judgement in the Corpus Christi Cycles and in Late Gothic Art," in *Homo, Memento Finis: The Iconography of Just Judgment in Medieval Art and Drama*, Early Drama, Art, and Music Monograph Series 6 (Kalamazoo, MI: Medieval Institute Publications, 1985), 123 [121–45].

91. Stevens and Cawley, eds., *The Towneley Plays*, p. 2:639 n300.

92. Anthony Gash, "Carnival Against Lent: The Ambivalence of Medieval Drama," in *Medieval Literature: Criticism, Ideology & History*, ed. David Aers (New York: St. Martin's, 1986), p. 78 [74–98].

93. Martin Stevens, "The York Cycle as Carnival," *Fifteenth-Century Studies* 13 (1988): 454–55 [447—56].

94. Justice, "Trade Symbolism," p. 56.

95. Sellers, ed., *York Mercers*, p. 92.

96. Beckwith, "Ritual Theatre, and Social Space," in *Bodies and Disciplines*, p. 76.

Conclusion: From Finchale to York: Are Merchants Respectable by 1500?

1. For a discussion of the Weber thesis and its limitations, see Edwin S. Hunt and James M. Murray, *A History of Business in Medieval Europe 1200–1550*, Cambridge Medieval Textbooks (Cambridge, UK: Cambridge University Press, 1999), pp. 242–44.

BIBLIOGRAPHY

Primary Sources

Anglo-Norman Dictionary [AND]. Ed. Louise W. Stone, William Rothwell, and T. B. W. Reid. London: The Modern Humanities Research Association, 1977–.

Aquinas, Thomas. *Summa Theologiae: Latin Text and English Translation, Introductions, Notes, Appendices and Glossaries*. 60 vols. New York: McGraw-Hill-Blackfriars, 1975.

Benson, Larry D. and Theodore M. Andersson, eds. *The Literary Context of Chaucer's Fabliaux: Texts and Translations*. Indianapolis: Bobbs-Merrill, 1971.

Biblia Sacra iuxta Vulgatam Clementinam. Ed. Alberto Colunga and Laurentio Turrado. 4th edn. Madrid: Biblioteca de Autores Cristianos, 1965.

Bowers, R. H. "A Middle English Mnemonic Poem on Usury." *Mediaeval Studies* 17 (1955): 226–32.

The Canterbury Tales: Fifteenth-Century Continuations and Additions. Ed. John M. Bowers. TEAMS Middle English Texts Series. Kalamazoo, MI: Medieval Institute Publications, 1992.

The Catholic Comparative New Testament. Oxford: Oxford University Press, 2005.

Chaucer, Geoffrey. *The Riverside Chaucer*. Ed. Larry D. Benson. 3rd edn. Boston: Houghton Mifflin, 1987.

———. *Variorum Edition of the Works of Geoffrey Chaucer: Volume II, The Canterbury Tales, Part One B, The General Prologue Explanatory Notes*. Ed. Malcolm Andrew. Norman: University of Oklahoma Press, 1993.

Consitt, Frances. *The London Weavers' Company*. Vol. I. Oxford: Clarendon Press, 1931.

English Towns and Gilds. Translations and Reprints from Original Sources of European History, vol. 2, no. 1. Philadelphia: Department of History of the University of Pennsylvania, 1902.

Glare, P. G. W. *Oxford Latin Dictionary*. Oxford: Clarendon Press, 1982.

Gower, John. *Complete Works*. Ed. G. C. Macaulay. 4 vols. Oxford: Clarendon Press, 1899–1902.

———. *The Major Latin Works of John Gower: The Voice of One Crying and the Tripartite Chronicle: An Annotated Translation into English with an Introductory*

Essay on the Author's Non-English Works. Ed. and Trans. Eric Stockton. Seattle: University of Washington Press, 1962.

Gower, John. *Mirour de l'Omme (The Mirror of Mankind)*. Trans. William Burton Wilson. Rev. Nancy Wilson Van Baak. Foreword R. F. Yeager. East Lansing: Colleagues Press, 1992.

———. *Confessio Amantis*. Ed. Russell A. Peck. 3 vols. Kalamazoo, MI: Medieval Institute Publications, 2000–2006.

Jefferson, Lisa, ed. *Wardens' Accounts and Court Minute Books of the Goldsmiths' Mistery of London, 1334–1446*. Cambridge, UK: Boydell Press, 2003.

Johnson, Charles, ed. *The De Moneta of Nicholas Oresme and English Mint Documents*. London: Thomas Nelson and Sons, 1956.

Johnston, Alexandra F. and Margaret Rogerson. *Records of Early English Drama: York*. 2 vols. Toronto: University of Toronto Press, 1979.

Kempe, Margery. *The Book of Margery Kempe*. Ed. Sanford Brown Meech; Pref. note Hope Emily Allen; Notes and App. Sanford Brown Meech and Hope Emily Allen. Early English Text Society o. s. 212. Oxford: Oxford University Press, 1940.

———. *The Book of Margery Kempe*. Ed. Lynn Staley. TEAMS Middle English Texts Series. Kalamazoo, MI: Medieval Institute Publications, 1996.

Kingdon, John Abernethy, ed. and intro. *Facsimile of First Volume of Ms. Archives of the Worshipful Company of Grocers of the City of London, A.D. 1345–1463, Transcribed and Translated with extracts from The Records of the City of London and Archives of St. Paul's Cathedral*. Part 1 of 2. London: Printed for the Company by Richard Clay and Sons, 1886.

Langland, William. *Piers Plowman: The B Version. Will's Visions of Piers Plowman, Do-Well, Do-Better, and Do-Best*. Ed. George Kane and E. Talbot Donaldson. Rev. edn. London: Athlone Press, 1988.

———. *Piers Plowman: A Parallel-Text Edition of the A, B, C and Z Versions, Volume I: Text*. Ed. A. V. C. Schmidt. London: Longman, 1995.

———. *Piers Plowman: The C Version. Will's Visions of Piers Plowman, Do-Well, Do-Better, and Do-Best*. Ed. George Russell and George Kane. London: Athone Press, 1997.

———. *The Vision of Piers Plowman: A Critical Edition of the B-Text Based on Trinity College Cambridge Ms. B. 15. 17*. Ed. A. V. C. Schmidt. 2nd Edn. London: J. M. Dent, 1995.

———. *Piers Plowman: A Parallel-Text Edition of the A, B, C and Z Versions, Volume II: Introduction, Textual Notes, Commentary, Bibliography, and Indexical Glossary*. Ed. A. V. C. Schmidt. Kalamazoo, MI: Medieval Institute Publications, 2008.

Latham, R. E. *Revised Medieval Latin Word-List From British and Irish Sources*. London: Oxford University Press for the British Academy, 1965.

Latham, R. E. *Dictionary of Medieval Latin From British Sources*. London: Oxford University Press for the British Academy, 1975-.

Lewis, Charlton T. and Charles Short. *A Latin Dictionary*. Oxford: Clarendon Press, 1879.

Libelle of Englyshe Polycye: A Poem on the Use of Sea-Power, 1436. Ed. Sir George Warner. Oxford: Clarendon Press, 1926.

McSparrow, Frances and P. R. Robinson, eds. *Cambridge University Library Ff. 2. 38.* London: Scolar Press, 1979.

Medieval English Political Writings. Ed. James M. Dean. TEAMS Middle English Texts Series. Kalamazoo, MI: Medieval Institute Publications, 1996.

Middle English Dictionary [MED]. Online edn. Ann Arbor: University of Michigan Press, 2001.

Miller, Robert P. *Chaucer: Sources and Backgrounds.* Oxford: Oxford University Press, 1977.

Niermeyer, J. F. *Mediae Latinitatis Lexicon Minus—Lexique latin médiéval-français/ anglais—A Medieval Latin -French/English Dictionary.* Leiden: E. J. Brill, 1976.

The Oxford English Dictionary [OED]. Ed. J. A. Simpson and E. S. C. Weiner. 2nd edn. Oxford: Clarendon Press, 1989.

Reginaldo monacho Dunelmensi [Reginald of Durham]. *Libellus de vita et miraculis S. Godrici, Heremitæ de Finchale.* Ed. Joseph Stevenson. Publications of the Surtees Society 20. London: J. B. Nichols and Son, 1847.

Remains of the Early Popular Poetry of England. Ed. and Coll. W. Carew Hazlitt. Vol. 1. 1864. Repr. New York: AMS Press, 1966.

Sellers, Maud, ed. *The York Mercers and Merchant Adventurers 1356–1917.* Publications of the Surtees Society 129. London: Bernard Quaritch, 1918.

Smith, Toulmin, ed. *English Gilds: The Original Ordinances of more than one hundred Early English Gilds.* Early English Text Society o.s. 40. London: N. Trübner & Co, 1870.

The Towneley Plays. Ed. Martin Stevens and A. C. Cawley. 2 vols. Early English Text Society s. s. 13. Oxford: Oxford University Press for EETS, 1994.

The York Plays. Ed. Richard Beadle. London: E. Arnold, 1982.

Secondary Sources

Adams, Jenny. "Exchequers and Balances: Anxieties of Exchange in *The Tale of Beryn.*" *Studies in the Age of Chaucer* 26 (2004): 267–97.

Adams, Robert. "Piers Pardon and Langland's Semi-Pelagianism." *Traditio* 39 (1983): 367–418.

"The Concept of Debt in *The Shipman's Tale.*" *Studies in the Age of Chaucer* 6 (1984): 85–102.

———. "Some Versions of Apocalypse: Learned and Popular Eschatology in Piers Plowman." In *The Popular Literature of Medieval England.* Ed. Thomas J. Heffernan. Tennessee Studies in Literature 28. Knoxville: University of Tennessee Press, 1985. [pp. 194–236].

———. "*Mede* and *Mercede*: the Evolution of the Economics of Grace in the *Piers Plowman* B and C Versions." In *Medieval English Studies Presented to George Kane.* Ed. Edward Donald Kennedy, Ronald Waldron, and Joseph S. Wittig. Cambridge, UK: D. S. Brewer, 1988. [pp. 217–32]

Aers, David. *Chaucer, Langland and the Creative Imagination.* Boston: Routledge & Kegan Paul, 1980.

———. "Representations of the 'Third Estate': Social Conflict and Its Milieu around 1381." *Southern Review* 16 (1983): 335–49.

Aers, David. "The Good Shepherds of Medieval Criticism." *Southern Review* 20 (1987): 168–85.

———. *Community, Gender, and Individual Identity: English Writing 1360–1430.* New York: Routledge, 1988.

———. "Reading *Piers Plowman*: Literature, History, and Criticism." *Literature and History* 1 (1990): 4–23.

———. "Class, Gender, Medieval Criticism, and *Piers Plowman*." In *Class and Gender in Early English Literature: Intersections.* Ed. Britton J. Harwood and Gillian R. Overing. Bloomington: Indiana University Press, 1994. [pp. 59–75].

———. "John Wyclif: Poverty and the Poor." *Yearbook of Langland Studies* 17 (2003): 55–72.

Aers, David, and Lynn Staley. *The Powers of the Holy: Religion, Politics, and Gender in Late Medieval English Culture.* University Park: Pennsylvania State University Press, 1996.

Alford, John A. "Haukyn's Coat: Some Observations on *Piers Plowman* B XIV 22–7." *Medium Ævum* 43 (1974): 133–38.

———. "The Design of the Poem." In *A Companion to Piers Plowman.* Ed. John A. Alford. Berkeley: University of California Press, 1988. [pp. 29–65].

Allen, Mark. "Mirth and Bourgeois Masculinity in Chaucer's Host." In *Masculinities in Chaucer: Approaches to Maleness in the* Canterbury Tales *and* Troilus and Criseyde. Ed. Peter G. Beidler. Rochester, New York: D. S. Brewer, 1998. [pp. 9–21].

Althusser, Louis. "Ideology and Ideological State Apparatuses (Notes towards an Investigation)." In *Lenin and Philosophy and Other Essays.* Trans. Ben Brewster. New York: Monthly Review Press, 1971. [pp. 127–86].

Andrew, Malcolm. "Context and Judgment in the *General Prologue*." *Chaucer Review* 23 (1989): 316–37.

Aston, Margaret. "Corpus Christi and Corpus Regni: Heresy and the Peasants' Revolt." *Past and Present* 143 (1994): 3–47.

Atkinson, Clarissa W. *Mystic and Pilgrim: The* Book *and the World of Margery* Kempe. Ithaca: Cornell University Press, 1983.

Axton, Richard. "Gower—Chaucer's Heir?" In *Chaucer Traditions: Studies in Honour of Derek Brewer.* Ed. Ruth Morse and Barry Windeatt. Cambridge, UK: Cambridge University Press: 1990. [pp. 21–38].

Bainbridge, Virginia. *Gilds in the Medieval Countryside: Social and Religious Change in Cambridgeshire c. 1350–1558.* Studies in the History of Medieval Religion 10. Woodbridge, Suffolk: The Boydell Press, 1996.

Baker, Denise. "From Plowing to Penitence: Piers Plowman and Fourteenth-Century Theology." *Speculum* 55 (1980): 715–25.

———. "The Pardons of *Piers Plowman*." *Neuphilologische Mitteilungen* 85 (1984): 462–72.

Baker, Joan, and Susan Signe Morrison. "The Luxury of Gender: *Piers Plowman* and *The Merchant's Tale*." *Yearbook of Langland Studies* 12 (1998): 31–63.

Barron, Caroline M. *London in the Later Middle Ages: Government and People, 1200–1500.* Oxford: Oxford University Press, 2004.

Barron, Caroline M. Review of *Wardens' Accounts and Court Minute Books of the Goldsmiths' Mistery of London 1334–1446*, edited by Lisa Jefferson. *Urban History* 32 (2005): 173–75.

Beadle, Richard. "The Shipwrights' Craft." In *Aspects of Early English Drama*. Ed. Paula Neuss. Woodbridge, Suffolk: D. S. Brewer, 1983. [pp. 50–61].

———. "The York Cycle: Performances and the Bases for Critical Enquiry." In *Medieval Literature: Texts and Interpretations*. Ed. Tim William Machan. Medieval and Renaissance Texts and Studies 79. Binghamton: MRTS, 1991. [pp. 105–19].

———. "The York Cycle." In *The Cambridge Companion to Medieval English Theatre*. Ed. Richard Beadle. Cambridge, UK: Cambridge University Press, 1994. [pp. 85–108].

Beadle, Richard, and Peter Meredith. "Further Evidence for Dating the York Register (BL Additional Ms. 35290)." *Leeds Studies in English* n. s. 11 (1980): 51–58.

Beckwith, Sarah. "Making the World in York and the York Cycle." In *Framing Medieval Bodies*. Ed. Sarah Kay and Miri Rubin. Manchester: Manchester University Press, 1994. [pp. 254–76].

———. "Ritual, Theater, and Social Space in the York Corpus Christi Cycle." In *Bodies and Disciplines: Intersections of Literature and History in Fifteenth-Century England*. Ed. Barbara A. Hanawalt and David Wallace. Medieval Cultures 9. Minneapolis: University of Minnesota Press, 1996. [pp. 63–86].

———. *Signifying God: Social Relation and Symbolic Act in the York Corpus Christi Plays*. Chicago: University of Chicago Press, 2001.

Bennett, Judith M. "The Village Ale-Wife: Women and Brewing in Fourteenth-Century England." In *Women and Work in Preindustrial Europe*. Ed. Barbara A. Hanawalt. Bloomington: Indiana University Press, 1986. [pp. 20–36].

———. "Conviviality and Charity in Medieval and Early Modern England." *Past and Present* 134 (1992): 19–41.

Beidler, Peter G. "Chaucer's French Accent: Gardens and Sex-Talk in the *Shipman's Tale*." In *Comic Provocations: Exposing the Corpus of Old French Fabliaux*. Ed. Holly A. Crocker. New York: Palgrave Macmillan, 2006. [pp. 149–61].

Bevington, David, and Pamela Sheingorn. "'Alle This Was Token Domysday to Drede': Visual Signs of Last Judgment in the Corpus Christi Cycles and in Late Gothic Art." In *Homo, Memento Finis: The Iconography of Just Judgment in Medieval Art and Drama*. Early Drama, Art, and Music Monograph Series 6. Kalamazoo, MI: Medieval Institute Publications, 1985. [pp. 121–45].

Bowden, Muriel. *A Commentary on the General Prologue to the Canterbury Tales*. New York: Macmillan, 1948.

Bowers, John M. "*The Tale of Beryn* and *The Siege of Thebes*: Alternative Ideals of *The Canterbury Tales*." *Studies in the Age of Chaucer* 7 (1985): 23–50.

Burrow, J. A. "Lady Meed and the Power of Money." *Medium Ævum* 74.1 (2005): 113–18.

Butcher, A. F. "English Urban Society and the Revolt of 1381." In *The English Rising of 1381*. Ed. R. H. Hilton and T. H. Aston. Cambridge, UK: Cambridge University Press, 1984. [pp. 84–111].

Bynum, Caroline Walker. *Fragmentation and Redemption: Essays on Gender and the Human Body in Medieval Religion*. New York: Zone Books, 1992.

Cahn, Kenneth S. "Chaucer's Merchants and the Foreign Exchange: An Introduction to Medieval Finance." *Studies in the Age of Chaucer* 2 (1980): 81–119.

The Cambridge Companion to Medieval English Theatre. Ed. Richard Beadle. Cambridge, UK: Cambridge University Press, 1994.

Carus-Wilson, E. M. "The Effects of the Acquisition and of the Loss of Gascony on the English Wine Trade." *Bulletin of the Institute of Historical Research* 21 (1947). Repr. in *Medieval Merchant Venturers: Collected Studies*. 2nd edn. London: Methuen, 1967. [pp. 265–78].

Carus-Wilson, Eleanora. "The Medieval Trade of the Ports of the Wash." *Medieval Archaeology* 6–7 (1962–63): 182–201.

Cave, Roy C., and Herbert H. Coulson. *A Source Book for Medieval Economic History*. New York: Biblo and Tannen, 1965.

Cipolla, Carlo M. "Currency Depreciation in Medieval Europe." In *Change in Medieval Society: Europe North of the Alps, 1050–1500*. Ed. Sylvia L. Thrupp. New York: Appleton-Century-Crofts, 1964. [pp. 227–36].

———. *Before the Industrial Revolution: European Society and the Economy, 1000–1700*. 2nd edn. New York: W. W. Norton & Company, 1980.

Cline, Ruth Huff. "Four Chaucer Saints." *Modern Language Notes* 60.7 (1945): 480–82.

Clopper, Lawrence M. *"Songes of Rechelesnesse:" Langland and the Franciscans*. Ann Arbor: University of Michigan Press, 1997.

———. "Langland's Persona: An Anatomy of the Mendicant Orders." In *Written Work: Langland, Labor, and Authorship*. Ed. Steven Justice and Kathryn Kerby-Fulton. Philadelphia: University of Pennsylvania Press, 1997. [pp. 144–84].

Coghill, Neville K. "The Pardon of Piers Plowman." In *Style and Symbolism in Piers Plowman: A Modern Critical Anthology*. Ed. Robert J. Blanch. Knoxville: University of Tennessee Press, 1969. [pp. 40–86].

Coldewey, John C. "Some Economic Aspects of Late Medieval Drama." In *Contexts for Early English Drama*. Ed. Marianne G. Briscoe and John C. Coldewey. Bloomington: Indiana University Press, 1989. [pp. 77–101].

Cole, Andrew. "Scribal Hermeneutics and the Genres of Social Organization in *Piers Plowman*." In *The Middle Ages at Work: Practicing Labor in Late Medieval England*. Ed. Kellie Robertson and Michael Uebel. New York: Palgrave Macmillan, 2004. [pp. 179–206].

Coleman, Janet. *Piers Plowman and the Moderni*. Rome: Edizioni di Storia e Letteratura, 1981.

———. *Medieval Readers and Writers, 1350–1400*. New York: Columbia University Press, 1981.

Coleman, Joyce. "Lay Readers and Hard Latin: How Gower May Have Intended the *Confessio Amantis* to Be Read." *Studies in the Age of Chaucer* 24 (2002): 209–35.

Crane, John Kenny. "An Honest Debtor?: A Note on Chaucer's Merchant, line A276." *English Language Notes* 4 (1966): 81–85.

Craun, Edwin D. *Lies, Slander and Obscenity in Medieval English Literature: Pastoral Rhetoric and the Deviant Speaker.* Cambridge, UK: Cambridge University Press, 1997.

Crépin, André. "Human and Divine Love in Chaucer and Gower." In *A Wyf Ther Was: Essays in Honour of Paule Mertens-Fonck.* Ed. Juliette Dor. Liège: Liège Language and Literature, 1992. [pp. 71–79].

Crouch, David J. F. "Paying to See the Play: The Stationholders on the Route of the York Corpus Christi Play in the Fifteenth Century." *Medieval English Theatre* 13 (1991): 64–111.

Dane, Joseph A. "The Wife of Bath's Shipman's Tale and the Invention of Chaucerian Fabliaux." *Modern Language Review* 99 (2004): 287–300.

Davidson, Clifford. "Northern Spirituality and the Late Medieval Drama of York." In *The Spirituality of Western Christendom.* Ed. E. Rozanne Elder. Kalamazoo, MI: Cistercian Publications, 1976. [pp. 125–51].

———. *From Creation to Doom: The York Cycle of Mystery Plays.* New York: AMS Press, 1984.

Davidson, Mary Catherine. "Code-Switching and Authority in Late Medieval England." *Neophilologus* 87 (2003): 473–86.

Delany, Sheila. "Sexual Economics, Chaucer's Wife of Bath, and *The Book of Margery Kempe.*" *Minnesota Review* n.s. 5 (1975): 104–15.

Delasanta, Rodney K. "The Horsemen of the *Canterbury Tales.*" *Chaucer Review* 3 (1969): 29–36.

Donaldson, E. Talbot. *Piers Plowman, the C text and Its Poet.* 1949. New Haven: Yale University Press, 1966.

———. "Chaucer the Pilgrim." *PMLA* 69 (1954): 928–36.

———. "The Effect of the Merchant's Tale." In *Speaking of Chaucer.* New York: W. W. Norton, 1970. [pp. 30–45].

———. "Patristic Exegesis in the Criticism of Medieval Literature: The Opposition." In *Speaking of Chaucer.* New York: W. W. Norton, 1970. [pp. 134–53].

Dorrell, Margaret. "The Mayor of York and the Coronation Pageant." *Leeds Studies in English* n.s. 5 (1971): 35–45.

Du Boulay, F. R. H. *The England of Piers Plowman: William Langland and his Vision of the Fourteenth Century.* Cambridge, UK: D. S. Brewer, 1991.

Duby, Georges. *The Three Orders: Feudal Society Imagined.* Trans. Arthur Goldhammer. Chicago: University of Chicago Press, 1980.

Dyer, Christopher. *Standards of Living in the Later Middle Ages: Social Change in England c. 1200–1520.* Cambridge Medieval Textbooks. Cambridge, UK: Cambridge University Press, 1989.

Echard, Siân. *A Companion to Gower.* Woodbridge, Suffolk: D. S. Brewer, 2004.

Edwards, A. S. G., and Derek Pearsall. "The Manuscripts of the Major English Poetic Texts." In *Book Production and Publishing in Britain, 1375–1475.* Ed. Jeremy Griffiths and Derek Pearsall. Cambridge, UK: Cambridge University press, 1989. [pp. 257–78].

Ellis, Deborah S. "The Merchant's Wife's Tale: Language, Sex, and Commerce in Margery Kempe and in Chaucer." *Exemplaria* 2 (1990): 595–626.

————. "Margery Kempe and King's Lynn." In *Margery Kempe: A Book of Essays.* Ed. Sandra J. McEntyre. New York: Garland, 1992. [pp. 139–63].

Epstein, Steven A. *Wage Labor & Guilds in Medieval Europe.* Chapel Hill: University of North Carolina Press, 1991.

Erler, Mary C. "Fifteenth-Century Owners of Chaucer's Work: Cambridge, Magdalene College Ms. Pepys 2006." *Chaucer Review* 38.4 (2004): 401–14.

Farber, Lianna. *An Anatomy of Trade in Medieval Writing: Value, Consent, and Community.* Ithaca: Cornell University Press, 2006.

Farmer, David Hugh. *The Oxford Dictionary of Saints.* 4th edn. Oxford: Oxford University Press, 1997.

Fichte, Joerg O. "Chaucer's *Shipman's Tale* within the Context of the French Fabliaux Tradition." In *Chaucer's Frame Tales: The Physical and the Metaphysical.* Ed. Joerg O. Fichte. Cambridge, UK: D. S. Brewer, 1987. [pp. 51–66].

————. "'For couetise after cros; þe croune stant in gold': Money as Matter and Metaphor in *Piers Plowman.*" In *Material Culture and Cultural Materialism in the Middle Ages and the Renaissance.* Ed. Curtis Perry. Turnhout: Brepols, 2001. [pp. 57–74].

Field, Rosalind. "January's 'Honeste Thynges': Knighthood and Narrative in the *Merchant's Tale.*" *Reading Medieval Studies* 20 (1994): 37–49.

Finlayson, John. "Chaucer's *Shipman's Tale*, Boccaccio, and the 'Civilizing' of Fabliau." *Chaucer Review* 36 (2002): 336–51.

Fisher, John H. *John Gower: Moral Philosopher and Friend of Chaucer.* New York: New York University Press, 1964.

Fitzgerald, Christina M. *The Drama of Masculinity and Medieval English Guild Culture.* New York: Palgrave Macmillan, 2007.

Fudge, John D. *Cargoes, Embargoes, and Emissaries: The Commercial and Political Interaction of England and the German Hanse 1450–1510.* Toronto: University of Toronto Press, 1995.

Fulton, Helen. "Mercantile Ideology in Chaucer's *Shipman's Tale.*" *Chaucer Review* 36 (2002): 311–28.

Ganim, John M. "Double Entry in Chaucer's *Shipman's Tale*: Chaucer and Bookkeeping before Pacioli." *Chaucer Review* 30 (1996): 294–305.

Gash, Anthony. "Carnival Against Lent: The Ambivalence of Medieval Drama." In *Medieval Literature: Criticism, Ideology & History.* Ed. David Aers. New York: St. Martin's, 1986. [pp. 74–98].

Gastle, Brian W. "Breaking the Stained Glass Ceiling: Mercantile Authority, Margaret Paston, and Margery Kempe." *Studies in the Literary Imagination* 36 (2003): 123–47.

Gates, Barbara T. "A Temple of False Goddis: Cupidity and Mercantile Values in Chaucer's Fruit-Tree Episode." *Neuphilologische Mitteilungen* 77 (1976): 367–75.

Giancarlo, Matthew. "*Piers Plowman*, Parliament, and the Public Voice." *Yearbook of Langland Studies* 17 (2003): 135–74.

Gibson, Gail McMurray. *The Theater of Devotion: East Anglian Drama and Society in the Late Middle Ages.* Chicago: University of Chicago Press, 1989.

Godden, Malcolm. "Plowmen and Hermits in Langland's *Piers Plowman*." *Review of English Studies* n.s. 35 (1981): 129–63.

Goldberg, P. J. P. *Women, Work, and Life Cycle in a Medieval Economy: Women in York and Yorkshire* c. *1300–1520*. Oxford: Clarendon Press, 1992.

Goodman, Anthony. "The Piety of John Brunham's Daughter, of Lynn." In *Medieval Women*. Ed. Derek Baker. Oxford: Basil Blackwell for The Ecclesiastical History Society, 1978. [pp. 347–58].

Green, Richard Firth. *Poets and Princepleasers: Literature and the English Court in the Late Middle Ages*. Toronto: University of Toronto Press, 1980.

———. "Legal Satire in *The Tale of Beryn*." *Studies in the Age of Chaucer* 11 (1989): 43–62.

———. *A Crisis of Truth: Literature and Law in Ricardian England*. Philadelphia: University of Pennsylvania Press, 1999.

Gross, Charles. *The Gild Merchant: A Contribution to British Municipal History*. 2 vols. Oxford: Clarendon Press, 1890.

Grove, Robin. "*The Merchant's Tale*: Seeing, Knowing and Believing." *Critical Review* 18 (1976): 23–38.

Hahn, Thomas. "Money, Sexuality, Wordplay, and Context in the *Shipman's Tale*." In *Chaucer in the Eighties*. Ed. Julian N. Wasserman and Robert J. Blanch. Syracuse: Syracuse University Press, 1986. [pp. 235–49].

Hanawalt, Barbara A., ed. *Chaucer's England: Literature in Historical Context*. Minneapolis: University of Minnesota Press, 1992.

———. *Growing Up in Medieval London: The Experience of Childhood in History*. Oxford: Oxford University Press, 1993.

———. "'The Childe of Bristowe' and the Making of Middle-Class Adolescence." In *'Of Good and Ill Repute': Gender and Social Control in Medieval England*. Oxford: Oxford University Press, 1998. [pp. 178–201].

Hanna, Ralph. *London Literature, 1300–1380*. Cambridge, UK: Cambridge University Press, 2005.

Harbert, Bruce. "Lessons from the Great Clerk: Ovid and John Gower." In *Ovid Renewed: Ovidian Influences on Literature and Art from the Middle Ages to the Twentieth Century*. Ed. Charles Martindale. Cambridge, UK: Cambridge University Press, 1988. [pp. 83–97].

Hardman, Phillipa. "Chaucer's Tyrants of Lombardy." *Review of English Studies* n.s. 31 (1980): 172–78.

Helmholz, R. H. "Usury and the Medieval English Church Courts." *Speculum* 61 (1986): 364–80.

Hermann, John P. "Dismemberment, Dissemination, Discourse: Sign and Symbol in the *Shipman's Tale*." *Chaucer Review* 19 (1985): 302–37.

Hicks, Michael A. *Who's Who in Late Medieval England (1272–1485)*. London: Shepheard-Walwyn, 1991.

Hilton, Rodney. *Bond Men Made Free: Medieval Peasant Movements and the English Rising of 1381*. New York: Methuen, 1973.

———. "Women Traders in Medieval England." *Women's Studies* 11 (1984): 139–55.

John Hines, Nathalie Cohen, and Simon Roffey. "Iohannes Gower, Armiger, Poeta: Records and Memorials of his Life and Death." In *A Companion to Gower*. Ed. Siân Echard. Woodbridge, Suffolk: D. S. Brewer, 2004. [pp. 23–41].

Hodges, Laura F. *Chaucer and Costume: The Secular Pilgrims in the General Prologue.* Chaucer Studies 26. Cambridge, UK: D. S. Brewer, 2000.

Holloway, Julia Bolton. "Bride, Margery, Julian, and Alice: Bridget of Sweden's Textual Community in Medieval England." In *Margery Kempe: A Book of Essays*. Ed. Sandra J. McEntyre. New York: Garland, 1992. [pp. 203–22].

Holmes, G. A. "The 'Libel of English Policy.'" *English Historical Review* 76 (1961): 193–216.

Homan, Richard L. "Ritual Aspects of the York Cycle." *Theatre Journal* 33 (1981): 303–15.

Howard, Donald R. *Chaucer: His Life, His Works, His World*. New York: E. P. Dutton, 1987.

———. *The Idea of the Canterbury Tales*. Berkeley: University of California Press, 1976.

Hoy, James F. "On the Relationship of the Corpus Christi Plays to the Corpus Christi Procession at York." *Modern Philology* 71 (1973–74): 166–68.

Hunt, Edwin S. and James M. Murray. *A History of Business in Medieval Europe: 1200–1550*. Cambridge Medieval Textbooks. Cambridge, UK: Cambridge University Press, 1999.

James, Mervyn. "Ritual, Drama and Social Body in the Late Medieval English Town." *Past and Present* 98 (1983): 3–29.

Jefferson, Lisa. "The Language and Vocabulary of the Fourteenth- and Early Fifteenth-Century Records of the Goldsmiths' Company." In *Multilingualism in Later Medieval Britain*. Ed. D. A. Trotter. Cambridge, UK: D. S. Brewer, 2000. [pp. 175–211].

Jefferson, Lisa, and William Rothwell. "Society and Lexis: A Study of the Anglo-French Vocabulary in the Fifteenth-Century Accounts of the Merchant Taylors' Company." *Zeitschrift für franzözische Sprache und Literatur* 107 (1997): 273–301.

Johnson, A. H. *The History of the Worshipful Company of the Drapers of London: preceded by an Introduction on London and her Gilds up to the close of the XVth Century.* Vol. 1. Oxford: Clarendon Press, 1914.

Johnson, Oscar E. "Was Chaucer's Merchant in Debt? A Study in Chaucerian Syntax and Rhetoric." *Journal of English and Germanic Philology* 52 (1953): 50–57.

Johnston, Alexandra F. "The Procession and Play of Corpus Christi in York after 1426." *Leeds Studies in English* n.s. 7 (1974): 55–62.

———. "English Guilds and Municipal Authority." *Renaissance and Reformation* n. s. 13 (1989): 69–88.

Johnston, Alexandra F. and Margaret Dorrell. "The Doomsday Pageant of the York Mercers, 1433." *Leeds Studies in English* n.s. 5 (1971): 29–34.

———. "The York Mercers and their Pageant of Doomsday, 1433–1526." *Leeds Studies in English* n.s. 6 (1972): 10–35.

Jones, Terry. *Chaucer's Knight: The Portrait of a Medieval Mercenary.* Rev. Edn. London: Methuen, 1994.

Joseph, Gerhard. "Chaucer's Coinage: Foreign Exchange and the Puns of the *Shipman's Tale.*" *Chaucer Review* 17 (1983): 341–57.

Jost, Jean E. "From Southwark's Tabard Inn to Canterbury's Cheker-of-the-Hope: The Un-Chaucerian Tale of Beryn." *Fifteenth-Century Studies* 21 (1994): 133–48.

Justice, Alan D. "Trade Symbolism in the York Cycle." *Theatre Journal* 31 (1979): 47–58.

Justice, Steven. *Writing and Rebellion: England in 1381.* Berkeley: University of California Press, 1994.

Kaminsky, Howard. "Estate, Nobility, and the Exhibition of Estate in the Later Middle Ages." *Speculum* 68 (1993): 684–709.

Kaye, Joel. *Economy and Nature in the Fourteenth Century: Money, Market Exchange, and the Emergence of Scientific Thought.* Cambridge, UK: Cambridge University Press, 1998.

Keen, William P. "Chaucer's Imaginable Audience and the Oaths of *The Shipman's Tale.*" *Topic* 50 (2000): 91–103.

Keiser, George R. "Language and Meaning in Chaucer's *Shipman's Tale.*" *Chaucer Review* 12 (1978): 147–61.

Kennedy, Kathleen E. "Changes in Society and Language Acquisition: The French Language in England 1215–1480." *English Language Notes* 35 (1998): 1–17.

Kerby-Fulton, Kathryn. *Reformist Apocalypticism and "Piers Plowman."* Cambridge Studies in Medieval Literature 7. Cambridge, UK: Cambridge University Press, 1990.

Kerby-Fulton, Kathryn and Steven Justice. "Scribe D and the Marketing of Ricardian Literature." In *The Medieval Professional Reader at Work: Evidence from Manuscripts of Chaucer, Langland, Kempe, and Gower.* Ed. Kathryn Kerby-Fulton and Maidie Hilmo. Victoria, BC: English Literary Studies, University of Victoria, 2001. [pp. 217–37].

Kermode, Jennifer I. "Urban Decline? The Flight from Office in Late Medieval York." *Economic History Review* s. s. 35 (1982): 179–98.

Kermode, Jenny. *Medieval Merchants: York, Beverly, and Hull in the Later Middle Ages.* Cambridge, UK: Cambridge University Press, 1998.

Kindrick, Robert L. "The Unknightly Knight: Anti-Chivalric Satire in Fourteenth and Fifteenth-Century English Literature." Ph. D. diss., University of Texas-Austin, 1971.

King, Pamela. "The Bolton Hours and the York Plays." Paper presented at the 31st International Congress on Medieval Studies, Kalamazoo, Michigan, May 9, 1996.

Kirk, Elizabeth D. "Chaucer and His English Contemporaries." In *Geoffrey Chaucer: A Collection of Original Articles.* Ed. George D. Economou. New York: McGraw Hill, 1975. [pp. 111–27].

Kittredge, George Lyman. *Chaucer and His Poetry.* Cambridge, MA: Harvard University Press, 1915.

Knott, Thomas A. "Chaucer's Anonymous Merchant." *Philological Quarterly* 1 (1922): 1–16.

Kowaleski, Maryanne. "Women's Work in a Market Town: Exeter in the Late Fourteenth Century." In *Women and Work in Preindustrial Europe.* Ed. Barbara A. Hanawalt. Bloomington: Indiana University Press, 1986. [pp. 145–64].

Ladd, Roger A. "Margery Kempe and her Mercantile Mysticism." *Fifteenth-Century Studies* 26 (2001): 121–41.

———. "The Mercantile (Mis)Reader in *The Canterbury Tales.*" *Studies in Philology* 99 (2002): 17–32.

———. "The London Mercers' Company, London Textual Culture, and John Gower's *Mirour de l'Omme.*" *Medieval Clothing and Textiles* 6 (2010): 127–50.

Lambdin, Laura C., and Robert T. Lambdin, eds. *Chaucer's Pilgrims: An Historical Guide to the Pilgrims in* The Canterbury Tales. Westport, CT: Greenwood Press, 1996.

Lassahn, Nicole. "Literary Representations of History in Fourteenth Century England: Shared Technique and Divergent Practice in Chaucer and Langland." *Essays in Medieval Studies* 17 (2001): 49–64.

Lawler, Traugott. "The Pardon Formula in *Piers Plowman*: Its Ubiquity, Its Binary Shape, Its Silent Middle Term." *Yearbook of Langland Studies* 14 (2000): 117–52.

Lees, Clare A. "Gender and Exchange in *Piers Plowman.*" In *Class and Gender in Early English Literature: Intersections.* Ed. Britton J. Harwood and Gillian R. Overing. Bloomington: Indiana University Press, 1994. [pp. 112–30].

Leicester, H. Marshall, Jr. "Structure as Deconstruction: 'Chaucer and Estates Satire' in the General Prologue, or Reading Chaucer as a Prologue to the History of Disenchantment." *Exemplaria* 2 (1990): 241–61.

Levy, Bernard S. "The Quaint World of *The Shipman's Tale.*" *Studies in Short Fiction* 4 (1967): 112–18.

Little, Lester K. *Religious Poverty and the Profit Economy in Medieval Europe.* Ithaca: Cornell University Press, 1978.

Lloyd, T. H. *The English Wool Trade in the Middle Ages.* Cambridge, UK: Cambridge University Press, 1977.

Maguire, Stella. "The Significance of Haukyn, *Activa Vita*, in *Piers Plowman.*" In *Style and Symbolism in Piers Plowman: A Modern Critical Anthology.* Ed. Robert J. Blanch. Knoxville: University of Tennessee Press, 1969. [pp. 194–208].

Manly, John Matthews. *Some New Light on Chaucer: Lectures delivered at the Lowell Institute.* 1926. Repr. New York: Peter Smith, 1951.

Mann, Jill. *Chaucer and Medieval Estates Satire: The Literature of Social Classes and the* General Prologue *of the* Canterbury Tales. Cambridge, UK: Cambridge University Press, 1973.

Martin, Loy D. "History and Form in the General Prologue to the *Canterbury Tales.*" *English Literary History* 45 (1978): 1–17.

Martindale, Wight Jr. "Chaucer's Merchants: A Trade-Based Speculation on Their Activities." *Chaucer Review* 26 (1992): 309–16.

Masschaele, James. *Peasants, Merchants, and Markets: Inland Trade in Medieval England, 1150–1350.* New York: St. Martin's Press, 1997.

Matthew, Gervase. *The Court of Richard II*. New York: W. W. Norton, 1968.

McClintock, Michael W. "Games and the Players of Games: Old French Fabliaux and the *Shipman's Tale*." *Chaucer Review* 5 (1970): 112–36.

McCulloch, D., and E. D. Jones. "Lancastrian Politics, the French War, and the Rise of the Popular Element." *Speculum* 58 (1983): 95–138.

McGalliard, John. "Characterization in Chaucer's *Shipman's Tale*." *Philological Quarterly* 54 (1975): 1–18.

McRee, Ben R. "Charity and Gild Solidarity in Late Medieval England." *Journal of British Studies* 32 (1993): 195–225.

Meredith, Peter. "John Clerke's Hand in the York Register." *Leeds Studies in English* n.s. 12 (1981): 245–71.

———. "The Fifteenth-Century Audience of the York Corpus Christi Play: Records and Speculations." In *"Divers Toyes Mengled": Essays on Medieval and Renaissance Culture/Etudes sur la culture européenne au Moyen Age et à la Renaissance: en hommage à André Lascombes*. Ed. Michel Bitot, Roberta Mullini, and Peter Happé. Tours: Publication de l'Université François Rabelais, 1996. [pp. 101–11].

Middleton, Anne. "Acts of Vagrancy: The C Version 'Autobiography' and the Statute of 1388." In *Written Work: Langland, Labor, and Authorship*. Ed. Steven Justice and Kathryn Kerby-Fulton. The Middle Ages Series. Philadelphia: University of Pennsylvania Press, 1997. [pp. 208–317].

Miller, Edward, and John Hatcher. *Medieval England: Towns, Commerce and Crafts, 1086–1348*. London: Longman, 1995.

Miller, Martyn J. "Meed, Mercede, and Mercy: Langland's Grammatical Metaphor and Its Relation to *Piers Plowman* as a Whole." *Medieval Perspectives* 9 (1994): 74–75.

Miller, Paul. "John Gower, Satiric Poet." In *Gower's* Confessio Amantis: *Responses and Reassessments*. Ed. A. J. Minnis. Woodbridge, Suffolk: D. S. Brewer, 1983. [pp. 79–105].

Mooney, Linne R. "More Manuscripts Written by a Chaucer Scribe." *Chaucer Review* 30.4 (1996): 401–7.

———. "Chaucer's Scribe." *Speculum* 81 (2006): 97–138.

———. "Some New Light on Thomas Hoccleve." *Studies in the Age of Chaucer* 29 (2007): 293–340.

Morgan, Gerald. "The Universality of the Portraits in the *General Prologue* to the *Canterbury Tales*." *English Studies* 58 (1977): 481–93.

Muscatine, Charles. *The Old French Fabliaux*. New Haven: Yale University Press, 1986.

Myers, A. R. *London in the Age of Chaucer*. Norman, Oklahoma: University of Oklahoma Press, 1972.

Newhauser, Richard. *The Early History of Greed: The Sin of Avarice in Early Medieval Thought and Literature*. Cambridge, UK: Cambridge University Press, 2000.

Nightingale, Pamela. *A Medieval Mercantile Community: The Grocers' Company & the Politics & Trade of London 1000–1485*. New Haven: Yale University Press, 1995.

————. "Knights and Merchants: Trade, Politics and the Gentry in Late Medieval England." *Past and Present* 169 (2000): 36–62.

Nissé, Ruth. "Staged Interpretations: Civic and Lollard Politics in the York Plays." *Journal of Medieval and Early Modern Studies* 28 (1998): 427–52.

Noonan, John T. *The Scholastic Analysis of Usury*. Cambridge, MA: Harvard University Press, 1957.

Olson, Paul A. "The Merchant's Lombard Knight." *Texas Studies in Literature and Language* 3 (1961): 259–63.

Ormrod, W. M. "The Peasants' Revolt and the Government of England." *Journal of British Studies* 20 (1990): 1–30.

Palliser, D[avid] M. *Tudor York*. Oxford: Oxford University Press, 1979.

————. "Civic Mentality and the Environment in Tudor York." *Northern History* 18 (1982): 78–115.

Pantin, W. A. *The English Church in the Fourteenth Century*. Medieval Academy Reprints for Teaching 5. 1955. Repr. Toronto: University of Toronto Press, 1980.

Park, B. A. "The Character of Chaucer's Merchant." *English Language Notes* 1 (1963): 167–75.

Patterson, Lee. *Chaucer and the Subject of History*. Madison: University of Wisconsin Press, 1991.

————. "Chaucer's Pardoner on the Couch: Psyche and Clio in Medieval Literary Studies." *Speculum* 76 (2001): 638–80.

Pearsall, Derek. "The Gower Tradition." In *Gower's* Confessio Amantis: *Responses and Reassessments*. Ed. A. J. Minnis. Woodbridge, Suffolk: D. S. Brewer, 1983. [pp. 179–97].

————. *The Life of Geoffrey Chaucer: A Critical Biography*. Oxford: Blackwell, 1992.

————. "Langland's London." In *Written Work: Langland, Labor, and Authorship*. Ed. Steven Justice and Kathryn Kerby-Fulton. Philadelphia: University of Pennsylvania Press, 1997. [pp. 185–207].

Peter, John. *Complaint and Satire in Early English Literature*. Oxford: Clarendon Press, 1956.

Petersen, Zina. "'As Tuching the Beyring of Their Torchez': The Unwholesome Rebellion of York's Cordwainers at the Rite of Corpus Christi." *Fifteenth-Century Studies* 22 (1995): 96–108.

Pigg, Daniel F. "Apocalypse Then: The Ideology of Literary Form in *Piers Plowman*." *Religion and Literature* 31.1 (1999): 103–16.

Pirenne, Henri. *Economic and Social History of Medieval Europe*. Trans. I. E. Clegg. 1933. Repr. New York: Harcourt, Brace & World, Inc., 1937.

Pounds, N. J. G. *An Economic History of Medieval Europe*. New York: Longman, 1974.

Powell, Raymond A. "Margery Kempe: An Exemplar of Late Medieval English Piety." *The Catholic Historical Review* 89 (2003): 1–23.

Power, Eileen. *Medieval People*. 1924. Repr. New York: Doubleday, 1954.

Reale, Nancy M. "A Marchant Was Ther With a Forked Berd." In *Chaucer's Pilgrims: An Historical Guide to the Pilgrims in* The Canterbury Tales. Ed. Laura

C. Lambdin and Robert T. Lambdin. Westport, CT: Greenwood Press, 1996. [pp. 93–107].

Reidy, John. "Grouping of Pilgrims in the General Prologue to the *Canterbury Tales*." *Papers of the Michigan Academy of Sciences, Art and Letters* 47 (1962): 595–603.

Richards, William. *The History of Lynn, Civil, Ecclesiastical, Political, Commercial, Biographical, Municipal, and Military, from the Earliest Accounts to the Present Time*. 2 vols. Lynn: W. G. Whittingham, 1812.

Richardson, Janette. "The Façade of Bawdry: Image Patterns in Chaucer's *Shipman's Tale*." *English Literary History* 32 (1965): 303–13.

Rickert, Edith. "Extracts from a Fourteenth-Century Account Book." *Modern Philology* 24 (1926–27): 111–19; 249–56.

Robertson, D. W. Jr. *A Preface to Chaucer: Studies in Medieval Perspectives*. Princeton: Princeton University Press, 1962.

Roberson, Kellie. *The Laborer's Two Bodies: Literary and Legal Production in Britain, 1350–1500*. New York: Palgrave Macmillan, 2006.

Rodger, N. A. M. "The Naval Service of the Cinque Ports." *English Historical Review* 111 (1996): 636–51.

Rogerson, Margaret. "External Evidence for Dating the York Register." *REED Newsletter* 1 (1976): 4–5.

———. "A Table of Contents for the York Corpus Christi Play." In *Words and Wordsmiths, a volume for H. L. Rogers*. Ed. Geraldine Barnes, John Gunn, Sonya Jensen, and Lee Jobling. Sydney: Department of English, University of Sydney, 1989. [pp. 85–90].

de Roover, Raymond. "The Concept of the Just Price: Theory and Economic Policy." *Journal of Economic History* 18 (1958): 418–34.

Rosser, Gervase. Review of *Medieval Artisans: An Urban Class in Late Medieval England*, by Heather Swanson. *Economic History Review* n. s. 43.4 (1990): 740–41.

Rothwell, W. "The Missing Link in English Etymology: Anglo-French." *Medium Ævum* 60 (1991): 173–96.

———. "The French Vocabulary in the Archive of the London Grocers' Company." *Zeitschrift für französözische Sprache und Literatur* 102 (1992): 23–41.

———. "The Legacy of Anglo-French: *faux amis* in French and English." *Zeitschrift für romanische Philologie* 109 (1993): 16–46.

———. "The Trilingual England of Geoffrey Chaucer." *Studies in the Age of Chaucer* 16 (1994): 45–67.

———. "Anglo-Norman at the (Green)Grocer's." *French Studies* 52 (1998): 1–16.

———. "Aspects of Lexical and Morphosyntactical Mixing in the Languages of Medieval England." In *Multilingualism in Later Medieval Britain*. Ed. D. A. Trotter. Cambridge, UK: D. S. Brewer, 2000. [pp. 213 33].

———. "English and French in England after 1362." *English Studies* 6 (2001): 539–59.

Russell, J. Stephen. *Chaucer and the Trivium: The Mindsong of the Canterbury Tales*. Gainesville: University Press of Florida, 1998.

Scanlon, Larry. *Narrative, Authority, and Power: The Medieval Exemplum and the Chaucerian Tradition.* Cambridge, UK: Cambridge University Press, 1994.

Scase, Wendy. *Piers Plowman and the New Anti-Clericalism.* Cambridge Studies in Medieval Literature 4. Cambridge, UK: Cambridge University Press, 1989.

Scattergood, V. J. *Politics and Poetry in the Fifteenth Century.* London: Blandford Press, 1971.

———. "The Originality of the *Shipman's Tale*." *Chaucer Review* 11 (1977): 210–31.

Shaw, Judith Davis. "*Lust* and *Lore* in Gower and Chaucer." *Chaucer Review* 19 (1984): 110–22.

Sheridan, Christian. "May in the Marketplace: Commodification and Textuality in the *Merchant's Tale*." *Studies in Philology* 102 (2005): 27–44.

Shoaf, R. A. *Dante, Chaucer, and the Currency of the Word: Money, Images, and Reference in Late Medieval Poetry.* Norman, Oklahoma: Pilgrim Books, 1983.

Silverman, Albert H. "Sex and Money in Chaucer's *Shipman's Tale*." *Philological Quarterly* 32 (1953): 329–36.

Simpson, James. "Spirituality and Economics in Passūs 1–7 of the B Text." *Yearbook of Langland Studies* 1 (1987): 83–103.

Smith, D. Vance. "The Labors of Reward: Meed, Mercede, and the Beginning of Salvation." *Yearbook of Langland Studies* 8 (1994): 127–54.

———. *Arts of Possession: The Middle English Household Imaginary.* Medieval Cultures 33. Minneapolis: University of Minnesota Press, 2003.

Solopova, Elizabeth, ed. *The General Prologue on CD-ROM.* Cambridge, UK: Cambridge University Press, 2000.

Specht, Henrik. *Chaucer's Franklin in the Canterbury Tales: The Social and Literary Background of a Chaucerian Character.* Copenhagen: Akademisk Forlag, 1981.

Spencer, H. Leith. *English Preaching in the Late Middle Ages.* Oxford: Clarendon Press, 1993.

Spufford, Peter. *Money and Its Use in Medieval Europe.* Cambridge, UK: Cambridge University Press, 1988.

———. *Power and Profit: The Merchant in Medieval Europe.* New York: Thames & Hudson, 2002.

Staley, Lynn. *Margery Kempe's Dissenting Fictions.* University Park: The Pennsylvania State University Press, 1994.

Stevens, Martin. "'And Venus Laugheth': An Interpretation of the *Merchant's Tale*." *Chaucer Review* 7 (1972): 118–31.

———. "The York Cycle: From Procession to Play." *Leeds Studies in English* n. s. 6 (1972): 37–61.

———. *Four Middle English Mystery Cycles: Textual, Contextual, and Critical Interpretations.* Princeton: Princeton University Press, 1987.

———. "The York Cycle as Carnival." *Fifteenth-Century Studies* 13 (1988): 447–56.

Stillwell, Gardiner. "Chaucer's 'Sad' Merchant." *Review of English Studies* 20 (1944): 1–18.

———. "John Gower and the Last Years of Edward III." *Studies in Philology* 45 [1948]: 454–71.

———. "Chaucer's Merchant: No Debts?" *Journal of English and Germanic Philology* 57 (1958): 192–6.

Stock, Lorraine Kochanske. "The Meaning of *Chevyssaunce*: Complicated Word Play in Chaucer's *Shipman's Tale*." *Studies in Short Fiction* 18 (1981): 245–49.

———. "La Vieille and the Merchant's Wife in Chaucer's *Shipman's Tale*." *Southern Humanities Review* 16 (1982): 333–39.

Strohm, Paul. "The Social and Literary Scene in England." In *The Cambridge Chaucer Companion*. Ed. Piero Boitani and Jill Mann. Cambridge, UK: Cambridge University Press, 1986. [pp. 1–18].

———. *Social Chaucer*. Cambridge, MA: Harvard University Press, 1989.

———. *Hochon's Arrow: The Social Imagination of Fourteenth-Century Texts*. Princeton: Princeton University Press, 1992.

———. *England's Empty Throne: Usurpation and the Language of Legitimation, 1399–1422*. New Haven: Yale University Press, 1998.

Sutton, Anne F. *The Mercery of London: Trade, Goods and People, 1130–1578*. Burlington, VT: Ashgate, 2005.

Swanson, Heather. "The Illusion of Economic Structure: Craft Guilds in Late Medieval English Towns." *Past and Present* 121 (1988): 29–48.

Szittya, Penn R. "The Antifraternal Tradition in Medieval English Literature." *Speculum* 52 (1977): 287–313.

———. *The Antifraternal Tradition in Medieval Literature*. Princeton: Princeton University Press, 1986.

Taylor, Karla. "Chaucer's Reticent Merchant." In *The Idea of Medieval Literature: New Essays on Chaucer and Medieval Culture in Honor of Donald R. Howard*. Newark: University of Delaware Press, 1992. [pp. 189–205].

———. "Social Aesthetics and the Emergence of Civic Discourse from the *Shipman's Tale* to Melibee." *Chaucer Review* 39.2 (2005): 298–322.

Thrupp, Sylvia L. *The Merchant Class of Medieval London 1300–1500*. 1948. Repr. Ann Arbor: University of Michigan Press, 1962.

Trotter, David. "Not as Eccentric as It Looks: Anglo-French and French French." *Forum for Modern Language Studies* 39.4 (2003): 427–36.

Tucker, S. M. *Verse Satire in England Before the Renaissance*. New York: Columbia University Press, 1908.

Turner, Marion. "'Certaynly His Noble Sayenges Can I Not Amende': Thomas Usk and *Troilus and Criseyde*." *Chaucer Review* 37.1 (2002): 26–39.

———. "Usk and the Goldsmiths." *New Medieval Literatures* 9 (2007): 139–77.

Vauchez, André. *Sainthood in the Later Middle Ages* [*La sainteté en Occident aux derniers siècles du Moyen Age*]. Trans. Jean Birrell. 1988. Cambridge, UK: Cambridge University Press, 1997.

Wallace, David. "Mystics and Followers in Siena and East Anglia: A Study in Taxonomy, Class and Cultural Mediation." In *The Medieval Mystical Tradition in England: Papers read at Darlington Hall, July 1984*. Ed. Marion Glasscoe. Woodbridge, Suffolk: D. S. Brewer, 1984. [pp. 169–91].

———. *Chaucerian Polity: Absolutist Lineages and Associational Forms in England and Italy*. Stanford: Stanford University Press, 1997.

Watney, Sir John. *An Account of the Mistery of Mercers of the City of London, otherwise the Mercers' Company*. London: Blades, East & Blades, 1914.

Weissengruber, Erik Paul. "The Corpus Christi Procession in Medieval York: A Symbolic Struggle in Public Space." *Theatre Survey* 38 (1997): 117–38.

White, Eileen. "The Tenements at the Common Hall Gates: The Mayor's Station for the Corpus Christi Play in York." *REED Newsletter* 7 (1982): 14–24.

Williams, Raymond. *Marxism and Literature.* Oxford: Oxford University Press, 1977.

Wilson, Janet. "Communities of Dissent: The Secular and Ecclesiastical Communities of Margery Kempe's *Book*." In *Medieval Women in their Communities.* Ed. Diane Watt. Toronto: University of Toronto Press, 1997. [pp. 155–85].

Winstead, Karen A. "The Conversion of Margery Kempe's Son." *English Language Notes* 32 (1994): 9–13.

Woolf, Rosemary. *The English Mystery Plays.* Berkeley: University of California Press, 1972.

———. "Moral Chaucer and Kindly Gower." In *J. R. R. Tolkien, Scholar and Storyteller: Essays* in Memoriam. Ed. Mary Salu and Robert T. Farrell. Ithaca: Cornell University Press, 1979. [pp. 221–45].

Wright, Laura. "Bills, Accounts, Inventories: Everyday Trilingual Activities in the Business World of Later Medieval England." In *Multilingualism in Later Medieval Britain.* Ed. D. A. Trotter. Cambridge, UK: D. S. Brewer, 2000. [pp.149–56].

———. "Social Context, Structural Categories and Medieval Business Writing." *Bilingualism: Language and Cognition* 3.2 (2000): 124–25.

Yeager, Robert F. "Aspects of Gluttony in Chaucer and Gower." *Studies in Philology* 81 (1984): 42–55.

———. "*Pax Poetica*: On the Pacifism of Chaucer and Gower." *Studies in the Age of Chaucer* 9 (1987): 97–121.

———. "Did Gower write Cento?" In *John Gower, Recent Readings.* Ed. R. F. Yeager. Kalamazoo, MI: Medieval Institute Publications, 1989. [pp. 113–32].

———. "Learning to Speak in Tongues: Writing Poetry for a Trilingual Culture." In *Chaucer and Gower: Difference, Mutuality, Exchange.* Ed. R. F. Yeager. English Literary Studies Monograph Series. Victoria: University of Victoria Press, 1991. [pp. 115–29].

———. "Gower's French Audience: The *Mirour de l'Omme*." *Chaucer Review* 41.2 (2006): 111–37.

INDEX

Olivi, Peter John, 24, 37, 51
Oresme, Nicholas, 22, 51

Paris, 57–58, 96–97
Pavia, 87, 98
Peverel, Thomas, Bishop of
    Worcester, 107, 109–10
Philpot, Sir John, 8, 10, 61, 86, 164
Philip the Good, Duke of Burgundy,
    114–15
Pinkhurst, Adam, see Scribes
Pole, de la
    Michael, Earl of Suffolk, 20
    Sir William, 20
pride, see Sins, Seven Deadly
promercantilism, see ideology
Prussia, 112
puns characteristic of
    antimercantilism, 27–30,
    40–43, 93–99, 124

readers, see audience
religious orders and foundations, 15,
    32–33, 45–47, 51, 81, 91–99,
    107
    Carthusians (Order of
        St. Bruno), 21
    Fountains Abbey (Cistercian
        Order), 4
    Franciscans (Order of Friars
        Minor), 27, 32, 111–12, 186
    Priory of St. Mary Overie (Order
        of Saint Augustine), 54, 74
    Reivaulx Abbey (Cistercian
        Order), 4
    see also hospitals
restitution, 13, 25, 27, 30, 34, 38, 71,
    119–25, 149, 156
Richard II, 8
Roman de la Rose, 97
Rome, 106, 110, 126, 129
Roos, Thomas, 21

St. Erkenwald, 4
St. Margaret's Parish Church, Bishop's
    Lynn, 104, 107–109

saints
    St. Catherine of Siena, 9
    St. Denis, 96
    St. Francis of Assisi, 9, 110, 127
    St. Godric of Finchale, 8–9, 16–17,
        158, 160
    St. Homobonus, 9, 106
    St. Ivo of Chartres, 96
    St. Martin of Tours, 96
    St. Nicholas, 8
    see also Aquinas, Thomas;
        Augustine of Hippo
scribes, 20–22
    Hammond scribe, 22
    Hoccleve, Thomas, 22, 168
    Pinkhurst, Adam, 21–22, 86
    Scribe D, 22
    Usk, Thomas, 22
servants, 70, 105–106, 123–25
Seville, 57
Sigismund, Holy Roman Emperor, 114
simony, 29, 36, 38, 46, 78, 154
Sins, Seven Deadly, 4, 24, 28, 31, 45,
    52, 105, 153, 163, 193
    avarice (greed), 4, 9, 16–17, 24–36,
        41, 45–46, 52, 59, 65–67,
        73–75, 83, 98, 105, 111, 113,
        119–25, 130–31, 133, 143, 145,
        147, 153–54, 157, 163, 166, 170
    envy, 105, 170
    gluttony, 29
    lechery (lust), 30, 59, 111, 153
    pride, 43, 45–46, 52, 59, 68, 71, 80,
        104–106, 110–11, 152–54
    sloth, 46, 171
    wrath, 52
sloth, see Sins, Seven Deadly
Sluys, 115
staple, wool, 63–67, 74, 79, 113, 115,
    160, 178
Statute of Laborers, 24
Stokdale, John, 146

1381 Rising, 7
Three Estates, 1–4, 59, 68, 84
    see also ideology